divorce

Rights of Passage

by
Dr. Gerald D. Alpern

PSYCHOLOGICAL DEVELOPMENT PUBLICATIONS
ASPEN, COLORADO

Published by: Psychological Development Publications
               Box 3198
               Aspen, Colorado 81612

First Edition: First Printing, January, 1983

Editor: Kay Eldredge

Cover Design: Carol Alpern

Author's Photo: Amelie DeBlois

Printed in the United States of America

ISBN 0-912397-00-4

Dedication

To Carol, my much loved ex-wife who provided 80% of this book's creative thoughts, 0% of the actual work, and who will receive 15% of the net profits. And so it goes... G.D.A.

Author's Notice

The aim of this book is to be a guide for those dealing with the emotional and legal complications of divorce. The book cannot and does not claim that the general information offered provides definitive help to readers' *specific* legal or emotional problems. Laws and legal terminology and precedence differ from state to state and are constantly being changed. People's mental lives are much too complex for a book to provide the comprehensive attention needed to those with significant emotional difficulties. Carefully chosen mental health or legal professionals should be consulted before making important life decisions.

This manual gives the reader what I consider the most useful information for those who are considering or dealing with divorce. The more one can predict about an experience, the more it can be controlled. This manual provides an understanding of the divorce process so that the reader gains the ability to manipulate its legal and emotional realities.

GERALD D. ALPERN, PH.D.

Preface

Divorce is a unique passage. It is a stage of development that about half of all adults will, at some time, pass through. Some choose it, others try to avoid it at all costs. The fact that our world has increasingly permitted it and accepted it has not much diminished the upheaval it causes, probably because one of man's deepest needs is to be in a commited, bonded relationship, and ending a marriage seems antithetical to meeting that need.

This book is aimed at reducing divorce pains through information about how to best get through its still archaic legal rituals and primordial human emotions. But the most experienced advice and brilliant technology can only be minimally effective without an attitude about the passage.

The attitude this book is dedicated to is that dead marriages do not mean the death of relationship possibilities with any child or adult. In fact, the debris of marriages, regardless of whether they expired for cultural or personal reasons, can provide the most fertile soil available for the production of hardier and richer relationships.

That attitude is as realistic as a pre-surgical belief that the removal of some malfunctioning organ will provide for the possibility of better health. Furthermore in the same way people who recover from illnesses can gain antibodies which leave them healthier than they were before the illness, divorce should render people better able to maintain nourishing relationships than before the experience of divorce.

CONTENTS

PART III
CHILDREN AND DIVORCE

PART IV
APPENDICES

CHAPTER 1

Introduction: Couple Changing

After all, my erstwhile dear,
My no longer cherished,
Need we say it was not love,
Just because it perished?
EDNA ST. VINCENT MILLAY

Divorces are typically hideous experiences. People expect them to be painful and ugly. The judicial system that regulates them has the reputation of exacerbating the trauma. The thesis of this book is that divorces needn't be a debilitating, humiliating life crisis. It is possible to go through all the emotional and legal complications, not only minimizing negative effects, but utilizing the potential of divorce to promote positive outcomes.

Americans in the 1980's are undergoing overwhelming cultural revolutions in which our shared beliefs, values and feelings concerning the most crucial aspects of our lives are radically changing. The 80's are a transitional age in which people are conducting bold and diverse experiments in their ways of working, having relationships, and finding meaning in their individual lives.

Daniel Yankelovich's 1981 book, "New Rules", presents a myriad of statistics which document the radical changes that have taken place in just the past few years. In the late 1950's, opinion polls determined that 80% of the people interviewed believe single adults to be either neurotic, amoral, or abnormal. Twenty years later the same inquiry testified to a radically changed view. Seventy-five percent of those polled in the late 70's considered singledom to be "normal".

A recent NBC poll indicated that a majority currently feels that couples wedded today will not remain married. Thus, the "forever" aspect of marriage which used to be commonly assumed, is no longer believed.

Moral viewpoints about relationships have also drastically changed. Twice as many people were living as couples without the sanctity of marriage in 1977 as in 1960. Opinion polls document this change with results that show the majority of people now reporting that living together arrangements are not morally wrong. Even the majority of parents of college age children now condone premarital sex; in 1967, 85% of them condemned it.

Another basic change involves attitudes toward childless marriages. There used to be tremendous pressures for married couples to have children in order to be considered "normal". Recent polls show that 83% now consider a childless marriage to be acceptable. A related belief which has recently toppled is that when marriages do produce children, the adults have an obligation to maintain the family in spite of marital difficulties. Now the majority feel that a couple should not stay together for the sake of the children.

The impact of these findings reported by Yankelovich, along with the collection of statistics reported almost weekly of increasing divorces, can be interpreted as a very pessimistic portrait of today's relationships in America. One hears philosophical or sociological opinions that today people are indulging in infantile, self-centered, me-now values. These commentators state that the desire for committed, long-term, intimate relationships has been replaced with an ethic in which the fulfillment of all of one's emotional cravings has been dignified to the level of a sacred responsibility. The fear expressed by such social critics is that all of the new demands for self-fulfillment actually represent a level of immaturity which undermines the possibility of quality, in-depth relationships.

The belief of this author is that although relationships may definitely be changing, their quality is increasing, not diminishing.

In 1970, the ideal of two people sharing a life together was subscribed to by 96% of Americans. A decade later the percentage was again 96%. Thus, the bias of the American majority and of this book is identical (i.e., having a long-term, committed, mutually nurturing relationship is the ideal). What is changing about relationships may not be reflected by the statistics indicating declines in marriages. What seems to be really changing is the old belief that coupling requires major sacrifices of one's individuality. Today martyrdom of one's personal growth is definitely not in vogue. The evolving belief, which like the physical fitness craze may be lasting and not just a fad, is that achieving one's own self actualization enhances one's capability for the deepest and most authentic relationships with others.

This book seeks to guide people not in ending relationships, but in coping with divorce in a manner to minimize the pains from changing personal commitments and present archaic legal realities. The underlying goal of the book is to help people learn to have rewarding relationships with others: friends, lovers, children, and even ex-spouses.

In a very important sense, divorce is not a unique event in anyone's history. From the time we begin to have relationships with other people, we learn about the ending of relationships. Relationships are begun for many reasons and under many circumstances. We begin with others because they are our neighbors, school classmates, romantic attractions, or colleagues. Very frequently some outlandish chance contact brings us together with a person with whom we form an important connection. Almost all of these relationships go through many alterations over time. People make geographical moves. Sport and interest patterns change. New romances lead to withdrawal of energy from old romances. Growth, or just change, renders formerly important connections less significant. Most of these relationship changes, which we all experience, do not result in a complete ending of the relationship. We simply regularly revise the form of our contacts with others.

These relationship revisions most often are an evolution into a more comfortable or useful form. Most of our major relationships do not end but rather continually change. For example, the form of contact people have with parents as children is very different from what it is as adults. We expect relationships with children to change with each year of their and our development. Most of these changes take place without much effort or training, but this natural evolution of relationships seems the most difficult with marital relationships.

Marriage historically has been an extremely unique connection between people traditionally formalized in an elaborate ceremony with publicly declared vows. There has been the binding stamp of formal religious approval. Its legal implications have been and remain immense. Very important has been the fact that traditional marriages are begun with the belief that the commitment being declared at the time of the marriage ceremony will last throughout a lifetime.

The institution of marriage has, however, rather quickly evolved over recent times, to be much less unique among relationships. The religious bonds are looser. Cultural and technological changes have erradicated earlier realities which practically mandated a male-female team in order to survive. Both females and males are, in today's world, more capable of having their financial, sexual, social, and home and heath needs met without marriage. These massive changes in our society now make it possible for people to begin and end marital relationships much more like all other relationships. Changes in shared interests, new career opportunities, important romances, personal growth, or a loss of that sense of a special, important connection are now more often valid reasons for divorce.

In some limited ways, our society has adapted to the needs of married people to make changes. Fault-free divorces, open marriages, prenuptial agreements arc all attempts to alleviate the pressures of the more traditional form of marriage which no longer serves many healthy developing people. However, the fact that our country is presently changing its view of marriage as a sanctified, permanent, unchanging, legally binding bond has caused a real problem. We are presently caught in a time in which we are faced with a clumsy and damaging, changing and untenable set of rules for ending marriages. Current divorce proceedings extract a very high financial and emotional price from people. An important part of the emotional expense is the fear most people have about the divorce process. In marriages with children, the legal complications and emotional concerns, and thus the fears about divorce, are usually multiplied. Historically, children could only morally and legally enter the world within marriage. Today, though laws and morals offer children an easier time, they remain extremely vulnerable to victimization by the legal and emotional complications of the typical divorce.

It is the formal court process of divorce which today's legal system mandates that produces much of the negative feelings about divorce. The legal process can easily turn a former loved one into a hated enemy. Divorcing couples already suffer financial worries, fears of isolation, anxieties about their roles in society. It is tragic that the courts add to the awesome list of fears. When there are children, the problems are multiplied because parents are afraid children will be emotionally crippled by divorce. When there are also fears of what judges, lawyers, and court procedures may do either directly to the children or to the parents' continuing relationship to their children, it can be positively terrifying. Parents fear they will lose children who are an essential part of their identity.

All of these problems of divorce can be easily avoided in spite of the way our courts are currently dealing with divorce. The techniques for achieving this make up the bulk of this book.

The motivation for producing this manual came from two sources. The first motivation was objective. Over twenty some years the vantage point of the therapist's chair has given me knowledge of the painful failures and joyful successes of others. It seemed that the things learned from these people could and should be passed on to others, especially since there are so many others now engaged in such similar struggles. My personal life provided the more subjective and undoubtedly major motivation for this work. After fifteen years of a solid and loving marriage, my wife and I thoughtfully designed a divorce which has enhanced our relationship and our individual lives. Appendix A, "My Relationship With Carol," describes that relationship.

COUPLE COUNSELING

An understanding of how couples change provides a framework for looking at one's individual divorce. The most formal approach used by couples seeking to change (not necessarily end) their relationship has been professional counseling.

The form and goals of the counseling available to couples have dramatically changed over the last 25 years. The changes, of course, mirror the cultural changes in the attitudes about relationships that have taken place over that same period of time. Through the 1950's and most of the 60's the label used for couple therapy was simply marital therapy. Because almost all who sought couple therapy were married. The clear goal of the 50's version of marital therapy was to resurrect a sick or tired or damaged marriage. If there was a renewal of the positive energy within the marriage, the therapy was a success.

If not, the therapist, the couple, and the marriage might all be labeled failures. By the late 1960's, marital therapy was more often called "relationship therapy". This change in titles offered a recognition that couples seeking help in maintaining a positive relationship might be homosexual couples, heterosexual couples living together, divorced parents, couples in multiple marriages, or any of the ever widening varieties of bonding that were becoming a part of our society. By the 1970's, it seemed that for significant numbers of people traditional marriage was becoming less necessary, less appealing, and much less popular. Divorce was becoming more popular not as a result of adultery, abandonment, or mental illness, but as a direct result of the disenchantment with the marriage lifestyle. Though more and more people were divorcing, the difficulties for those seeking to end marriage remained so great that it led to a form of relationship therapy which never before existed—divorce therapy. In 1978, Dr. James L. Framo defined the goal of divorce therapy: "to help a couple disengage from a marriage with a minimum of distructiveness to themselves, their children, and with the personal freedom to form new relationships." This definition implies that ending a marriage means that new primary relationships are planned. Although most divorces still involve a desire to end most mutual interrelating, a substantial number of people are seeking divorce simply as a way to end certain legal, living, or financial involvements; they still intend to continue some important aspects of their former marital relationship. Love, sex, friendship, financial or emotional supports are not dependent on marriage. Furthermore, such basic ties as a shared history or shared offspring are strong justification for maintaining a good relationship with a former spouse.

Readers convinced they want to end as much contact with their marriage partner as possible need not fear that this manual will discourage that path. Most people today share the belief that a divorce primarily offers a welcome relief from a bad situation. This book offers specific instructions on easy ending tactics though there is also exposure to the advantages of non-bridge burning techniques.

My style of counseling couples contemplating divorce reflects a belief that they should examine the vast number of options available to enhance them individually and as a couple. In the 1980's, couples can still choose to have a traditional exclusive marriage where they live together essentially all of the time and meet all of each other's nurturance, social, supportive, stimulation, friendship, sexual, financial, spiritual, romantic, intellectual, emotional, recreational, vocation, and avocational needs. Many people are capable of and content with this lifestyle and regardless of any current trends should engage in traditional marital therapy to help them maximize the quality of the exclusive relationship they prefer.

Options to the traditional relationship can be explored by listing which of the fourteen needs can be met by others. Can, for instance, friendship or recreational needs be met by someone other than the spouse? A couple could agree that one spouse could have certain needs met by their children, relatives, same-sexed friends, friends of the opposite sex, or new or old acquaintances of one or both spouses. The possibilities expand further when you consider that there may be certain times or certain places when the rules can change for who can meet what needs.

Now consider altering another aspect of the basic couple format. If the couple decided not to live together, then we can further multiply the already listed possibilities. For example, a couple might decide to live separately one or two or fifty-one weeks each year, and live together the rest of the year.

Once couples can be taught to realize the many options they actually have, they can begin to explore which possibilities they want to investigate to enhance their relationship. If, for instance, they discover that they thoroughly enjoy each other only when on vacations, then they could decide to end their formal marriage and enjoy vacations together. On the other hand, they may decide that they enjoy each other in a working, live-together relationship but do not recreate very well together. That knowledge may lead them to a lifestyle where they live and work together, but recreate separately, save their marriage and create genuine happiness. The basic notion is simply that a fantastically wide variety of relationship possibilities are available. The goal of couple counseling in the 1980's is to guide the couple towards reaching a set of agreements (a constantly alterable contract) as to how they wish to fashion their unique relationship.

In a certain number of cases couples will decide that in order to best enhance their relations or individual lives they need to obtain a divorce. The essential point now is to realize that there exists as wide a variety of post-divorce styles of relationships as there are marriage styles. When and if the couple decides on divorce, then "divorce therapy'' has as its goal helping the couple disengage from the legal status of marriage in a manner designed to maximize the quality of their lives as individuals *and* as a continuing couple.

As has been noted, much of this book has come from experience gained guiding many couples who came for counseling with relationship problems. Over the last quarter of a century, increasingly higher proportions of such couples opted for a divorce as part of their problem solution. The experience has been that when divorces were planned during counseling, the divorce decision, procedures, and post-divorce relationships were much more positive than among the non-counseled divorces.

The usual, non-counseled divorce proceeds by people dealing with the usual ambivalence about ending the relationship by eventually using anger. That is, the ambivalence that most people feel when considering divorce is painful. If, however, it is clear that the other person is a son-of-a-bitch then it is easier and less painful to separate from them. The ambivalence disappears and you can feel good about ending the relationship. So anger serves; it makes things easier. The trouble, however, is that because the legal system is an adversarial system it can so easily multiply the anger expotentially. Then the court system not only ends the legal bonds between the people but also destroys most hope for a continuing relationship between two people who formerly loved and cared for each other. The usual anger/court procedure is very destructive, wasteful, and in so many cases, unnecessary.

Reviewing the methods used in good relationship counseling will explain how you can reach the goal of divorcing to enhance your individual life, while maximizing the possibility for a positive relationship between you and your spouse.

RELATIONSHIP THERAPY

The possibility of relationship therapy can only be considered after determining that neither of the people are in need of individual psychotherapy. Relationship therapy can usefully proceed only when both people are within normal mental health limits. Preliminary meetings, or formal psychological testing given at the outset is used to discover if either person suffers from emotional problems serious enough to undermine their relating to anyone. If this is the case, the relationship counseling must be delayed until the individual psychological problem is under control. Having to delay relationship therapy for individual counseling is a rather rare occurance.

The vast majority of the time people who come for relationship therapy are seen as a couple. Furthermore, almost all sessions are conducted with them together. Initially, however, the two may be seen individually to allow them privacy in which to describe their personal goals for the counseling. The individual sessions frequently lead to the discovery of one person's hidden agenda which represents their major reason for seeking therapy and which is unknown to their partner. The most common two hidden agendas are the fact that one person has an outside relationship which they either wish to keep secret from the other or deal with only in the safety of counseling sessions. The second most commonly found hidden agenda is the fact that they have already made the decision to end the relationship and are only seeking counseling to provide an atmosphere in which to do this in the most gentle or constructive manner. These hidden agendas must be dealt with at the outset of counseling. The methods with which the secret agendas are resolved, of course, are as varied as the problems and the people themselves, but they are always handled early in the counseling.

What is to be described next is couple counseling, not divorce counseling. The latter is but one possible outcome of couple counseling and will be outlined later. The difference between the two kinds of counseling is simply that the couple counseling has as its goal to clarify and enhance the relationship while divorce counseling applies when a married couple decides on divorce and wishes to go through the procedure in a manner which is as beneficial and as least destructive to them and their family as possible.

The general procedure for couple counseling is for the two people to be together. If either requests to see the therapist individually, this request is honored, but the preferred method for dealing with all issues is with open communication between the two people in the relationship. Clearly, being able to work out any issue openly with one's partner provides the atmosphere ideal for building trust. From the beginning, the couple is taught to engage in honest communication which involves learning confrontive techniques necessary for effectively dealing with the issues.

This same procedure of the two parties seeing the therapist

together also applies where divorce is being considered and attorneys enter the picture. The same open communication between the couple with the third party present serves whether the third party is therapist, attorney, priest or children and the skills gained by doing this with a counselor have a great transfer value if the couple later requires attorneys and/or mediators. Thus, the advantages of being able to discuss, reveal and deal with all issues in the presence of the partner is important training offered in relationship therapy. To be able to do this requires skill, guts, willingness to learn, and with couples in trouble, a talented therapist. Note that what was asked for is a skilled therapist rather than a skilled, gutsy, or even willing partner. That is because it is a good bet that if you can be responsible for providing your own skill, guts, and willingness, you can create a willing partner.

Another necessity for successful couple counseling involves the atmosphere. It is important, if not essential, to provide an atmosphere of friendship. Frequently, couples come to counseling hoping for the counselor to judge their arguments to determine who is right. Couples need to learn how to deal with issues between themselves, and that the initially essential step for this involves, if not a friendly, then at least a courteous atmosphere. Some feel that if a courteous working atmosphere could be created, counseling would be over and they could get on with their marriage. The feeling is that once they are able to be friendly or even genuinely civil, the rest will work out. However, friendship itself does not solve problems such as conflicting values, sexual disinterest, or basic goal differences. What friendship does do is provide for a type of communication where each person is rooting for the other person to get what they want from life. Because the easiest feeling to have during a marital crisis is not friendliness, but anger, it is common for the creation of a sincerely friendly environment to take the major amount of time and effort in the counseling sessions.

There are times when the establishment of a friendly atmosphere simply cannot be accomplished between badly alienated spouses. If a friendly atmosphere is impossible, a courteous-civil one is almost always possible. The importance of a non-hostile environment for achieving anything outside the potentially destructive legal system is crucial. If a genuinely friendly environment cannot be established, then simple courtesy must be taught. Being courteous can emulate friendship sufficiently to permit effective communication. Even rival statesman from countries at war frequently initiate peace negotiations through ritualized etiquette (a formal version of politeness) only to conclude with useful agreements and sometimes even limited friendships.

Emotionally strained couples can be guided toward beginning useful interactions and communications with courtesy, and if the counseling is very successful, the couple could end with mutual respect and even viable friendships. Friendship may not be an essential pre-requisite for a torrid love affair, but it may well be the best guarantee for an enduring love relationship.

Once the atmosphere of nonhostility has been created, the next step in couple counseling deals with that overused, poorly understood term, communication. Communication is simply making authentic contact with another. For couples in trouble, it actually begins when each can clearly articulate dissatisfactions with their partners. The problem is that though they are very anxious to communicate, they express things in destructive ways and frequently to the wrong person. They want to list their partner's crimes to the therapist. Effective couple counseling teaches how to express ideas or feelings *in a way that they can be heard.* An outpouring of sadness or anger or a collection of strongly felt ideas about how they are being abused in the relationship is usually the antithesis of useful communication because it is not heard and generates anger, defensiveness, and a desire to counter-attack or avoid confrontation. Although therapy does establish an accepting atmosphere for outpourings of logical or illogical emotions, feelings, and ideas, these are not valid communications in the problem solving sense. The most useful communications are those in which the sender's message is heard by the receiver and responded to, not defensively, but in a way designed to meet the needs of both. The easiest way to understand this concept of useful communication is to follow the mechanical way it can be learned in the counseling situation.

A technique used for teaching couples effective communication is to have each person independently write a list of the issues in their relationship. The couple is instructed to state their issues clearly, concisely, and in non-accusatory language. The usual 5 to 10 issues which occur in the lists involved financial matters, sexual needs, childrearing styles, quality time alone, quality time together, outside marriage friendships and/or loves, vocational demands, avocational interests, and inside the marriage roles, responsibilities, and expectations. Lists usually will contain items such as, "Julie gambles too much;" "Alfred no longer excites me sexually;" "Phyllis' job takes too much time;" "Phillip is too strict with the kids;" "I feel stifled by the relationship and need more time to myself."

The purpose of writing down the issues is so that during counseling sessions they can discuss one by one while being monitored by the therapist who is teaching them the kind of communication skills necessary to resolve issues. Theoretically, if all the issues are resolved, the couple should be able to go off hand in hand into the sunset. That's not really the goal. The real goal is not to solve the particular issues, but to have them learn how to resolve issues. If they can learn how to honestly approach and deal with issues, they will have come a long way toward effectively communicating with *any* other human being.

Once each person has produced his list of issues, the technique proceeds by having one person present to their partner their easiest-to-resolve issue first. The counselor informs them that they can talk to each other only as long as things are going well. As soon as one of them makes a communication error, such as switching topics, not letting the other person finish, begin too accusatory, becoming too long-winded, or any other error that hinders the useful exchange, then the counselor points out the error, teaches how to avoid the error, and then lets them continue. Thus, the procedure is to have the couple talk to each other with the counselor carefully listening for any mistakes which could hamper the communication. Hypothetically, as the counselor corrects each mistake, the couple is learning how to competently deal with issues.

To illustrate, let's say the man makes as his first statement: "Julie gambles too much." The counselor offers the instruction that the husband should not address the therapist, but his wife. Direct eye contact will also be encouraged. Furthermore, it will be pointed out that his accusatory statement is liable to produce a defensive response. The counselor will work with the introductory statement until the husband is able to rephrase it in a way that maximizes a potentially positive response from Julie. The statement might be worked over until the presenter says something such as, "The amount of money you gamble, Julie, makes me feel really uncomfortable." Julie is then allowed to respond. She will be helped to understand how important it is not to find an accusation in the issue and thus become defensive. If Julie, for example, would respond by saying, "I only gamble with the money I saved from the sewing work I do on the side," the defensiveness of this statement would be pointed out. Julie might make an even more disastrous communication error by responding with a counteraccusation, "You're the one who wastes the money in our family! Who bought that overpriced stereo?"

The counselor, through all of the interruptions of the couple's ongoing discussion, is attempting to guide each of them to (1) recognize the concerns of their partner, and (2) display a commitment to making the partner more comfortable without sacrificing their own needs, thus producing resentment. Julie might take a half an hour before she can understand enough to be able to respond with something like, "I know my gambling has been a problem for you. I really am sorry you are unhappy about it, and I'd really like to make things more comfortable for you. I think I need to know what it is that makes you so upset. Sometimes I think it is the money that you worry about and other times I think you don't like my going to the track because of the people I meet there. Maybe it's just how much time going to the races takes, and that you feel I'm not with you enough. I need to know more about what you're feeling because I want to be able to enjoy my recreation without having it cause problems between us."

Such stylized and overly idealistic responses may well be perceived as both unbelievably saccharine and artificial. At first, the "corrected" statements tend to be guilty on both counts. However, with time and practice, the way rational and considerate responses work becomes clearer, and the statements sound more natural.

As with life, humor is essential and renders counseling bearable. It provides an antedote for the necessary artificiality in this kind of training.

The work gets very tricky. Even though the couple may begin with the issue believed to be the simplest to resolve, it can evolve that the apparently superficial problem represents the very essence of one person's basic dissatisfactions with the relationship. In discussing the gambling issue, it could become clear, after just a few exchanges, that Harry really feels that whether Julie gambles or not, she never spends enough time with him, which supports his feeling that she no longer loves him or, perhaps, that she is passionately in love with her co-gambler. Or Julie may feel that she must gamble because Harry's objection to her gambling is, in reality, his mother's objection to gambling, and it is Julie's anger about her mother-in-law's role in her marriage that is the real issue.

The use of a superficial issue as the calling card for dealing with a very deeply important issue is but one problem in the working-through-issues technology. It is the dealing with just such problems that makes grist for the counseling mill.

Dealing with dissatisfaction is *not* a process in which the people somehow come to a compromise in which neither person gets what they really want. Julie cannot give up gambling if Harry gives up smoking in the house. The counseling must lead the couple towards solutions—experiments for the couple to live with and later evaluate. The couple may decide that Julie will only gamble under certain conditions. Then at some later date, the two of them must communicate on whether this solution has been satisfactory to both of them. If it is, fine. If not, they continue their commitment to coping with the dissatisfactions by experimenting with another possible solution. There are, of course, no relationships without continuing conflicts. There are only, in successful relationships, the skills and commitment of both people working for solutions that are satisfactory to both partners.

How does this counseling technique promote such essentials as mutual joy, individual fulfillment, spiritual unity, family commitments, and/or any other ingredient essential to a proper marriage? It doesn't. It cannot. Each person has their own ideal and practical recipes for successful marriages. The relationship counselor does not provide a cookbook with directions for satisfying each appetite. What the relationship counselor does provide is a method for clearly determining whether the ingredients brought by the couple can be blended to satisfy their particular tastes, however bland or exotic they may be.

Whether or not their relationship survives, the techniques learned in counseling are extremely valuable for dealing with the conflicts that are inevitable when one is, for any length of time, in close contact with another human being. Whether they choose to continue the relationship with the particular person with whom they're in counseling is ultimately based on variables too complex for the skills or techniques of any counselor. All counseling can hope to do is to provide a couple with a clear understanding of what is going on between them and allow them to make the decisions about what path their lives should take. Communication skills can be learned, but love cannot be created.

If relationship counseling leads to the decision to end the marriage, relationship counseling evolves into divorce counseling. The most crucial aspect of divorce counseling involves the attempt to resolve as many issues as possible outside the emotionally and financially expensive judicial system.

DIVORCE COUNSELING

Divorce counseling is a relatively new addition to the therapies being offered by mental health professionals. The same conditions which produced the need for this divorce book have also produced the need for professional divorce counseling. There is now a widespread realization that couples can substantially ease the difficulties of divorce by using counselors either as arbitrators or helpers in settling differences.

Even when people feel they are ready for divorce counseling, relationship counseling may be well worth considering. That is, before deciding who gets the family silver, they might feel much clearer about the decision to divorce after putting forth the kind of effort demanded by relationship counseling. The skills learned during relationship counseling serve as a good background for avoiding the multitude of traps usually in the path of those seeking divorce.

The word "traps" is important to understanding how this manual serves as a divorce counseling guide. The word "traps" implies pitfalls *which are avoidable*. Some divorce related traps are obvious, such as the material losses. This trap can be avoided. Some divorce traps are less visible, like losing many of the social contacts enjoyed by married couples. This trap can be avoided. The book is also about avoiding traps of jealousy, loneliness, loss of identity, depression, and a hundred other emotional or legal consequences typically expected by those who have or are facing divorce.

Children are often thought to be the most vulnerable victims of divorce. Children can very often be as much helped as hindered by divorce.

Financial losses are not at all inevitable.

The feeling of failure usually expected is primarily a self-fulfilling myth.

Perhaps the most hidden trap that divorcing couples regularly and unnecessarily trip into is the trap of further alienation from each other. It would be foolish to deny that there are times when one needs to minimize contact with the other person. However, it is equally foolish to forget that, at one time, the couple did enjoy love, friendship, passion, or common goals during the course of their relationship. Discarding what has been nourishing in the marriage is unnecessary. It is probably not the belief or desire of most people that a divorce serve as a way of enhancing a relationship, but it is worth considering as a possibility.

Part I
Psychological Aspects of Divorce

CHAPTER 2

Adult Development and the Tyranny of Habit

Some divorces are simple happenings, a graceful parting in which two people go off in different directions to new lives. Other divorces occur so gradually, over so many years, that the divorce process is not a deeply felt experience. For others, the marriage involved a connection so casual that a legal divorce is but a formality.

However, the majority of divorces are very powerful experiences which, for many, are devastating. For most people, divorce necessitates major revisions in life goals, expectations, and personal identities. People involved in divorce find themselves acting in unfamiliar ways. They may behave irrationally, become vicious or promiscuous, or suddenly plan to desert loved children. These unfamiliar actions and feelings are very frightening and cause grave self-doubts which exacerbate the depression so common to divorcing men and women. The most disorienting experience is the wide mood swings which accompany the vacillating positive and negative feelings about the divorce. At one moment the person is high on thoughts of being independent, of being free of a spouse no longer loved. The next moment or day the same person may be crying, longing for the missing spouse and planning an attempt at reconciliation.

Understanding the emotional aspects of the divorce allows one to predict and, to an important degree, control one's psychological state during the divorce process. A later section of the book will teach about the legal realities of divorce in order to prepare the divorcing person to best be able to deal with the courts. This section discusses the psychological aspects of divorce in order to teach people how best to deal with themselves throughout the ordeal.

Adult Developmental Passages

Appreciating the basic facts concerning adult development provides the necessary framework for understanding the emotional tendencies and experiences of those who undergo divorce. For decades psychologists produced textbooks and taught courses on *child* development, documenting the regular and predictable developmental phases from infancy through adolescence. Relatively new to psychological literature are similar descriptions of *adult* development. The development of 30, 40 and 50 year olds is more subtle than that of 1, 6 or 16 year olds, but it is equally significant. With young children, we can notice almost weekly developmental changes. A one year old is clearly very different from a three year old. The differences between adults 31 and 33 years old are less than dramatic.

To understand adult development it is necessary to understand the concept of developmental tasks. Each stage of development has certain tasks which are accomplished as a pre-requisite to further development. During the first year of life, a person's developmental tasks center around physical accomplishments. Parents applaud and are thrilled to watch as their children learn to sit unsupported and later creep and crawl and then eventually walk. The second year of life sees most children begin the developmental task of speaking language. At these young ages, the first developmental changes are obvious and fairly universal. During the pre-school years, learning to be a social animal dominates the developmental tasks as the child learns to relate to friends. During these years, the child also learns appropriate sex role behaviors and begins to develop a sense of right and wrong. The elementary school years involve developmental tasks leading to growth of intellectual, moral, and academic skills. When children become teenagers, they begin to form individual identity and establish sexual preferences. All of these developmental tasks beginning with infancy and stretching through adolescence are reasonably easy to observe. If there existed no other clues to this dramatic development, there are, of course, the obvious changes of physical growth. It doesn't take a degree in psychology to see that a helpless infant who cannot move, communicate, or survive without help, does, with time, evolve into a grown person with all of the physical and mental skills necessary to function as an independent being. It also seems apparent that somewhere between the ages of seventeen and twenty-one, most humans have completed their growth and development. Very apparent, but *very* wrong.

New psychological and sociological insights impressively point out patterns of development past young adulthood and through the middle and later years. I vividly recall the personal shock of recognition that came in 1977 when I read *"Passages."* In the previous two years, I had given up a tenured professorship at a university where I had spent the previous fifteen years. At age forty-four, I moved to a new town where I had no job just because I decided that it was where I wanted most to live. I began carving out a new career and felt uniquely courageous. In fact, I had a whole list of self-congratulatory adjectives for myself until I had the ego-sobering experience of reading in Gail Sheehy's book that somewhere between forty and forty-five men commonly perform a re-evaluation of their life and frequently make major life changes at that time. Not only wasn't I unique, I was even a bit retarded. Had I made the changes at say thirty-seven, I might have considered myself accelerated in my mid-life development. Age 42 would have been average. I wasn't able to get it together until 44, thus placing me in the slightly retarded category. Furthermore, my changes were not even as adventuresome as many others who made major career changes. A university professor who evolves into a private practitioner, still in his field of psychology, seems paltry compared to corporate attorneys who become free-lance artists or housewives who become corporation attorneys.

I consider it mandatory to understand some of the major concepts of adult development in order to understand the psychology of divorce. Without the proper perspective of adult development, divorce can too easily be viewed as a failure of a life task. The underlying assumption with the "failure" hypothesis is that once a life mate is chosen (at age 16, 26 or whatever), the fully mature adult should be able to continue to grow and find contentment in that relationship until death do part. A simple appreciation of how adults develop shows how unrealistic that assumption is. A man before twenty may well have needed a wife-mother type mate to meet his sub-twenty needs. At a later age, this same man should mature to a state where he requires less mothering and a more intellectually stimulating, recreationally energetic companion-mate. Likewise, women who at younger ages may appropriately desire a protective provider during the time of having and raising children, later may develop a distaste for caring for others and feel a deep desire to find meaning through a career outside the home. If people happen to develop (change) at similar times *and their new needs continue to be compatible,* the couple could continue to be satisfactory partners.

However, just as people differ in their physical growth rate, there are also differences in rates and directions of psychological change. Adult development involves changes in values, morals, energy patterns, life goals, styles of relating, focus of interests and activity levels. There are certain trends which most people generally follow. There are ages at which most people focus on establishing financial security and/or parenting and usually later ages when most people begin to focus more on community needs or dealing with their individual life problems. However, there are more differences between people's adult development changes than there are similarities. Think of your high school friends. While your lives and goals may have been rather similar at age 15 or 20, there are probably now wide differences in lifestyle and ambitions between the members of your high school class.

It is no one's fault that Janie and Johnny's deep friendship from age four to age twelve ended when Janie became a head taller than Johnny, and had changed her social preferences. Jane simply no longer wanted to spend most of her free time with baseball and Johnny had no desire for Jane's new interests. Similarly there is no failure involved when Jane and John's marriage of nineteen years ends when at age forty-three, Jane no longer feels her identity as a mother and homemaker is meaningful, and she seeks a new career. If John is also ready, and even needs for Jane to alter the goals and role preferences she had at twenty-four, then the relationship can continue with some changes that will enhance their marriage. If Jane's or John's developmental changes are not mutually compatible, then a major change in the relationship, such as a separation, divorce, or altered marital style, may be necessary.

Viewed in this light, a divorce (as one solution to the John-Jane tale) does not represent any failure, but rather an example of a couple continuing to support each other positively. It is crucial to look at why this logical explanation for divorce is, at this point in our cultural history, no more widely known, to say nothing of accepted. The reason most people can not consider divorce a positive developmental step is because in the recent past it simply wasn't true. People did, in fact, choose their spouse and their career for life, because until recently, our culture and society produced strong pressures demanding that careers and spouses be maintained throughout life.

Toffler's *"Future Shock"* and *"The Third Wave"* document ever faster rates at which our culture is not only making dramatic changes, but insisting on change. Technologically produced changes have rendered all curriculums but those in our elementary schools largely irrelevant. We live during a unique time in history when adults can no longer predict what the future will be like and so cannot plan what skills school children should be taught. It has become essentially impossible to predict what our schools can offer children that will not be obsolete ten years hence. That was not the case for our parents. They know that basic math, physics, auto mechanics, business machinery skills would be as useful in 1980 as in 1950. They were wrong. But they didn't know it. Our parents knew that a person who held one job for twenty years would be a more valued employee than one who had five or ten related jobs within a twenty-year period. They were wrong about that, too. The flexible, adaptable person who has not been stifled by doing things the same way for twenty years enjoys many employment options in this technologically fast changing world.

For a long time the sociological changes in our society had lagged behind the technological ones. But now, our world has been drastically altered through social changes in which there have been drastic re-evaluations of men and women's roles, work ethics, and moral, spiritual, sexual, and ethical values. One major consequence of these recent cultural changes has been to force adults toward continuing change and growth throughout life. This push toward continual adult development is resulting in changes in the form and structure of all human relationships.

The institution of marriage, like the institution of the family, has already gone through drastic cultural changes and is now becoming essentially obsolete in the forms known to our parents. Though family life and marital commitments will certainly undergo further revisions, some things cannot change. The human needs for air, food, and intimate relationships will remain realities.

Intimate relationships already have changed from those experienced by our parents. Marriages do not last for decades as they once did. Families used to have an extended form in which three or four generations and innumerable relatives lived close together. Today, the nuclear family is more typical, where only the mother and father and children live together, often geographically separated from family roots and relatives. Furthermore, families no longer stay in a single location. Today, families relocate at least once a decade. The most current trend is a further limiting of family life. The nuclear family of mother, father, and children is being replaced by increasing numbers of single parent families or open marriages or households which consist of live-in friends and lovers rather than blood relatives.

Society is changing faster than ever and with it adult roles and lifestyles. It follows that the patterns for intimate relationships must also change.

Divorce is now a very common experience. Although divorce may never be considered a normal developmental task, such as learning to ride a two-wheel bicycle, that may be because the whole institution of marriage in its present form will be obsolete even before the ten-speed is replaced by the solar variable speed helio-autoplane. Whatever unpredictable future lies ahead for committed, intimate relationships, today we still live in a culture in which marriage is a way of expressing commitment.

The point is that the end of a marriage today should not be considered as it was in the past, a failure at best, and a criminal, punishable action at worst. Consider the possibility that divorce is just our current awkward style of changing good and growing relationships. The life-long classical marriage may no longer be viable for our current culture now that our world offers a myriad of relationship styles potentially as rich and fulfilling as the older style marriage till death. One should not suffer guilt or recriminations from a need to end a marriage which no longer meets the individual's or the couple's relationship needs. When people realize that ending one formerly satisfactory relationship can be an indication of positive development, then there is no need for the anger or hate which are too frequently the mechanisms by which people justify divorce. Couples who understand the parting as development can maintain friendships and even love relationships with former marriage partners. Divorce rarely means that one or both individuals have failed to mature. Divorce may rather testify to the growth of individuals who can celebrate the divorce as the beginning of a needed new chapter in their lives.

Because we no longer need to depend so totally on another to cook or bring home the bacon, we have the luxury of being with a mate who meets current emotional needs. It is a rarity to choose someone who serves those needs for a lifetime and whose needs we meet for a lifetime. As necessity is the mother of invention, we can rest assured that future relationship styles will encourage easier methods for making and breaking important, though nonpermanent contacts with others.

The Tyranny of Habit

An aspect of divorce which is often misunderstood is the pain associated with changing from the marital to the single state. This pain is misunderstood when it is thought to come from some need or longing for a partner. Actually, much of the suffering results simply from changes required by a new lifestyle. Many emotional struggles surrounding divorce can be avoided by appreciating the unbelievable amount of power that habit has in our lives.

Physical separation from a spouse forces changes in a thousand aspects of one's daily routine. Much of the trauma attributed to divorce, in reality, is the painful breaking of entrenched habits. It serves the divorcing person well to know the difference between the suffering caused by the loss of a relationship and the suffering due simply to living under drastically new circumstances. When these crucial differences are understood, the hurt can much more effectively be remedied.

It is probably impossible to overestimate the role habit has in our lives. People are blissfully unaware of how much their comfort is dependent upon having things the way they are used to having them. Consider revising all your habitual ways of doing things for just one day. If you changed only the majority of how you normally go through a day, you would feel grossly disoriented and physically ill. The feelings are not unknown to the newly separated. The problem is that the newly separated usually attribute such negative feelings solely to their needs for the estranged other. In fact, what is missing is not a person but their own usual routines.

Imagine waking up at a new time to a different alarm, getting out of a strange bed in a strange room, and dressing in different clothes. Further, consider preparing a breakfast of new foods, eating it at an unusual pace in different surroundings, going to some unfamiliar work, involving different people with different views of reality from those to which you're used to. It is difficult to imagine the strangeness such circumstances would lead you to feel. It is wrong to assume that all of the strangeness would be felt as negative. Many daily routines are happily altered with vacations which are usually pleasant, although they certainly involve drastic changes in routinized ways of being. However, many people become slightly ill on vacations. Vague anxieties or actual physical upsets are common on vacations. These are due to habit changes even though such changes were voluntarily chosen to enhance the quality of life. Vacations usually offer sufficient relief from daily responsibilities that the ill effects, caused by changing habits, are offset. If, on the other hand, the habit changes occur non-voluntarily (e.g., being fired or injured) then the negative effects of the change are strong and exaggerated. Vague anxiety can be translated into concrete fears which the person cannot stop worrying about.

It is not that people can allieviate the pains of divorce by looking on its brighter side, but it helps to be able to realistically distinguish between difficulties of separation and the difficulties associated with major habit alterations.

An example: Imagine a situation where a wife, by her own choice, separates from her husband of 20 years. Even though she may have been tormented for years by the marital conditions, almost everything written on divorce will warn her to expect periods of questioning her divorce decision and to expect to suffer aches for the missing husband. Divorce seminars, divorce counselors, and divorce support groups offer help to get over "the death of the relationship." All such divorce aids are designed to teach that the majority of pains, fears, and strange disorientations evolve from a natural mourning over the loss of the bastard. It takes a lot of brainwashing to convince her that she is suffering from lack of contact with someone she knows was not very nourishing to her. But because "experts" tell her it is true, and she is keenly aware of some kind of suffering, she finally believes she must endure months of mourning as if a cherished loved one had died.

The danger in this is that of any incorrect diagnosis: it leads to inappropriate treatment. The "experts" may advise her to concentrate on more effectively killing the relationship so that the quicker death can cause the period of mourning to end sooner. She may be taught to concentrate on all the negatives of the relationship, to have no friendship with her former husband, and certainly not any continuing sexual intimacies. Why are such techniques inappropriate? Because:

1) Her former husband is not dead and there most probably will be a continuing relationship with him and certainly an important one if they have children.

2) If she is successful in convincing herself that her former husband is a villain, then she may experience a diminished self-concept since she fell in love with, married, lived with and could not help change such a rotten human being.

3) She must deny herself the positive aspects of the relationship which may either always have existed, or more usually, are capable of being resurrected in a relationship that at one time involved such valuable aspects as love, respect, nurturance, friendship, and deep caring. There is also the extremely valuable aspect of long term relationship, a shared history, something that no new relationship can duplicate.

In spite of the objection to the death-like interpretation of divorce pain, it is undeniable that divorce does generate some legitimate grieving. There are genuine losses connected with most divorces and so sadness, tears, yearnings should be expected. The important thing is to distinguish between grieving for real losses and the artificial mourning for a dead relationship. The relationship need not be dead and certainly should not be killed in order for the person to effectively cope with the emotional changes that come with adapting to a new life as a single.

The reason the "experts" can sell the period-of-mourning is that undefined but clearly deeply negative feelings are usually experienced with divorce. Many of these are best dealt with by knowing how much discomfort is due to habit changes. Soldiers returning home from war, long hospitalizations, or even prisoner of war camps go through a long readjustment period of stress and despondency. These soldiers are like divorcing people who are confused by the negative mental state that accompanies what is certainly a positive, wanted change. The fact is that changing any habitual patterns involves anxieties and periods of despondency. How to best deal with the negative response to divorce is the topic of the next chapter.

CHAPTER 3

Strategies for Dealing with the Psychological Stresses of Separation

The concepts of adult development and habit strength described in Chapter Two, are the theoretical underpinnings for the techniques described in this chapter for minimizing the negative emotions suffered by many as they leave a long term relationship.

The emotional hazards that come with divorce are rooted in very real handicaps and stresses. For example, a divorced woman whose only career has been her family may have a very difficult time getting financial credit. In addition, learning all the necessary steps in order to gain credit will promote the additional anxiety which accompanies establishing any new set of habits. The degree to which this woman realizes that her pain is caused by anxiety specific to learning new skills (i.e., doing things in non-habitual ways) and not by missing Harry, the easier the solution to the pain becomes.

There is another major aspect of adult development which is promoted by the divorce process. Learning to deal with credit, laundry, new social situations, or any other task required for independent functioning provides a move away from dependency and a positive adult developmental task. Achieving more effective self-sufficiency does not mean no longer being capable of enjoying or needing intimate relationships. What it does mean is losing the undesirable need to have another person take care of you. Dependency is a characteristic of children rarely charming in adults. The healthiest and most satisfactory relationships between adults occur between independent, capable people. It is much more satisfying to have a stimulating, contributing companion rather than a needful childlike adult. Divorce does provide an invaluable opportunity for becoming a more independent and better functioning adult.

Sex Linked Problems of Divorce: Writing this section gave me a strong sense of optimism. It became very obvious while outlining typical male and female problems that today's trends indicate that in the forseeable future people will look at the listed problems as incomprehensible. It will seem ludicrous that people once lived in such an "unnatural", sexist culture in which men required mother-like figures to provide them with meals and laundry and freshly made beds, or women needed some father-like figure to pay the bills and protect them from the politics and problems of the market place.

In the 1980's many newly separated women still suffer problems associated with entering the world of commerce. Their poor knowledge of finances and lack of economically rewarding careers are the result of a world where females were raised to be homemakers and child rearers. Male victims of divorce often still present themselves as dependent cripples who require someone, wife or housekeeper, to cook their food, launder their clothes, and provide all those home-centered comforts essential to daily living. Not only have males not been raised to deal with homemaking tasks, but they've been considered effeminate if they did enjoy such tasks.

One aspect of our current sexist culture which is not changing quickly enough is the inequity that exists in the search for appropriate romantic partners. Men have the far more favored position in a world that cherishes youth and beauty. A fifty year old male can date women half his age without suffering much disapproval. In fact the man of fifty dating women in their twenties is likely to be praised for his virility. On the other hand, women dating men twenty-five years or even fifteen years their junior are likely to be credited only with picking up all the bills.

In other areas, society is harder on men. Men, who traditionally have a very hard time gaining custody of their children, are expected, nevertheless, to accept not having real life contact with their children. Fathers who have only limited visitation rights are asked to pay the bills yet forfeit opportunities to expand their emotional attachments with their children.

There is a wide range of problems linked to the sex of the newly single person. Rather than listing them all, consider the following sexist points that apply to both sexes.

First, society needs to eliminate the differential incapacitating expectations based on the sex of an individual. Sex linked expectations have produced artificially dependent beings who need to pair off to survive. Society is slowly making changes which discourages the need for anyone to *have* to couple in order to meet basic needs. When two people decide to become a couple so they can gain a stimulating, loving lifestyle, it enhances personal growth: when it is done as a survival technique it impedes personal growth.

Two: divorce is not necessarily a negative thing today. It pushes both men and women toward becoming more independent, fully functioning adults. If the change thrust upon divorced people were understood as both the man and the woman giving up dependency habits that have been handicapping them, it would be less likely for them to frantically seek out new versions of their former mates. To quickly find a live-in replacement disallows the golden opportunity for what is probably the best adult education course available— singledom.

Non-Sexist Problems: Many problems suffered by newly divorced people have nothing to do with any culturally imposed limitations, but are the resurrection of the individual's pre-marital problems. All who marry have not chosen marriage for the best reasons. Frequently, people marry as a solution to a serious life problem. Some of the more classic problem-solving reasons for getting married are:

- Escaping from oppressive parents.
- Finding a parent surrogate.
- Needing a partner to perform unwanted life chores.
- Providing a parent for wanted or existing children.
- Avoiding loneliness, boredom, sexual frustration, or jealousy.
- Forming a social unit more acceptable to one's business, peer group, or family expectations.
- Proving one's worth by attracting and "catching" a satus or sexual symbol.

In any combination these could provide justifiable reasons for matrimony, however, they more often, at best, are poor solutions for developmentally arrested adults. Marriages based on these reasons are very limited in their capacity to offer long term contentment.

Although many people have dealt with these limitations in marriages of long duration, such marriages tend to perpetuate rather than solve the individual's developmental problems. When such marriages end in divorce, the person is faced with having to either grow or again marry to avoid the same problem which necessitated the last marriage.

Those characteristics of dependency which force people to marry should be considered genuine mental health problems. They are impediments to successful living which may be eliminated through formal psychotherapy, maturing life experiences, or a number of other forms of education. Marriage can alleviate certain dependency symptoms in the same way that enough pain medication can relieve a severe toothache. But alleviating symptoms is not a cure.

One problem of the newly single comes from the fact that the marital state can actually cripple otherwise healthy individuals. Consider how marriage typically works. Imagine a marriage between mentally healthy adults who decided to marry for all the positive reasons people can choose for the intimate sharing of life. They loved waking up together, solving problems together, raising children together, and gaining the intellectual and physical gratifications they consistantly received from each other. However, even for this hypothetically ideally matched couple, marriage has some built-in disadvantages. The major one is that the natural division of labor that comes with marriage can establish rigid habits and dependencies. After a relatively short time, it's easy to get hooked on having another person assume responsibility for roughly half of life's tasks. The effects of such dependency habits are witnessed when the newly separated make statements like, "I really thought I was losing my mind." The reasons for this mental disorientation comes from taking on the vast number of tasks that used to be performed by the mate.

Another disadvantage of marriage is revealed when the newly separated state, "I can't believe how much I miss X." This cry testifies to a confused mental state in which the person believes it is the spouse's absence which underlies their pain when, in fact, it should be correctly attributed to any or all of the following:

- Not as easily or automatically being able to have money, sex, a social partner, babysitter, tax consultant, housekeeper, decision maker, grocery shopper, etc.

- Having to do many new tasks without having the skills or inclination, or time to do them.
- Not being able to enjoy many familiar things while having all the skills, inclinations, and time to do them; for example, having a partner for bed, tennis, book reviewing, experience sharing.

People long married tend to misinterpret these needs or desires as due to a missing mate. Unmarried adults develop the skills necessary to deal with such needs.

Some of the most difficult aspects of being single again have to do with very subtle functions—not the obvious yard work or taxes, but rather that collection of responsibilities given unconsciously to a life partner. Take the spending and saving of money. Couples usually strike a delicate financial balance by, without discussion, delegating the role of spender to one and the role of saver to the other. The spender learns to depend on their spouse for the necessary financially conservative force in the family. Likewise, the saver learns that all of life's wonderful little extravagances will be produced by their spouse. Even if there were continuing battles over money management and this was, in fact, a major impetus for the marital split, the newly single spender will find it painful relearning financial responsibility, and the prudent partner may discover problems in learning to spend money without needless guilt and worry.

The many subtle and usually unconscious roles adopted in marriage become hardened into very potent habits. For example, the role of being the partner who usually initiates sexual activities may be much more ingrained than is realized until dealing with a new sex partner.

Many major functions in life are divided between a couple, and all the duties assigned to one's mate must be newly relearned when a person becomes single. Having to change so many of one's established habits has a higher potential for causing pain after separation than missing the particular personality that had been responsible for handling those tasks.

Another collection of important habits are those associated and traditionally celebrated with the family. Thanksgiving, Christmas, Easter, and birthdays are all very difficult to enjoy solo. The solution lies in past experience. Most of us left our parental home for school, camp, or some job away from home where we celebrated holidays with friends rather than family. At first, the prospect of celebrating personally important events with new people seems unworkable. However, the alternative of being alone is much worse. Being alone on holidays provides fertile ground for feelings of being abandoned and unworthy.

This section of the book gives specific advice on how to deal with emotional traps awaiting the ill-prepared divorced person. In alphabetical order, the primary negative feelings to which the newly divorced are vulnerable are: abandonment, anger, envy, failure, guilt, insecurity, jealousy, loneliness, loss (children, material goods, non-romantic and romantic friends). Most of the other negative emotions experienced are sub-topics of those listed. Social awkwardness for instance, is a subtopic of friendships. Remorse can be very strongly felt, but it is considered here as a subtopic under failure. Feelings of being worthless, a loser, a reject, are all classified under the more general heading of insecurity.

Before discussing the usual negative emotional traps, it must be acknowledged that there are also a collection of very positive emotional experiences which regularly accompany divorce. Joy, exhilaration, feelings of fantastic freedom, optimism, excitement are all emotions which the newly separated usually feel at one time or another.

The fact that both sets of emotions, the negative and the positive, are both present creates a poignant and almost universally experienced phenomenon for the divorcing person. This phenomenon consists of an emotional see-saw in which people feel optimistic and terrifically energetic one moment and pessimistic and deeply depressed the next. These drastic mood swings can best be coped with if they are expected. Being forewarned about the emotional swings minimizes the feelings of going crazy because of such erratic moods. The mood swings are the emotional equivalent of one's intellectual ambivalence about the divorce.

Almost all who end a marriage have some ambivalence about the decision. Most of us have the foresight to predict the readjustment problems, child care problems, financial problems, and legal problems that automatically come with the decision for divorce.

In addition to these foreseeable difficulties, there is the uncertainty related to separating one's life from the person one was once committed to. Questioning if one has tried hard enough to make the marriage work plagues many. These questions go on: what if only X happened? (X refers to such events as the spouse stopping drinking, dating, being financially irresponsible, becoming more sexually responsive, or more understanding.) No matter how bright and shining the new single life appears, there are enough negatives about divorce to create the conflict which is the basis for the severe emotional ups and downs.

The reason the uncertainty is frequently felt as negative emotions rather than negative thoughts is that making the divorce decision leads to conscious repression of reasons which do not support that decision. Long after people become intellectually committed to divorce, emotions continue the ambivalency battle.

The best thing to do with these vacillating emotions is exactly what is best done with all life decisions which are not 100%. You weigh the pros and cons of each decision for an amount of time and with an amount of vigor you consider adequate. Whatever means you use to make a decision, as long as they are sufficient by your standards, it's important to energetically implement the decisions you reach. You increase your comfort by using all available energy in going in one direction, rather than two. It also helps to remember that you have the power to reverse most every decision you'll ever make. If the divorce doesn't work out you can always get a remarriage.

Helping people realize their ability to alter most decisions is very rewarding to psychologists. It's wonderful to observe the change in personal confidence that comes when people learn about all the life options they have. It's even more wonderful to watch the powerful feeling people gain as they learn how to exercise those options.

The remainder of this chapter offers specific information on each of the listed negative emotions.

Abandonment:

Abandonment involves a collection of fears that are most appropriate during the time one is a helpless child. The usual connotation of abandonment is an incapable child being deserted by a capable adult. Child abandonment is a legal offense. Young children are incapable of coping independently. They cannot fend for themselves and left without a protective adult could perish for lack of food, shelter, warmth, or guidance. Adults who respond to divorce with feelings of abandonment are expressing some belief that they need their spouse for their very survival.

It is not unusual for a capable adult to feel abandoned. Frequently, fully functioning adults experience the feeling upon the death of a parent, especially if it is their last parent. The *feelings* of abandonment that can come with a parent's death, or when losing a spouse are both understandable and inappropriate. In reality, adults do not need another to tell them when to go to bed, what to eat, or what activities will bring them pleasure or are too dangerous. Adults are able to make all these decisions for themselves. Any adult who is unable to make such decisions requires professional help rather than any parental surrogate.

With men, feelings of abandonment are usually connected to concerns about who will take care of them as their mothers once did. If these problems are not squarely faced, the man may, in fact, regress by actually going home to his mother, or by quickly finding a mother substitute with whom to live. Either solution is, of course, less than ideal. When a man's dominant relationship need is for mothering, it not infrequently becomes the issue which leads grown women to leave grown men. There are those who are satisfied by serving as a parent to their spouse. Such relationships can work. They represent complimentary neurotic need systems like a match between a sadist and a masochist. However, most people are not seeking a partner to indulge their most neurotic needs. Most people want to enhance the healthiest parts of their personalities with relationships which stimulate the best part of themselves.

Women frequently demonstrate the mirror image of the male abandonment problem. Women may need a protective father who proves their loveability by paying bills and providing directions. More and more, women's severe dependency is becoming an underlying reason for the end of marriages. The make-me-alive syndrome is one in which the woman feels secure only when her husband tells her what to do, how to do it, and she maintains the expectation that all her recreational, vocational, and all stimulation needs should be provided by him. Without clear direction from a man, the abandonment-prone woman is incapable of enjoying herself. This syndrome is a very sad one in which the woman makes tremendous demands on her spouse because without him she simply does not know what to do with herself.

When abandonment is keenly felt for any extended period of time, the underlying reason is inappropriate dependency. Inappropriate is the key word. It is appropriate to frequently depend on a partner for support, nurturance, love, and understanding. It is, in fact, crucial in a mature relationship to be able to depend on our loved ones during times when fatigue, illness, or frustrations and disappointments render us something less than the energetic, lovable, sparkling personalities that would be attractive to anyone.

Inappropriate dependency can usually be recognized by the anger it generates, strangely enough, toward the person depended upon. The technical psychological term for this is "hostile-dependency." Hostile-dependency is seen regularly in adolescents. Most adolescents, for example, are dependent on their parents for money. The very knowledge of this financial dependency makes the adolescent angry with the parent. The adolescent hates having to ask, beg, or steal for funds and this produces real hostility toward the parents. Hostile dependency is also created because the adolescent knows he or she needs the parent's discipline, approval, guidance and other non-materialistic needs.

Many adults form hostile-dependency relationships with mates, but it creates an unhealthy course of events. The sooner the dependency can end, the better the relationship between the parties can be. Over-dependency of one spouse is a common problem, and if the couple faces it together as a problem, it can be solved and the relationship vastly improved. Alcoholism, drug abuse, promiscuity, over-spending, over-eating, over-working, over-dependency on anyone, over-indulgence with children, are all habits which can, with proper motivation and direction, be changed.

If feelings of abandonment are strong, the best path is to face any inappropriate dependency habit that exists and overcome it. It may be a painful process, but it leaves one with an increased capacity to enjoy relationships, with much less potential for hostility.

Anger:

Anger is *the* emotion of divorce. Folk wisdom encourages it. "Get angry, think of all the dastardly things they did to you." Shockingly, this "common sense" advice is supported by many divorce authorities. Advice from too many attorneys is to generate as much anger towards the former spouse as possible. Lawyers operate, after all, in the adversarial arena and so encourage or even demand anger as a prerequisite to being a "good" client. How to cope with such urgings or one's own inclination to get fighting mad is explained in the following analysis of the reasons, benefits and detriments of anger.

Frustration leads to aggression. Any time one is frustrated there is an impulse to strike out against the source of the frustration. A hungry infant throws the empty bottle. A child kicks the chair he tripped over. An adult bangs down the hood of a car that won't start. The socialization process which civilizes all of us as we mature teaches us not to physically attack the source of our frustration. We musn't hit. Swearing at the car is considered a bit better, but real maturity would be exemplified by simply closing the hood quietly and searching for the best solution to the transportation problem.

However, no matter how civilized we become, when we are frustrated our most basic response is the primative one of striking out angrily at the source of our frustration. A terrible relationship can be a tremendous source of frustration which, therefore, impels one towards the expression of aggression or feeling anger.

There are three ways to manage anger: extrapunitively, toward an outside person or object; intrapunitively, towards the self; or impunitively, toward neither self or another, but with a non-hostile attitude toward the frustration source. The philosophical position in the inpunitive approach is that the event happened and though someone or something may be responsible, no one is to blame.

The intrapunitive approach, blaming oneself, often causes depression, which can be defined as anger turned inward. Newly separated people often suffer depression with its symptoms of sleep difficulties, low energy and feelings of sadness and finding little pleasure in life. It is this depressive syndrome which seems to respond to the friendly folk wisdom of getting angry. Well meaning friends, seeing this suffering of a divorcing buddy, advise them to get angry at their former spouse to turn the anger outward. Be extrapunitive, they are saying.

Striking out at the spouse does work to alleviate the feelings of depression. It is a way of manufacturing energy. It does get the person moving and gives a direction for action. Get the bitch or bastard. Society even provides a formal vehicle for venting of one's spleen: the courts. The settlement and sometimes even the custody arrangements can be the blunt instrument used to bash the head of the one you once loved. And it works. That is, using anger in all its legally allowed forms is liable to effectively relieve the sufferings of the depressed person. The friends are happy that they offered the advice when they see their formerly depressed friend so energized. The attorney is likely to be delighted, and the divorcing person is feeling much better for having escaped the horrors of depression.

But the rub of externalizing anger to avoid depression is similar to that of provoking a war to end a sluggish national economy. War has too many disastrous effects to justify it as a solution, especially if you lose. In divorce wars, everyone loses.

Those who use anger this way tend to exaggerate all hostilities. They decide they have, for years, been ripped off, psychologically abused, and unfairly treated by their spouse. The newly discovered anger not only leads to seeking of revenge on the spouse, but can easily provoke a resolve to never be treated that way again. One danger, therefore, is that they develop the belief that they can trust no one. In extreme, not uncommon cases, these angry people project hostility towards everyone of the opposite sex. We have all experienced being in the company of chronically angry people. The hostility given off is abrasive. Such people are not attractive as neighbors or business associates, to say nothing of friends or lovers.

Perhaps the most hazardous aspect of turning the anger outward is the long term loss of the former spouse. Vicious attacks on a spouse are hard to forget even with time. Such battles cause scarring that hampers chances for valuable post-divorce relationships. Again, ending a marriage does not necessarily mean ending the relationship. If there are children, the relationship automatically must continue. Even if there are no children, businesses, or other reasons for maintaining the association, there are still those reasons which initially attracted you to one another. These can still serve as the basis for a good relationship.

In addition to the use of anger as a defense against depression, there is the fact that anger can serve to maintain a flagging resolve to end the marriage. The ambivalences experienced when divorce is being considered (should I? shouldn't I?) are painful. If one can maintain a head of anger, then emotions in favor of maintaining the marriage are held at bay. The problem with this strategic use of anger is that it is often so intellectually manufactured that it, in the end, causes more ambivalence than was originally present. A person who is angry by design does it awkwardly. Rather than frustrations flowing naturally into anger, the person consciously picks something to believe they *should* be angry about and then simulates rage. It doesn't feel right. Its artificiality bleeds its effectiveness.

Another type of anger misfiring comes to those people who have always been uncomfortable with anger. Perhaps as children they were taught that anger was destructive or evil. Others require massive justification before they allow themselves any expressions of displeasure. Whatever dynamic underlays the habit of repressing anger, when these people ventilate anger, it backfires. Such people tend to store up frustrations until the dam bursts and then an overpowering, inappropriate, and frightening rage erupts. Often, the outburst is so violent that it further inhibits them from a healthy response to frustrations.

Anger, when not artificially designed to avoid depression or to maintain a divorce resolve, can be a very useful and normal response to the frustrations of a poor relationship. Healthy anger can produce the energy required to reduce the frustrations as well as offer appropriate directions for using the energy. If you get furious at your car for continually failing you, kicking it or swearing at it may make you feel better temporarily, but it doesn't achieve the necessary carburetor readjustment or lead to the information that the essential components are in such bad shape that you should replace the vehicle. If you get furious at your relationship for continually failing you, ventilating your anger may mollify you for a while, but it is more useful to expend the anger energy by investigating whether the relationship needs work or whether the essential parts of the marriage are in such bad shape that the relationship in its present form should be replaced.

A careful analysis of chronic anger rarely leads to the discovery that the anger originates from one source, such as repeated late arrivals without phone calls. Rather it comes from more basic matters like meeting one's need for respect, or affection. Once the sources of the anger are identified, then try various ways of better meeting the frustrated needs within the relationship. Continuing anger means that either you have incorrectly diagnosed your frustrations, you haven't found effective ways to satisfy your frustrated needs, or you need a different partner.

Anger, at its best, offers energy and direction. There is a difference between aggression and assertiveness. Both involve the positive characteristic of forcefulness, but aggressiveness involves hostility which produces abrasive and frequently ineffectual actions. Assertiveness involves direct, effective action.

The existence of anger, then, is a natural response to frustration. When its thrust is exclusively directed towards oneself (intrapunitive) or others (extrapunitive) it becomes handicapping. The trick is to make it as impunitive (blaming no one) as possible. When anger is created by a long term relationship, it's important to direct the energy into an analysis of the relationship and make the moves necessary to end the frustrations.

This constructive use of anger involves using the energy and motivation produced by the anger to systematically investigate positive solutions to ending your frustrations. The advantage of this inpunitive approach is that it makes you responsible for the anger without depressing you, the way the intrapunitive approach does or turning you into a vindictive hostile person like the extrapunitive approach does. Anger, therefore, can be not only the most valid emotion of divorce but, if appropriately managed, the most useful.

Envy:

Envy is an emotion which arises from coveting something belonging to someone else. It's a bitter or longing contemplation of another's better fortune. Envy must be differentiated from jealousy. Jealousy, discussed later, is a collection of negative feelings about rivalry for affection. Envy will be analyzed in terms of the two very different circumstances in which it occurs in divorce: envy of others and envy of the former partner.

People who are prone to envy will find their envy increases with stress. Psychologically, envy comes from anxiety about one's self worth. An envious person's anxiety that they are not as worthy as someone else is allayed by believing that the only difference between them and the other person is that the other person has "X." The "X" can be anything—more money, greater height, a prestigious job, good luck, the right parents or car. These envied differences can be real or imagined, large or small, objects or attitudes. The dynamic underlying the envious personality are feelings of unworthiness. "I'd be just as worthwhile as Alice if I were a physician like she is, but since I'm not, I'm not very worthwhile."

Envy is frequently one of the aspects of depression. In depression, the envy focuses on *all* the negatives in one's life. Every life has positive and negative aspects. There are dozens of good and bad things at every point in time which anyone can bring to consciousness and think about. Our health, home, job, finances, family, toothbrush, houseplants, and washing machine are just a few of the thousands of things that can be either going particularly well or particularly not well at any particular time. We have the choice of focusing on the positive or negative aspects of these things. The envious-depressed personality focuses on his or her negative life aspects while at the same time seeing only the positive aspects of other's lives. When the divorcing person suffers a significant increase in envy of others, it usually reflects this envious-depression approach.

The second form of envy produced by divorce is that directed towards ex-spouses. Men may be envied because they have a career which gives them money, purpose, and adult contacts. Women may be envied because they have no career and so enjoy money without work, freedom from a continuing daily schedule, and time for social contacts with adults. This kind of envy encourages anger toward the spouse by fostering the belief that one is still getting the short end of the stick.

Envy can also perpetuate a dependency problem. If only I had him/her, I'd still have the home, social position, silverware, friends we shared that I need to feel worthwhile. If dependency underlies the envy then it indicates that the person needs to develop the capability and beliefs that they can provide for their own needs.

Envy is a difficult emotion because it can dominate a person's thoughts. Sufferers are obsessed with what others have. The best long-term solution involves learning to believe that one can acquire whatever one needs. Working toward an academic degree, earning money, gaining friends or lovers are all therapies which reinforce personal worth and therefore lessen feelings of envy.

Failure:

If 43 of one hundred public high school seniors received an F in the required English course and could not graduate, there would be a furor. The English teacher would probably be informed in no uncertain terms that failing 43% of a class was unacceptable and more reflective of the quality of teaching than the ability of the students to learn. The 43% figure approximates today's divorce rate. This figure alone should convince divorced people that they are not unique failures, but many still believe that they are.

Divorcing people have an exaggerated sense of failure because of the notion they were brought up with that marriages were to last forever. Despite statistical information to the contrary, newly divorced adults feel they flunked the most important course they ever took. Those who suffer the worst feelings of failure find no comfort in facts that 20% of all U.S. households consist of a single adult or that 25% of America's urban children are raised by a single parent. Statistics shouldn't relieve anyone of the responsibility for examining the reasons their marriage was no longer viable, but statistics do justify addressing the cultural as well as the individual reasons.

Each individual involved undoubtedly has some responsibility for the ending of most relationships, and it is certainly productive to recognize that responsibility. But to automatically label oneself a failure because a relationship ends is simply wrong. A person examining their contribution to the end of a marriage might, for example, decide they have characteristics which make a long-term, live-in relationship difficult. If a live-in, long-term relationship is a person's choice, they then need to remedy or circumvent the offending characteristic. Realizing the need to change or modify some aspect of one's personality doesn't justify thinking of oneself as a failure anymore than learning to cook fish in a better way means all former food preparation was a failure.

Instead, marriage today will often end because it didn't allow one or both parties to meet changing needs. Personal failings are rarely the primary causes of marriages not lasting, and selfblame is usually the incorrect reaction. Some people should even be praised for having the foresight and courage to squarely face incompatibilities and undergo the difficult, complicated divorce procedure with the motivation of raising the quality of both lives.

There is a more valid application of the failure-success concept. If one wants to label oneself a winner or loser, a success or failure, then do it by taking measure of *all* of one's close relationships. If you value close relationships then it's important to examine your ability to form and sustain them. How many satisfactory relationships have you been able to enjoy with friends, lovers, or relatives with whom you desire such closeness? If the number or quality of your intimate relationships is unacceptable to you, then you may consider seriously working on your relationship skills. Having to declare bankruptcy is certainly not desirable, but it does not prove that you cannot or should not conduct further business. You may well learn so much from the experience that led to the bankruptcy that you become a much more valuable business associate than a person with greater financial assets but less experience.

In sum, the feeling of having failed is more commonly felt by the divorced than necessary. Statistics demonstrate that it is the concept of lifelong marriage that is faltering. Statistics, however, rarely mollify emotions. Avoiding the trap of feeling a failure is best accomplished by evaluating the marital relationship to determine why the couple's or individual's needs were not being met in the marriage. The best antidote for any feelings of failure are experiences and feelings of success. So, if what one learns from the divorce relationship fosters more successful subsequent relationships, then whatever former sense of failure existed becomes an instructive bit of history.

Guilt:

Guilt is a very powerful emotion most typically experienced by the partner who instigated the ending of the marriage. Guilt can be one kind of anger turned inward—a punishment resulting from a belief that one has or is doing something reprehensible. Labeling oneself an evil-doer in a marriage is difficult because there are few methods of penance available. One less than satisfactory form of penance is staying in the marriage. This act of contrition works in a sense because the person does experience the pain sought to cleanse the guilt.

The problem is that maintaining a relationship which is painful for one person is rarely nourishing to the other person. So the sinner also punishes the victim. Continuing a bad marriage produces a vicious circle of discomfort. If "A" feels guilty about what they've done to "B", then "A" will not like to be around "B" who constantly reminds him or her of the guilt. However, to assuage the guilt,

"A" stays with "B" someone they do not enjoy being with. "B", of course, senses the negative vibrations and somehow expresses a reaction which increases "A's" discomfort with "B" and so on, and so on.

What is needed is not penance, but confession. "A" needs to tell "B" what is making them feel guilty and together, as a team, they ideally should figure out what initially caused the transgression. If the marriage can fulfill or deal with the need expressed by the "sinner," then all is well. If not, the relationship, if it is to survive, must be altered in some way.

Any act which causes guilt should be looked at not as proof that the person is a sinner, but rather that there is something lacking in the marriage. The frequency of the transgressions are indicative of the importance of the needs not being met. One lie about a late afternoon trip to the bar is different from chronic distortions of where one is spending their late afternoons. The latter situation needs to be openly confronted or the guilt alone can be expected to cause destructive alienation between the spouses.

The guilt which divorce counselors hear about most are guilt feelings expressed by one who feels they are deserting a needful spouse. In truth, believing that another cannot survive without the sacrifice of your happiness is much more often arrogance than reality. In spite of the emotional blackmail frequently used by the rejected spouse (I'll die, starve, drink, be unable to cope without you), staying to nurse a dependent invalid serves no one. The one who stays builds up resentments which will certainly be expressed. The spouse becomes increasingly dependent and eventually hostile-dependent.

The question is how much time and effort should a person expend on helping another over dependency before being able to guiltlessly say "enough." A lifetime is too long. The right amount of time is a period which both partners agree to. After mutually agreeing that an over-dependency problem exists, the couple should agree on an amount of time and a procedure for dealing with the problem. If, when that time has expired, insufficient progress has been made, the spouse who leaves should have no reason for guilt unless they stay longer. Clearly, their presence has not been helpful and staying on would only enable the dependent person to maintain those habits which are detrimental to any relationship.

Another form of guilt comes with, of all things, happiness. One person finds joy in some activity that does not involve their spouse and that produces guilt. Understanding that no one should be made responsible for another's happiness is a hard lesson to learn. Certainly taking someone to Disneyland can provide momentary joy. Likewise, lying to someone to make them feel better can produce some artificial happiness. At that simple, temporary level we do effect others' emotional climates, but meaningful, long-lasting happiness is something that comes from within. You can produce happiness in others for a while with acts of generosity. However, there are limits. The ability to be happy cannot be bought for another, either with money or personal sacrifices.

There is no doubt that there is appropriate guilt. Constant stealing, lying, cheating, deliberately hurting another person are all things which should prod our conscience into punishing us with feelings of guilt. The experience of appropriate guilt can be helpful if it serves as a cue for analyzing the reasons for acts which are unacceptable to ourselves. Analyzing the unacceptable behavior with one's partner can be a very productive, loving activity. Figuring out together why one felt they had to lie, cheat, or steal produces the openness that brings closeness as well as leading to the necessary corrective realignments within a marriage. Chronic transgressions without analysis is a crime for which both members ultimately pay. Transgressions of the marital agreements always involve lying and lying involves stealing another person's most precious possession—their reality.

Freedom from guilt causes a surge of joyful energy, and all of us have the right to a guiltless existence. Freedom from guilt belongs to those who know that their right to enjoy life to the fullest involves relationships where each person is capable of pursuing and finding their own joy and is interested in having the other person do the same. Any relationship not capable of producing freedom from guilt should be ended.

Insecurities:

Every human being is periodically the victim of insecurities. This is because all humans share the history of having been needful children who knew that we could not survive without help. In addition to the universal experience of infantile dependency, everyone has undergone a number of personal frightening events that stamped into memories documentation of terrifying inadequacies.

The divorce situation has certain built-in elements which automatically produce an emotional recall of early insecurities. The experience of being without someone who has provided some basic needs recalls, perhaps unconsciously, our most dreaded childhood fear: desertion. Three-year-olds are keenly aware that they cannot, themselves, obtain or prepare needed food or shelter. Young children are terrified by the thought of being abandoned by their parents. So they cling to parents and panic when they lose sight of them sometimes even for an instant.

Even though a person may be a very self-sufficient adult and not a helpless child, the divorce experience can resurrect the old fear of abandonment. The insecurity related to abandonment is much more potent for those partners who did not want divorce and thus experience more the feeling of having been left. The spouse being left further compounds the feelings of desertion by judging themselves a loser, or worse, an unloveable creature whose inadequacies have finally resulted in having to fend for themselves.

In divorce insecurity orginates from unconsciously equating the absence of someone who met some of one's needs with the desertion fears of childhood. To deal with the insecurities that come with divorce, you must recognize that you are quite capable of learning to acquire for yourself the things formerly provided by your spouse. Even better is the realization that you can meet your needs better than was possible in the non-working marriage. You may have to work to change some habits to do so. It helps to realize that the necessary habit changes produce a growth that will make you a happier, more independent person whose very independence makes for a more desirable partner. You need to know that you can learn to handle taxes, run a washing machine, create a satisfying social evening, shop for socks or provide a playmate for yourself. Not being able to do these things as an adult is only a result of not having gone through the learning process. A pre-school child doesn't yet have the physical or mental capabilities to accomplish the tasks of independent daily living. Adults do and the sooner they get past the initially awkward steps of learning, the sooner the insecurities dissipate.

Another positive result of overcoming insecurity is that when you become less dependent and learn you don't *need* another's help, you can avoid the disastrous solution of finding another parent surrogate to meet those needs. Some people advise recently separated people to quickly form another close alliance. The warning about quick re-alliances, however, is that they should not be where they are made to meet certain immature needs. That permits a continuation of arrested development which prevents reaching the desirable goal of being a fully functioning adult. This does not suggest that the newly separated should not find someone to enjoy socially, sexually, or any other way that meets one's *adult* needs. The danger being pointed out is using someone to fulfill needs once satisfied by parents that one feels incapable of fulfilling themselves.

Without sounding "Pollyannaish" about divorce, it is simply true that a major benefit of divorce can be the push toward achieving one's individual adult potential. The correlary to this is that it is more difficult to achieve and maintain one's individuality within a couple relationship. In the ideal couple the attraction comes from the exper-ience of each offering the other a range of creative and stimulating input, a commitment to the other's expressing their individuality, and a reluctance to meet the other's inadequacy needs.

There is an important lesson to be learned from couples in which the death of one results in the death of the other shortly thereafter. Typically, this happens with older couples who over the years have become exclusively dependent on each other for certain needs. Perhaps the most primary of these needs is the one for intimate companionship. When one dies, the other is left without the capacity to form intimate connections with others. Without someone to understand, care, and touch you, and you them, you are liable to die. Younger adults just feel as if they will die or that they want to. At advanced ages, the malady is, in fact, fatal.

Maintaining the capacity for building and sustaining intimate relationships is much like building and maintaining physical health. It must be worked on regularly or, with years, it becomes increasingly difficult and eventually impossible.

Insecurity as felt at the time of a divorce, involves a collection of minor fears such as not being able to get your taxes or laundry done, but the major insecurity is of not being able to achieve rewarding intimate relationships. The point being reiterated here is that the more functional you are (able to meet your own needs) the better your chance of finding mature, stimulating people with whom to share your life. Conversely, the more dependent you are, the less appealing you are to others.

One other type of insecurity is that referred to in that old joke in which the psychologist announces to his patient that he is not suffering from any inferiority complex, it is just that he *is* inferior. That is, in addition to the many valid developmental reasons for two people splitting up (e.g., different development growth rates, changing life goals, identity conflicts, new loves, or conflicting life directions), there is also the possibility that one person has genuine inadequacies no longer tolerable to the other. In this case, the feelings of insecurity are legitimate responses to psychological limitations. The question is how to determine if feelings of inadequacies are grounded in reality. It is always difficult to be aware of our own weaknesses. However, when there is a stressful, life-changing event such as a divorce, the rational assessment of personal problems becomes even more difficult. Egos weakened by the stresses of divorce may well exaggerate minor personality problems way out of proportion. There are two useful steps to follow to determine whether there are significant inadequacies that should be addressed.

First, gain an objective evaluation of any suspected negative characteristics. Your estranged spouse may be more than willing to provide you with an extensive list of your inadequacies, but they cannot be considered objective. Nor are most parents or close friends able to be truly objective. Mental health professionals, encounter group experiences, or appropriately trained physicians or ministers can frequently offer the objectivity needed. Mental health professionals may be the best source as they not only have expertise at diagnosing personality problems, but further can offer a variety of treatment strategies. Furthermore, there are mental health professionals specifically trained and experienced in dealing with the problems of divorce.

Second, decide if you are, at this time, motivated to deal with any objectively determined problems. Every human being at any given time has a large collection of less than perfect ways of being. We are overweight, under stress, over drinking, under sleeping, over working, or under-sexed. Only the individual can decide when and if they want to expend the energy required to remedy any problems.

Some expert may be able to determine the significance of a problem, but only a motivated individual is capable of successfully coping with it.

To summarize; experiencing insecurities during divorce is common and in most cases can be traced to childhood fears of desertion. If the insecurities are rooted in inappropriate adult dependencies then changing dependency habits is the best solution and helps prepare one for fuller, more satisfactory future relationships. For problems other than dependency, it's important to gain objective assessment of one's personality and then make decisions about where and when to get help.

Jealousy:

Jealousy is one of the most painful of all human emotions. It will be described, its source explained and treatment strategies offered.

Jealousy is an excrutiating feeling which is a complex mixture of loss, resentment, anger, sadness, and deep hurt. It is sparked when a person one loves is suspected or known to have an affectionate/romantic interest in another. Some people feel jealous only when sexual activities are involved or predicted or expected. For others, friendship, shared activity, or a glance toward another is sufficient to produce jealousy.

Both the acts that produce jealousy and the responses to it are quite variable. Like anger, jealousy can be externalized, as in a jealous rage, or internalized, as in a suicidal depression. Jealousy, therefore, cannot be defined by what provokes it or how it is expressed. Jealousy can be defined by two underlying causes; fear of loss to a rival, or actual loss to a rival. This definition demonstrates that jealousy can be a quite rational emotion. The possibility of losing someone you love to a rival is a legitimate fear. There is also an irrational form of jealousy which will be discussed later.

The degree to which the rational form of jealousy is felt is usually determined by the degree of insecurity in the relationship. The more insecure you are, the more jealous fear you are prone to feel. If you are unsure of a partner's love, then every contact they have with potential rivals promotes the fear that they will find the other person more attractive and choose to leave you for them. There are two sources of insecurity in a relationship: first, the overt or covert actions of the loved one, and second, the person's own beliefs about his or her lovability.

A loved one acting as if they are seeking a replacement, flirting, or having an affair, is the first source of jealousy. Being ignored or receiving less affection often stimulates jealousy. Coping with jealousy stimulated by the actions of the loved one involves open communication. Through honest discussions it is determined if their actions are, in fact, indicative of a weakening bond between you. In some cases, the simple communication that it would please you if they were less flirtatious is enough to sufficiently limit the behavior on their part and the pain of jealousy on your part. Other times this open communication leads to complicated discussion of both party's needs, expectations, and interpretations of life events.

Simple or complex, jealousy created by another's behavior requires good communication. Jealousy is too painful to suffer silently, and keeping your fears to yourself doesn't work because the fear incubates and grows. If you don't trust what is communicated or the words don't calm your fears, then seek a professional's help. Counselors can help open the communication between couples whose habits prevent useful give-and-take discussions.

The second source of jealousy springs from an individual's belief that they are insufficiently lovable to retain their loved one's attachment. Again, the most straightforward approach for dealing with this apprehension is through communication. In "Fiddler On The Roof" it took the husband over thirty years to ask his wife in song, "Do You Love Me?" When one experiences jealous pangs it is a good idea to find out if you are loved. To find out, ask. All of us possess an uncanny ability to know if another person is telling the truth. If we trust our feelings we can be human lie detectors. Everyone always knows how another person feels about us. The trick is to allow ourselves to really ask ourselves how another person feels about us. It takes some courage to face the truth, but it is better than living with unaddressed doubts.

In order to effectively get the information, the communication between the two people needs to be clear and direct. It is very easy to tell if any communication has been useful. If the communication has been useful, the jealousy will disappear. You will either be convinced of your lovability or begin dealing with the loss of the relationship. If the jealous fears remain, again, some form of counseling may be necessary to clarify the situation.

So the first kind of rational jealous fear is the anticipation of loss of a loved one to a rival. Its cause is insecurity and its cure is based in direct confrontation of the insecurity. There is always some hesitancy about direct confrontations, but like a fear of a dread disease the most appropriate step is to confront the fear with a diagnostic visit to a physician. If you want to rid yourself of the fear of losing your loved one, that is, jealousy, then confront the fear.

The second kind of rational jealousy is an actual loss rather than a fear of loss. It occurs when you, in fact, discover or know that a loved one loves someone else in a way that is unacceptable to you. Here, the relationship loss is real rather than imagined, suspected, or feared, and the emotion felt is actually envy, not rational jealousy. The process for understanding and dealing with envy has been discussed in an earlier section. The distinction between the two emotions is very important. If your loved one, in fact, is involved with someone else, but loves you also, then the emotion is jealousy. That is, you are afraid you will lose your loved one because of their love for someone else. If, on the other hand, the person loves someone else and not you, then the emotion is envy and should be dealt with as such.

Whatever label is assigned to it, envy, jealousy, or green-eyed monster, there is no question that the cruelest pains of all occur when one discovers a loved one is involved in a romantic-sexual relationship with another. The blind violent reactions known to occur with such discoveries and the sympathy evoked for one who suffers such pain has lead to a uniquely sympathetic legal defense: crime of passion. The uniqueness of this defense is apparent in the reversal of opinions concerning the perpetrators and victims of such crimes. The victims of crimes of passion are treated as if they deserve to be beaten or shot, while the term "injured party" is reserved for the husband or wife who committed the violent act. This reversal of the usual approach toward the commitors and victims of other violent crimes testifies to the understanding of the suffering of those whose loved one chooses another romantic mate.

There is also a strange, or at least illogical, aspect of this very strong emotion of jealousy. An overwhelming majority of both husbands and wives who engage in extramarital affairs state that *they* are capable of having additional sexual partners without it having any meaning at all for the primary relationship. The same people claim, however, that if their spouse would engage in extramarital sex, it would be catastrophic to the primary relationship.

In other words, many people feel that they can have casual love and/or sex relationships and maintain their primary commitment toward their partner, but that their partner is incapable of multiple sexual-love relationships without threatening the primary relationship. Furthermore, many people act on this assumption. They decide not to reveal an extramarital activity because of the belief that it would cause *unwarranted* concern from their spouse. However, a revelation of a spouse engaging in the same acts with the same motivations, is greeted with some green-eyed monstrous response.

Though jealousy itself may be illogical, it's important to learn how to deal with it effectively. The first rule is not to dwell on the specifics. Spending hour after hour obsessively visualizing one's spouse in a romantic/sexual situation with a rival only increases suffering a thousand fold. Difficult though it may be, distraction is the best method for mimizing jealousy-envy pain. One has absolutely no control over things that have already occurred so no amount of thinking can change the past.

All of us are really quite experienced with distracting our minds from certain unpleasant thoughts. We tend to forget dental appointments and very infrequently contemplate our own deaths. However, distracting one's self from thoughts which seem to think themselves, without our permission, can be very difficult. Jealousy epitomizes the kind of compulsive thoughts over which we have little control. One method of distraction is to keep extremely involved in ego enhancing activities, activities that make you feel better about yourself. Engaging in sports at which you excell can produce "winner" feelings as well as giving you confidence in a healthier, more attractive body. Egos can be enhanced through adult education courses to increase vocational or avocational skills.

Athletic and academic pursuits do work to promote feelings of self-worth, but the most helpful activities are social. To feel socially viable, to have friends, especially friends with romantic potential, helps one feel wanted, desirable and capable of meeting these important social needs. Social activities may not eliminate the hurts, angers, or disappointments of envy or jealousy, but they will provide the most effective diversion from the pain of obsessing on the specifics of the loss.

Irrational jealousy, when the fear of loss occurs without realistic basis, can be characterized as "over-jealous," and requires a different method of coping. The underlying cause of overjealousy is a deeply rooted sense of unlovability which prevents reasonable reassurances from curing jealousy. If a person doesn't like himself, he believes that anyone who knows them intimately could not possibly maintain an affection for him.

The treatment of irrational jealousy based on lack of self-regard must be individual psychotherapy. Deeply rooted dislike of self simply cannot be effectively altered by ordinary life events. Massive doses of love offered by another (the common approach so often attempted by mates of the overjealous) are incapable of reassuring the person who believes themself to be unlovable. The only effective cure is "uncovering psychotherapy" in which the original reason for not feeling loved as a child is revealed and discarded.

A common case of a less serious form of irrational jealousy is one person misunderstanding the actions of their partner as meaning rejection. In this case, one partner believes certain behavior doesn't affect the couple's commitment, while the other reacts with extreme jealousy. Couples benefit by being very clear with each other about what constitutes acceptable or unacceptable behavior since people tend to have widely different ideas as to what is or is not acceptable within a relationship. Some people suffer irrational jealousy when their mate joins a once-a-month club which has only members of the same sex. Other people do not feel any jealousy if their partner has sex with a variety of others, but do become jealous if their partner begins to have repeated sex with one other person.

In other words, jealousy is subjective and no one can say what would be just cause for another's jealousy. Each person, therefore, needs to let his partner know the things that are tolerable and intolerable to them. Those actions which are threatening to either partner should be carefully discussed to avoid irrational jealousies.

Irrational jealousy is very dangerous because of its self-fulfilling nature. When a mate's behavior is perceived as threatening, the threatened person can easily act in ways which, in fact, make them less attractive. They may inappropriately demand more of the other person's time or affection, and this pressure lessens the quality of the relationship. When their partner begins to pull back from the increased demands, the jealous one is convinced their fear of the partner leaving is real. In this way, the prediction that one's partner cares less can be turned into a reality.

The best prevention is, once again, communication. When one begins to feel even a twinge of jealousy, they must promote a threat-free discussion of their concerns. A clear agreement as to what is and is not acceptable must be worked out.

It may seem that this discussion of irrational jealousy is not relevant for a divorce manual and, rather, belongs in a marriage manual, but as people go through separations and divorces, emotional feelings run rampant, and many forms of jealousy are keenly felt at one time or another. The more you are acquainted with the forms of jealousy, the better prepared you are to deal with it.

Divorcing people are often shocked by their own jealous feelings about a spouse whom they were sure they no longer cared for at all. This form of irrational jealousy reveals the often unconscious truth that they do retain important positive regard for the person they once chose as a mate. Viewed this way, the positive feelings and, therefore, the jealous feelings that arise are not so irrational. Such feelings can be understood not as a reason to resurrect a relationship that no longer serves, but as a positive aspect of the relationship which argues against complete disregard of it. Positive regard may not be a basis for continuing the marital relationship, but it may be the basis for some future genuine friendship and/or love with a former spouse.

There is another approach that not only works for all forms of jealousy, but works to improve the quality of all important relationships. It is a way of reducing fear of loss of another. If you can reduce this fear you automatically undermine the potency of jealousy. The way to accomplish this does *not* involve devaluing any relationship, rather it involves enhancing them. Nor does the method include or even encourage watering down primary relationships by having other important, intimate relationships. It simply involves gaining security through the knowledge that you do enjoy such high level skills in relationships that you are confident in your capacity to create them.

The connection with jealousy is obvious. Knowing you can build meaningful relationships reduces the dread of not having relationships and this minimizes jealousies. Compare it to the business world.

To feel secure that your economic needs will be met by a business does not require a collection of businesses which may only hinder you because you are too scattered and inefficient to give any one business the attention it requires. What is important is the confidence that your business acumen is so high that even if your present business failed for any reason, you could successfully start and run another business.

The way to gain a high level of security in relationship skills is by having more open, authentic, and deeper contacts with present partners. A law you can apply to relationships is that in general they either improve or they deteriorate. Relationships, like businesses, seldom remain at one level. They grow or die. Thus, it's important to do the work necessary to make your relationship increasingly meaningful.

Working on relationships means improving your ability to relate verbally and physically. Practice hearing and responding to others, as well as making yourself clearly heard and getting your needs met. These are the talents which increase capability in all relationships. If you lose an important partner for any reason, you should mourn and understand the loss, but high skills in relationships guarantee that you won't be incapacitated by the loss because you know you have the ability to create other rewarding contacts. Skill at relationships offers the basic security for current relationships because it diminishes the fear of loss which fuels the destructive emotion of jealousy.

Loss and Loneliness:

Loss and loneliness are said by many divorce experts to be its most dominant feeling. Mel Krantzler, author of "Creative Divorce," describes divorce as an emotional crisis triggered by loss. This strong emphasis on the aspect of loss is the result of the number of people who seek professional help to help them overcome their suffering. Few of those exhilerated by their new freedom seek out mental health professionals.

For many people, most often the ones who initiated the divorce, their only loss is a frustrating relationship. Rather than feelings of loss, these people are in touch with gains. The freedom to be able to make independent choices is thrilling to many newly divorced people who are happy to be able to say, "I can be myself again," or "Now I'm free to find someone who cares about the real me."

Exclamations over the pleasures of divorce are not limited to those that instigated a divorce. Frequently, those who out of tenacious habit clung to a non-nurturing relationship and fought to avoid divorce are the very ones who after the separation admit to feeling great. "Since I discovered I do not need another person, I feel freer and happier than ever. I found out who the hell I am, and I prefer my own ways of doing things."

This positive introduction to the analysis of loss and loneliness in divorce is offered as a reminder that while losses can be very strongly felt, they are by no means universally experienced. In cases where the negative emotions of loss and loneliness are experienced, they should not continue on for months and certainly not years. If either loss or loneliness persists beyond a few months, then professional help is needed. There is life after divorce. The divorce professionals help long suffering victims by guiding them through breaking the habits or initiating the changes that are necessary to provide for a better life after divorce.

The four areas of loss after divorce are: (1) loss of material goods and possessions, (2) loss of children, (3) loss of friends, and (4) loss of a love partner. There are other losses, such as loss of direction, purpose, or happiness, but these are actually related to the four primary losses.

Material Losses:

During the extended period most people are married, they gain material goods in two ways. First, they acquire certain things to be shared, such as a home and its furnishings. Second, they acquire things as individuals, but because of living so closely with one another, the objects for all practical purposes seem jointly owned. An automobile, or simply a phonograph record bought for oneself gets used by both.

The legal division of material goods is discussed in the property settlements section of this book. This is the consideration of the *emotional* response to the fact that about half of what is felt to be one's own is lost in a divorce. Some of the things lost seem essential to living. The loss of a home or the income one has learned to expect are losses very hard to handle.

The most important thing to remember during the division of material objects is that *both* people are losing about half of their material goods. The problem of working out a property settlement so that neither person feels ripped off is very difficult. Fighting over property can serve as an excellent battle ground for maintaining anger, and there are many who use anger to help them deal with the separation from a spouse. A mutually agreeable settlement is almost impossible when done through the legal system. People are often advised by their attorneys not to even talk to their spouses about property. They advise that bargaining be done by the attorneys who usually do not know the emotional value attached to the objects, are committed to the most advantageous distribution that they can obtain for their client as opposed to "fair" distribution, and are usually limited to court precedents for dealing with disputes.

I'll illustrate this last point with an example from my personal settlement. When Carol and I worked on dividing our things, we did it as described in the section on property settlements in this book. That is, we discussed how much each person valued each object and then worked out trades that made sense to us. It went relatively smoothly, and when it didn't, we decided to wait a day or two and try again. Eventually we reached decisions on all of the personal property with the exception of two objects highly valued by both of us, our backpacking tent and a buddha. Our final decision was to continue to jointly own them. The tent is used by whoever is backpacking and the buddha alternates between our two households. Although courts have no precedent for such a property settlement, they are quite willing to agree to most settlements to which the parties *and their attorneys* agree. The trick is to have attorneys willing to aid you in implementing settlements you reach based on *your* evaluation of material goods and not on the market value of objects. People's feelings of loss are rarely limited to dollar value.

Regardless of how the settlement is handled—with love, kindness, and a sense of fairness or with hostility and revenge—there is still the fact that you have to deal emotionally with losing half your property. One thing to remember is that you have done it before and loved it.

Almost everyone has had the experience of leaving their parent's home. Usually that home contained many material things which were ours to use and enjoy. TV sets, dining room furniture, kitchen utensils were just a few of the hundreds of things we used daily. We took those comforts of home for granted but happily left when it was time for us to find our own identities. Most people were delighted to be free of parental domination no matter how subtle or velvet gloved it may have been. Not many left feeling great pain over the living room chair that was no longer regularly available to them.

Certainly, there are major differences where the analogy between separating from parents and spouse doesn't hold up. Most of us knew that we could, at times, return to our parent's home and those material comforts. We may even know that we'd inherit the silver or crystal. The differences do not detract from the point that when most people leave their parental home, they leave behind a lot of material possessions and that those losses are barely felt because of the elation over the gains in independence. If the newly separated can celebrate that same gain, the sting of material losses is reduced.

There are other positive attitudes which help deal with the material losses, such as having fewer things to maintain. Possessions can be burdens and having less of them allows indulgence in the now popular vogue for living lightly in the world. But the leaving-the-parental homesite analogy is the most useful insight for dealing with two concepts: "breaking habits" and "furtherment of adult development." Divorcing adults are hopefully more mature than when they left their parents which means the learning of new habits can be done with less awkwardness and more dramatic leaps in personal development than are possible as an adolescent.

Loss of Children:

When young children are involved in a marriage that's ending, there is usually a custody arrangement which makes one parent the live-in custodial parent and the other the visiting parent. How these awesome legal arrangements are best accomplished is covered elsewhere in this book. Again, the focus of this section is the emotional aspects of the loss.

First of all, as is true with material possessions, both parents suffer considerable losses. The primary parent who may be considered the "winner" in any custody battle loses, for instance, the day-to-day freedom of having a second parent to take over or at least provide adult contact for some part of the time. The primary parent is also in danger of becoming the basic disciplining parent which can present such an unfavorable contrast to a visiting "Disneyland" parent. The primary parent further loses the children's special sense of anticipations of visits gained by a loved non-custodial parent. So the custodial parent has the burdens of all the regular responsibilities of childrearing with less relief, help, or specialness. There is the further problem that children tend to blame the custodial parent for the loss of the visiting parent. That is, the custodial parent is often viewed as the villain who ended the happy family fantasy many children maintain in spite of whatever unhappiness they witnessed.

The obvious losses of the visiting parent often include one not so obvious special pain. Although they may have a strong desire to separate from their spouse, they rarely have a strong desire to lose regular contact with their children. I know of no words to describe the anguish I have seen in and out of my office or the courts when a parent realizes that they are going to be living without children they cherish.

There is a strong source of solace available for dealing with the losses both parents experience. This is the determination to develop deeper and more meaningful relationships with their children than they had prior to the divorce. Doing so is a very constructive, healing accomplishment, and it is equally feasible whether you live with or across the country from your children. It does not require studying books or taking intensive courses in order to vastly improve the quality of contact with your children. It can be done by activating the five ideas about to be offered. They are not difficult and they make sense. They can make the difference between a divorce causing painful loss for both you and your children, or leading to a change in your relationship to them which provides everyone with a genuine sense of gain.

1. Children as Friends: For most of your lives your children will be non-dependent adults rather than needful children. In fact, the time may come when they are the more competent adults. Witness the usual needs of people in their 70s or 80s requiring at least physical help from their children. Because of this, we should all work on developing genuine friendships with our children. Too often, circumstances require that as responsible parents we must authoritatively direct our children's lives. Those times should be balanced by times when the authority is set aside. We may play, talk, or even work together, *but as equals.*

For example, every child has some game or activity they particularly enjoy. Let the child direct you in doing their preferred game or activity. It can be enlightening to allow your child to be the leader or teacher for a change. One of the most powerful experiences in my life was having my 13-year-old boy teach me to rock climb. My son generously and patiently talked me through my considerable fears about heights and climbing. I was amazed at his sensitivity and knowledge. The whole experience taught me genuine respect for him, the lack of which had been part of our not getting along. Shared recreational activities can be a prime road to friendship with children especially when you can give up the role of director, teacher or leader.

Talking *with* our friends is, of course, an important activity. However, we tend to just talk *to* our children. It is a bad habit. When adults talk to other people's children, it is often with respect and an obvious desire to listen and communicate on a fairly equal basis. Yet when these same adults talk to their own children, their tone and manner communicates their feelings of superiority.

I was shocked one evening during a special night out with my 8-year-old son. My wife and I had had a quarrel which I was unsuccessfully trying to forget so that I could mentally, as well as physically, really be with Tyler. For the first twenty minutes I tried nodding my head and "uh huhing" my way through our time together. Then my preoccupation with the quarrel prompted me to say, "I'm sorry I'm so distant tonight. I can't seem to stop thinking about a fight I was having with your mother." Tyler then looked directly at me and like the most mature and insightful friend sincerely explained how he understood and said he felt I should go back home, deal with mother, and reschedule our special evening for another time. What was most astounding to me was not his clear understanding or wisdom, or even his non-selfcentered solution. It was the change in him while he was explaining his ideas to me. I saw there was a real person inside of this child's frame who was able to make a surprise appearance once I stopped treating him as an immature inferior.

Working with children can also promote friendships. While children are young, the best work experiences involve preparing for an immediate event. Making ice cream for dessert or packing a family picnic are ideal tasks for young children. Older children are capable of working with parents for non-immediate goals. Planting a garden, building an addition to a home, or earning funds for a family vacation can all involve older children and foster a comradery with parents. When working with children to promote parent-child friendships, it is best if the adult can create the atmosphere in which the parent is not in the role of "boss."

Dramatically improve your friendships with your children and the divorce may only hasten the loss of dependent and distant children and the gain of more meaningful relationships with your own children; a prize not won by many parents, married or divorced.

2. Children as Individuals: Parents with more than one child have a detrimental, though understandable, tendency to deal with their children as a group. Meals, rides, vacations, any times that include children tend to be times when all the children are included. Parents act like camp directors, and the children's group response eventually leads many parents to behave like concentration camp directors.

Understand that siblings ae natural rivals. Furthermore, children in the company of other children relate to the adult present in a more infantile fashion than if they were with the adult in a one-to-one situation. This is true whether the child is six, seventeen, or twenty-two. The solution is simple. Spend time with each of your children individually. Whether such quality times are fifteen minutes a day or a month, they are the prime times for getting to know children as rewarding individuals.

The fact that one-on-one time works magic for improving parent-child relationships is really not so unusual when you think about it. Imagine trying to become intimate with someone when a third, fourth, or fifth person is around. A group presents almost unsurmountable difficulties for getting close to one other person because you and the other person must be constantly aware of other ears, sensitivities, and needs.

To enjoy the many advantages of the one-on-one relationship, the custodial parent should make sure there are regular times with each child (meals, trips, recreational events) in which *all* other people are eliminated.

The visiting parent should do the same. It may be very difficult to find times to be with each child individually when you have only limited visitation time for all your children, but if you are aware of how essential one-on-one time is, you will be able to create such times. The loss of one's children comes not from divorce, but from not experiencing them as individuals. To find your child, separate them from others.

3. Children as Priorities: To a child the loss of divorcing parents comes from two sources. There is the obvious physical absense of one parent and the less obvious loss of the live-in parent caused by that parent's added responsibilities, draining emotions, or a new social life. Whatever the reasons for reduced parent availability, the child's perception of loss can be dramatically reduced if the parents give the child information as to exactly when the absent parent will be totally present.

If a child circles a date on a calendar and depends on that for their next contact with a parent, then insecurities born of parental absence are drastically dissipated. Physical hunger is most manageable when you know when you will be eating. Not knowing when you will eat again psychologically increases the hunger pangs. The same is true when the pangs of desire are for contact with one's mother or father.

Furthermore, when the child knows that the parent has reserved a special time for them, it reassures the child that they, in fact, are an important priority in the parent's life.

It works for adults in much the same way. Knowing when you will really spend time with your child again—not just feed them, get them to school or to the dentist—brings adults a similar sense of security about their relationship with their child.

Frequently, divorcing parents undergo painful guilt reactions because they feel they have deprived their children of some essential parenting. When this happens, parents worry that their children may withdraw their love, respect, or liking for the parents. Reserving private times to be with each child provides for both parent and child a structure for mutual reassurances of a continuing affectional bond.

Two aspects of scheduled contact times between parent and child are of utmost importance. The first is a logistical matter. If the parent needs to reschedule, the rescheduling should be done for an earlier rather than for a later time. Rescheduling for later often seems to the child like a cancellation, which can bring on fears of desertion. If plans must be changed, you should inform the child as soon as possible and reschedule for an earlier time. The closer the planned event, the higher the anticipation and the worse the disappointment.

The second, and most important aspect of reserved times is that they be of a frequency and duration which allows them to be positive. If either parent or child is tired, preoccupied, or bored the basic purpose of enhancing the relationship is defeated. Everyone always knows if another person is truly enjoying a contact. It is, therefore, essential to plan for amounts of time and types of events that can realistically be expected to provide for good times. Don't let guilt or any pressures lead you to spend more time with your children than you expect to actually enjoy. It is better to underestimate the amount of time you and your child might enjoy together and leave with a hunger for each other than to overestimate and part with a sense of relief that the contact is over.

Careful time scheduling gives your child the important message that you are with them because you plan and choose to be with them and not because of an obligatory responsibility forced on both of you.

4. Children as Communicators: Communication involves alternating between being a sender and being a receiver of messages. Effective communication requires the capacity to accurately receive messages and effectively send clear messages.

Most adults have a collection of seriously bad habits for communicating with children. Consider the fact that children, from a very young age—perhaps as early as three—feel their messages are better understood by peers than by adults. Given the option, most six-year-olds would rather communicate with another six-year-old than with a sixty-year-old. It is true children will seek out adults to have certain needs met, but for real give and take they are likely to choose another child. It isn't true that this preference is primarily based on mutual interests. Children simply are able to make themselves better understood with other children rather than with adults.

One reason for poor adult-child communication is that many adults talk to children in stylized, infantile ways that underestimate children's level of understanding. This typical adult error is usually coupled with the belief that although children can be cute, they surely have nothing to say that adults don't already understand better. These adults talk at, not with, children. They believe that anything more complicated than, "Pass the salt," is beyond the comprehension of anyone under 12. This serious under-estimation of children's capacity seems to come from some pompous need to always be the "teacher" with the young. Adults are constantly giving children lessons, directions or orders of some kind or another.

Many children, after years of getting only primary instructions from grownups, learn not to listen when adults speak. They eventually tune out, just as any adult would do with anyone whose messages were limited to instructions or commands. All people have this understandable tendency to ignore people whose dominate messages are directions on how they should be, act and behave.

In addition, adults too frequently do not hear the messages children send. Children use a different language than adults. Children's language style is more direct, more emotional and less verbally articulate. Adults are generally unable to interpret the body language which is a major source of messages sent by children. When my first child was less than twenty-four hours old, I picked him up for the first time and he began to cry. My wife, from the bed across the hospital room, said, "You are too tense. Relax." I relaxed, and he stopped crying. That was my first and rather complicated communication between myself and my day-old son. The two-way communication began when I informed him that I was tense. He received the message that I was tense and sent back his message that my tension made him uncomfortable. Through that magic of maternal understanding, even across the room, his crying and body language was translated for me by his mother. I then sent him the body message that I was able to give up the tenseness and he, in turn, let me know that he felt more comfortable.

It is not that children speak in some language that rational adults cannot understand. It's adults, unfortunately, who often speak an irrational language. They lie. As people mature, they seem to learn to use language to mask their real feelings. I was doing this when I had pretended to respond to my son while I was really obsessed with thoughts and feelings about an argument with his mother. As soon as I stopped lying and verbalized my true feelings, my son understood. Children are better able to authentically experience and communicate emotional truths than adults. Or rather, adults suffer from being highly skilled at using language to hide their emotions. Whatever impediments to useful communication between adults and children exist, there are four techniques that help overcome many of the difficulties:

1. *Verbalize, as best you can, your authentic feelings.* Children can usually sense your feelings anyway, and when they recognize the consistency between what they hear you say and what they feel is happening with you, they begin to trust you and expect to be able to communicate with you.

2. *Much of your talking with children should be unauthoritative and non-directive.* With children, engage in conversations that are more entertaining than informative. A great conversational exercise with children is to tell stories about the dumb things you have done recently or as a child. This allows children to see you as more like themselves—human, and it gives you practice at being less defensive and more open with children.

3. *Create an atmosphere in which your child can talk to you about anything with no chance of its resulting in a lecture or a punishment.* Children don't believe adult statements that they should feel free to talk to you any time about anything. Telling them that this is a special time when they can confess to anything without fear of consequences sometimes allows them to open up. Sometimes children respond to a challenge to tell you things they think or do that they are sure you would not approve of. Be prepared to be shocked. Be prepared to stick to your no-consequence promise, and be prepared to know your child better.

4. *Sometime ask them to explain why they can talk to a particular friend, maybe a particular adult, more easily than they can talk to you.* If you don't get defensive and are able to convince them of your genuine curiosity and desire for better communication, you can learn a lot. If you list for the child what they do that makes communication tough for you, you'll be most successful if you limit yourself to one critical point for each three critical points that they share about you.

If you can gain improved communication with your children, it will be easier to deal with the loss of their daily presence or with the burdens of being the live-in parent.

5. Children as Love Objects: Psychotherapists hear from patients about their depressions, physical ailments, inability to deal with realities, difficulties in relationships. But the most frequent problem underlying all these symptoms is that they feel unlovable. Then,

therapy commonly works through the collection of superficial reasons patients feel underlay their unlovableness. Initially, the reasons are superficial: they say they are unlovable because they are too fat, too thin, dependent, independent, angry, sad, or suffer from a severe case of ring around the collar. As therapy progresses, however, they discover that they feel unlovable because one or both of their parents conveyed the terrible message that they weren't good enough to love.

Perhaps the parents didn't spend enough time with them, or criticized and never praised them, or demonstrated more concern for a sibling. Maybe they overpunished the child, or sent the child away too early or too often, or used the child as an extension of themselves and pushed the child toward a particular achievement. The parents might never have bothered to know the child as an individual, or blamed the child for something and made him feel unworthy, or shamed the child and made him feel guilty about existing, or used withdrawal of love as a punishment device. Parental disapproval may exist in many subtle forms and every human experiences it, but if it is strong enough and constant enough, it finally impairs the functioning of the child and the adult that grows from the child.

There is no doubt that almost every parent has at some time been guilty of some of these things toward children whom they really loved. It just isn't possible to be a parent without occasionally making your child feel inadequately loved. However, parents need to be aware that each time they reject their child, it affects the child's belief about his or her lovability. To compensate, there needs to be many times when parents do things to reassure the child about his or her worth and lovability.

Some important ways parents make children feel loved:
1. Choosing to spend quality time with the child.
2. Praising children and letting them know what you value about them.
3. Making special efforts with children who have a reason to feel unfavored (on a short or long-term basis).
4. Learning about your child's expectations, ambitions, and goals for themselves, then supporting those so that the child understands that you respect their individuality.
5. When you are correcting children, take the time to make sure they know that you are teaching something you have confi-

dence they are capable of learning well. Emphasize their positive capabilities, not their mistakes.

6. Instead of using shame, guilt, or withdrawal of love as a way of disciplining, work out with the child *ahead of time* what "punishments" the two of you should use to help them learn to change.

7. Try to use rewards to change behavior as often as you use punishments. Rewards are not bribes. Bribes are used to motivate people to do something they shouldn't do—like policemen not issuing tickets. Rewards are a form of praising children when they do what they should do.

Giving children a feeling of being worthwhile is not a complicated procedure. I once worked at a child guidance clinic where families typically traveled for hours to bring their "problem" children. During the first three visits, background information was gathered, and no advice or treatment was offered. By the second or third visit, it was common to hear parents report a dramatic improvement in the child. This was, of course, before the clinic team had "done" anything that could be considered treatment.

The thing that caused the improvement in the child was that the child was getting a clear message that their parents cared about them. The child felt that the parents were taking time and expending energy for them. Such attention is no minor matter. It made many children feel loved enough to significantly reduce the symptoms that brought the family to the clinic.

Another way of helping children feel loved is the opposite of the carefully scheduled times previously described. A child feels loved through small, spontaneous gestures. Children, like adults, are pleased when someone, for no specific reason, surprises them with a gesture of caring. One way to remember to indulge your children with a surprise is to make a special mark on your personal calendar, say once every other week, and when you come to such a mark, do some unexpected small thing for your child. Telephone or write them a note saying that you're thinking about them. You could purchase an inexpensive token to let them know that they were in your thoughts. You could plan an unexpected visit, send an unbirthday gift, write a note to put in the child's pocket, prepare a special dessert, buy a record or tape in *their taste* in music. Any spontaneous thing will do. If you don't use a personal calendar, use some periodic event in your life to serve as a spur. Your haircuts, menstral cycle, dental appointments, exercise class, or times you have contact with Aunt Molly can serve as reminders that you should do some unexpected thing for your children, so when Aunt Molly calls or you get a haircut, you will remember to reach out warmly to your child.

Let your children feel your love, feel lovable, and their relationship with you and everyone else in their lives will be better. It is by far the best gift, the most precious inheritance, you can give your children.

Loss of Friends:

There can be a negative feeling of separateness and loneliness that comes with the physical separation from a long-term mate. One easily becomes used to having another person around regardless of the quality of that relationship. A new pet, a constantly playing TV, and temporary roommates are common, quickly acquired substitutes for the missing spouse. The newly separated adult who is living with children may experience a very severe loss of and need for adult company. Most often, separated adults feel alternately both the joy of having space to themselves and a desperate longing for companionship. Some crave romantic involvements, others do not. Some seek solitude, some do not. But most all newly separated people scarch for and need the companionship of friends.

The loneliness experienced by divorcing people is not as compassionately understood by most friends as the loneliness suffered after a loss by death. Divorced people, even though divorce is so common, are often stigmatized. They may be treated as if they have done something evil, as if they have a disease, or as if they have damaged the community. People who have insecurities about their own relationships fear single people as competitors for their partners, or as frightening demonstrations that their own marriage could end. So though the newly separated may be in special need of support and reaching out by friends, it is frequently not offered.

There are ways to understand and overcome the reluctance of our friends to be with us, and there are ways to deal with loneliness. When people live as a couple, the majority of their friends tend to be other couples because they are very convenient social units. There are the correct numbers for bridge games and balanced dinner parties.

When couples have children, there are built-in conveniences and compatibilities that allow you to exchange babysitting and ideas about schools.

Even without children, there is a feeling of compatibility with other couples who have chosen to be part of a committed couple, as you have. There are common grounds for discussions about relationships, lifestyles, money matters, or vacations. In part, this compatibility between couples exists because there is freedom from the potentially threatening presence of unattached singles.

When you separate, you suddenly become an unattached single, and you can expect a certain awkwardness to develop with your coupled friends. First, they may be confused as to whether to offer congratulations or condolences. Second, you no longer fit easily into the convenient social unit. You may be shocked to find that, as an unpaired adult, you might suddenly be seen either as a romantic rival or as an unwanted advertisement of the advantages of being single.

Furthermore, you may discover that it was your former mate and not you that the other couple enjoyed. Or you may newly realize that you've never enjoyed an independent friendship with either member of the couple and that for you they were primarily a social convenience.

There is also that phenomena labeled loyalty, as applied to divorcing couples. If your divorce involves alienation between you and your spouse, then those friends who knew you in your married state may decide they must choose sides. They fear that any friendly times with you will be interpreted as an affront to your former spouse. Even if you had a divorce like mine—one specifically planned and executed to enhance an already good relationship—your friends may not believe it or understand it. Whether the divorce is friendly or not, many former friends steer away from the newly separated in order to avoid taking sides.

But none of these reasons need deter you from approaching them. With effort and understanding, you can maintain any friendship you wish. You may choose not to relate to old friends as a couple. The same rationale for becoming closer to children by spending individual time with them also applies to adults. Genuine friendships are most liable to arise out of one-on-one time. The procedure for dealing with couples who have been friends is to select those individuals you want as friends, then *you* initiate the contact. You can, of course, also maintain friendships with couples. Although there are potential difficulties, they should not discourage you from any relationship you are enjoying as a newly single person.

Not only friends but relatives can offer rewarding support systems. People ignore the rich potential for friendships with former in-laws; and if you are really adventurous, you might consider making an overture of friendship toward your former spouse.

Sexual and Asexual Friendships:

All friendships can have an erotic facet, expressed or unexpressed. Also, there can be erotic relationships which are not friendships. All relationships are living things which can change. A former love affair can evolve into a non-sexual friendship or visa versa. All friendship and/or lover relationships tend to be worked out anew once the habits one has had with a former spouse no longer provide the rule book for your relationships.

There are many pressures impelling the newly separated or divorced towards sexual-romantic friendships. The habits or appetite for regular sexuality can be one source of pressure. The need to see one's self as desirable in the eyes of another is a strong need for some. Long frustrated desires for a truly supportive intimacy is a major impetus for some. Today's sexual freedom may be another pressure. Face-saving motives and the need for status motivate many toward a publicly visible romance. And then there is the relief from loneliness. Some people believe that the only way not to be lonely is to be romantically involved.

There are no all-purpose formulas for avoiding these pressures that make so many feel they must quickly seek a romance. The best solution is to work at being a good, supportive, and understanding friend to yourself while experiencing those early gyrations of separation. Understand that you may respond to the stresses and pressures of divorce by doing things you later will not do.

Overdependency on parents, revival of ancient relationships, homosexual encounters, promiscuity, and drastic changes in dress, social styles, drug or alcohol use, financial or religious habits may all be explored by those living through the pressures of divorce. Sympathetic tolerance and a sense of humor are needed while learning new life styles. The wide emotional swings already discussed are matched by vascilating ideas and behavior. Expect them, and be non-judgmental, especially of your wilder flights. Think of drastic behavior changes as proof of your bravery, as your appropriate risk-taking courage, rather than as indications of how deranged or lost you are.

Self-friendship or self-respect, in addition to self-tolerance, involves taking care of oneself. A common way of expressing caring for friends is to help them get what we know they will enjoy. Develop self-friendship by doing the same thing for yourself. Think about what would please, stimulate, relax, or excite you and then be an indulgent, generous friend and help yourself explore each possibility. You needn't, for instance, be seen out on the town to impress others with your lively social schedule if you realize that the most loving thing you can do for yourself is to luxuriate in a bath and go to sleep early.

The primary strategy for combating the loss of friendships some suffer with divorce is to make sure you are friendly with yourself.

The second line of defense against loneliness is the ability to have a good relationship with others. Non-romantic intimate relationships will be discussed first since the longest lasting romances start with deep friendships. It is certainly possible to have an erotic-sexual liaison evolve into a friendship or love, but it is rarer.

Knowing what pleases you will help you better choose friends who have the qualities, skills, or interests that can engage you. Good friendships consist of mutual respect, stimulation, trust, courtesy, and shared interests, but the most important ingredient is that you like the other person. It is a kind of magical connection: you enjoy spending time with them, root for their well-being, and feel you can trust them to care for the real you. People simply feel more comfortable about themselves when in contact with friends.

A friendship in which *all* these qualities exist is relatively rare. People with healthy personalities usually have several friendships, each one of which is valuable because of a special blend of ingredients. There can be one friend with whom it is easiest to discuss intimate and personal information. Another friend could be your best rock climbing buddy in whom you have infinite trust with a rope but not with a confidence. Your goal should be to have a variety of friendships because you want to be able to be with the friend whose company, at that moment, nourishes you.

Friendships are not things that happen, they are things you build. They can be built on a foundation of shared experiences. They can be built quickly, on a foundation of open communication. Talk with people who have been at a well-run encounter group, and you'll hear a testimonial to the depth of contact that can occur between strangers within a very short time. The key is open communication.

Picture yourself at a social gathering largely populated with strangers or slight acquaintances. When you engage in conversation with a relative stranger, *you* choose the level at which you will relate. There exists a continuum which ranges from very closed communication in which you exchange impersonal information, such as ball scores, to open communication in which very personal feelings are revealed. Between these open and closed extremes there are the levels of contact in which subjective ideas or opinions about politics, books, or social trends are discussed. At typical cocktail parties people exchange rather impersonal information and some minor personal information. People tell others where they live, their occupations, or some major interests. That level of contact, at best, will allow you to arrange for a squash game or concert date. Unless there are strong, nonverbal messages being transmitted during the conversation, that level of verbal contact is too superficial (too closed) to make adequate judgments about the potential for a friendship.

In order to investigate most effectively and enjoyably the possibility for meaningful relationships, one needs to move as rapidly as possible towards open communication. Practice giving up the introductory information in favor of an early sharing of personal opinions, moving toward the open expression of current feelings. Openly communicating the real and unique aspects of yourself certainly does not guarantee the creation of a friendship. There is at least an equal chance that you will discover that this is a person you don't care to know better. If your needs are for a squash partner, you may decide to plan a game despite this; athletic compatability might provide an enjoyable two hours every month. But, if you are looking for other, deeper qualities of friendship, you need to move on.

The advantages of using open communication are that it spares you the boredom of small talk, allows you to quickly estimate the chances for a meaningful contact, and trains you in a communication style that builds and maintains intimate relationships. The simple chart on the next page represents a rating scale of the quality of your conversations to test how openly you converse with any other—stranger, acquaintance, friend, or lover. You can determine where your conversation began and how deeply it developed. Do your contacts produce the level of contact you want? As basic as the scale may seem, it can serve. The closer you approach the open communication end of the scale, the deeper the contact, and the less isolated your life.

Most people who are capable of close relationships prefer making genuine contact with people and find cocktail talk disagreeable. To be sure, there are times when travel directions or a cake recipe is exactly what is wanted. This section, however, deals with loneliness and hunger for friendship. If you're experiencing social deprivation, then developing more open communication skills will be helpful. Risk moving along the scale at your next opportunity. If you are unable to make the kind of contacts with people that make both of you want more contact, you may decide you need the help that a sensitivity, therapy, support, or consciousness raising group offers.

The worst attitude is that being divorced automatically hampers one from developing friendships. It doesn't. You need to be confident that you can develop friends at any level you choose—at the level of shared hobbies, occupations, social backgrounds, ideas, or at the more intimate levels of shared feelings. About half of newly separated people have a strong need to communicate at the more intimate end of the scale. The other half loves the aloneness and tends to luxuriate in the freedom from dealing with anyone but themselves for awhile.

Another dimension of friendship, in addition to intimacy, has to do with give and take. The three essentials about giving are: 1) don't keep score; 2) be generous; and 3) give even when it is not expected. The three essentials about taking are: 1) risk by *clearly* asking for what you want; 2) allow yourself to receive; and 3) don't interpret unfulfilled requests as rejection.

One should also avoid the questions which can undermine friendships: 1) Why don't you call me as often as I call you? 2) Why don't you know what I want without being told? 3) How does this friendship rank with your other friendships? 4) Who is getting the most out of this friendship? 5) What is the future of this friendship? Friend-

Figure 1—Quasi-Quantification of Quality of Conversations

CLOSED TO OPEN VERBAL COMMUNICATIONS

CLOSED - OPEN

INFORMATION	**IDEAS**	**OPINIONS**		**FEELINGS**	
Non-Personal - - - - - - - -	Personal - - - - - - - -	Common - - - - - -	Original - - - - - - - -	Past - - - - - - - - - - -	Current
				Others - - - - - - *Self*	
Reports:	Occupation	Political	Drugs	Fears	
Weather	Vocation	Educational	Friends	Ambitions	
News	Residency	Economic	Life Styles	Desires	
Public Information	Marital Status		Peeves	Weaknesses	
	Religion			Pleasures	
Directions:					
Travel					
Cooking					
Health					

0	25	50	75	100

CLOSED COMMUNICATION   OPEN COMMUNICATION ships are demeaned when evaluated in these ways and are richer when they are free of measurements and comparisons.

Sometimes non-romantic friendships become romantic and sexual. Folk wisdom warns that sexual encounters can ruin a good friendship. Folk wisdom is wrong—or, at least, often inaccurate. Newly separated people tend to experiment with many new ways to meet many new needs. Things may be tried that don't work out. It is better to risk meeting needs in a new way than to do nothing and be miserable. Divorcing people need to be able to experiment with the knowledge that they will not ruin their lives by some action which later turns out to be undesirable. Attempting to include sexuality in a formerly non-sexual friendship may or may not work out. But if it doesn't, it needn't destroy the previous friendship. It can be another shared experience that enhances the friends' mutual understanding.

All important friendships contain the element of love, but when you add the erotic aspect, the nature of that love is altered. And what is love? The English language is inadequate when its single term "love" defines a wide variety of positive feelings. I love my mother, skiing, English muffins, my dog, Mozart, my wife, and Saturday Night Live (the original cast). These are clearly not all the same emotion. Regardless of the differences, most people can easily differentiate between loving a friend and loving a lover. Almost everyone feels that without a lover something important is missing from their life.

The natural desire for intimate, loving sexual partners eventually motivates a divorced person to seek romantic contacts. No matter how discouraged about the complications, that basic desire for a romantic connection can usually be counted on to overcome the pain of previous unsuccessful relationships. Statistics say three out of four divorced people remarry. It may be that the popularity of formal marriages will decline, but there is little doubt that the human desire to couple will continue.

Another failing of our English language is certainly documented by the words available to define the mate seeking procedure. "Dating" sounds like a cute adolescent form of socialization. "Courting" produces a feeling of antiquity comparable to somebody noting how "spry" you are. "Cruising," definitely has the connotation of someone looking for a one-night stand. "Affair" implies that some kind of secret sexuality has begun. "Having a relationship" is so overused that it hardly describes anything. A proper term for the procedure should accurately describe it. What people are engaging in is "Actively Investigating Relationships With A Potential Partner." As AIR-WAPPing probably will not catch on ("who are you AIR-WAPPing"), this book will settle for the term dating.

Also needed is an acceptable term for the people who are selected to AIR-WAPP, or, rather, date. Most of us are uncomfortable with terms like suiter, boyfriend, mistress, paramore, beau, lover. As friendship is such a fine start for a romantic relationship, friend seems the closest appropriate word. Furthermore, only slight voice inflections are necessary to change the word "friend" in ways which clearly communicate the exact nature of the relationship.

Successfully dating again as single person requires new attitudes, a sense of purpose, and guidelines. A helpful attitude to have is that you will be learning new dating skills. You should not think that you're resurrecting old skills that may go back to your adolescence, since both you and society have changed.

The sense of purpose when dating can be understood by comparing it to that in adolescence. Dating at that time is done without pressures for long-term commitments. The major motive for going out as a single adult, as with adolescents, is because you are anticipating a pleasant time. You should feel free to go out with a particular person for as long as there are more positive than negative aspects. Dating, initially, is a time to discover who you are *now* and what you enjoy about spending time with another.

Of course, before you can begin the discovery, you need to find potential partners. "Where can I find likely men?" "Where are all those available women I heard about while I was married?" Everyone comes in contact with scores of men and women everyday in super-markets, church, concerts, business, school, or just walking down the street. Yes, you say, but how can I actually meet those of the right age, marital status, lifestyle, or appearance that I might want to investigate further?

By sending out signals.

It's most often non-verbal communication that is used to make others aware of one's attraction and availability. I have had patients who believed they wanted to date but who unconsciously were not ready. They were, perhaps, too anxious, or still emotionally involved with their former mate or feeling too unlovable to risk it, so they just couldn't seem to come across any likely prospects. However, when they became really ready for a relationship, then out of nowhere appeared eligible partners.

What, in fact, had happened was that they began sending out signals of interest and availability, and others had responded to those signals. In whatever way the signals are sent—a glance or a friendly remark—they were correctly interpreted as an invitation indicating a desire for further contact.

There are two dangers associated with extending invitations; acceptance and rejection. Acceptance can be dangerous if you feel you have to meet someone's unknown expectations. How charming, sexual, clever, sophisticated, educated, athletic do you have to be to win further acceptance? The best answer is that you should be just as charming, sexual, clever, sophisticated, educated and athletic as you really are. To pretend to be somebody that you are not is setting yourself up for severe stress. It takes a tremendous amount of energy to maintain a facade, and it keeps you from finding somebody who is attracted to who you really are. Furthermore, when the real you does show up (and inevitably that will happen) the chances of rejection are doubled because you are rejected for not really having the qualities feigned and for being a phony. Therefore, acceptance of someone's interest is really only dangerous if you do it with the intent to defraud. Most people understand your trying to put your best foot forward. What they won't tolerate is when you put forward someone else's foot.

Rejection, much more than acceptance, is the danger feared when one person sends out come-on signals to another. It hurts when someone you find attractive and approach says, "No thanks." Divorced people may already suspect themselves of being a loser or failure, so the possibility of a negative response is just too much to risk.

Motivate yourself to take the risk of sending out signals of interest by realizing that any rejection you might get at the very beginning of a relationship has very little or nothing to do with you. The other person may be in a committed relationship, gay, in mourning, afraid of new relationships, shy or fearful of rejections themselves. They may have prejudices about your age, educational level, motives, skin color, shoe size, or family background. Even if their reasons for not taking you up on your invitation are more personal, such as their not liking what they have heard or seen of you, you still should not feel that you have been adequately judged. The question to ask is did they know enough about the real you to make a sound judgment. And even if they did make a genuine judgment about you as a person, it was based on the decision that the two of you were not compatible. In that case, you should be grateful to them for saving you the considerable time and energy it can take to determine if a relationship has a future.

But chances are that rejection by a relative stranger is done on grounds that have nothing to do with your real self. Figure that you will need to extend ten invitations for every one that is accepted. The nine turn downs are best regarded as a shame that the other person missed the opportunity of meeting you. Send the signals. Make the invitations. It's the way to exercise your choice to be with people you find, at least initially, attractive.

Beyond the dating-for-pleasure principle are the attitudes needed to explore relationships that may involve greater degrees of commitments. The most useful attitudes for exploring committed relationships are not versions of your previous marital commitments. Marriage can produce habits antithetical to an individual's freedom. The best relationships are ones in which both people are devoted both to the other person and to their own individual freedom. This is not a paradox. It is possible to couple and yet maintain one's own life rhythms. To do it, most people have to break certain marital habits.

For example, it is common in a marriage to play a certain sexual role—e.g., to always initiate sexual activities. With post-divorce dating, you will have to work at trying new behavior instead of automatically following previous patterns. Those who had very long marriages tend to suffer from automatic feelings of commitment toward anyone they date. These people have a difficult time realizing that they are not owned by someone they slept with, made dinner for, or with whom they have become friends. One Christmas does not a tradition make.

Wanting to try out different levels of contact should and can easily be explained to potential partners. You need to be as clear as you can about who you are and what you want. Chances are very high among single adults for painful misunderstandings. People have all kinds of beliefs about what it means if you spend time with them or choose them as a sexual partner. It is necessary for couples who have *any* important feelings to openly discuss present and future commitments, feelings, and plans. Declaring feelings of love in a moment of passion may represent a long-term promise to one person while to another it is merely an involuntary, instinctual response, easily made and forgotten. People who don't discuss their relationship goals and feelings are in danger of confusing and often alienating someone they really care about.

It may be that everyone, at some level of their consciousness, is aware of how others regard them. We frequently choose to fool ourselves for one reason or another. Relationships develop the least number of distortions when both people regularly verbalize their feelings about and plans for the relationship.

Implementing the attitude of learning about one's self through dating involves spending a lot of time with potential partners. As an adult, spending a lot of time with a potential partner automatically brings up questions about the sexual part of the relationship. Dating typically begins with social activities, but if the sexual chemistry is there, there will be pressure to have a sexual relationship. How quickly and to what extent the sexual aspect evolves, of course, depends on the two personalities. Sex for the newly single can be fraught with complications if sex is an artificial performance, rather than a genuine expression of feeling, if the excitement of new sex is misinterpreted as a sign of enduring love and compatibility, or if sexual fears are misread as sexual disinterest.

Because these can so easily cause misunderstandings, sex should be an on-going topic of discussion in the process of "Actively Investigating Relationships With Potential Partners." Most adults like to discuss sex, so the trick is to promote authentic discussions of sexual anxieties, desires, and feelings.

If the initial social and physical aspects of a relationship work for both people, then the next phase is a kind of settling in. Continuing pleasant sexual and social times lead to a reduction of those first pressures to sparkle for the other person. It becomes easier to share disappointments, depressions, problems and longer-term goals, hopes, plans, financial aims, life ambitions.

Some people so enjoy this phase of a relationship that they, very early, tell everything to each new person. There are as many who are very private and prefer to show others only their most sparkly side and, further, prefer it if that is what others display for them. Some thrive on the excitement of new sex. Others feel uncomfortable about it. Some like knowing who they'll spend New Year's Eve with by Thanksgiving or even Easter. Others want no definite plans beyond next Wednesday. The newly separated are very changeable about all of these issues. Those going through a divorce need to be prepared to experience rapid shifts in mood and beliefs. It's helpful to consider these changes as natural experiments with different ways of being, rather than as indications of basic instability.

The style or pace of post divorce dating is less important than the inviolate rule to not remarry for at least two years after divorcing. This time allows for emotional ups and downs, changes in life plans, and sufficient *AIR-WAPPing* to take place. What you are looking for is a relationship in which there is mutual enjoyment, stimulation, trust, love, intimacy, support, sexuality, and sharing of goals. But the best relationships are when these qualities can be yours *without sacrificing your own growth.*

In order to develop their own individuality, adults should be able to eat, sleep, read, vacation, work or pursue personal interests according to their own rhythms and needs. If a relationship demands serious compromises which prevent this, then the viability of the relationship should be questioned. Two years seems a minimal amount of time for finding and developing a relationship with the elements that foster mutual contentment and individual growth. Some people can only find the combination they want in a sexually exclusive legal marriage. Others find satisfaction with a series of more or less permanent friends and lovers. The best combination for any individual simply cannot be known during the turbulent times following a divorce.

Furthermore, what worked for your parents or even for you at a younger age under different social rules probably no longer fits. Take the time to evaluate former habits, establish personal developmental goals, and openly explore relationship styles. The better you know your new self, the better prepared you will be to create a satisfying and exciting relationship.

Part II
Legal Aspects of Divorce

CHAPTER 4

Legal Realities of Divorce

There's good news. Getting a divorce is becoming an easier and more rational process almost every day. The cumbersome, laborious court processes loaded with religious and legal traditions are changing. The days when those seeking a divorce were treated like criminals brought to court for punishment are pretty much over. Society's attitudes towards divorce have changed so radically from those held during the times of most of our parents' lives that even the tradition-bound courts have been forced into major reforms. Under the old system, the mere numbers of people now seeking legal separations and divorces would so bog down the courts that no other "justice" could be dispensed. Therefore, there have been drastic liberalizations and simplifications of all procedures dealing with divorce. Yet despite the changes, a recent Wall Street Journal article reported that the courts are still swamped with disputes over money and children as a result of dissolving marriages. It's hoped that this manual can help the reader avoid confusing information about divorce so that the court interference in your personal life is kept to a minimum.

The reason a psychotherapist considers it crucial to include basic information about the legal aspects of divorce is because such matters significantly effect people's mental health. In the same way environment, physical health, and economics are relevant to a person's mental wellbeing, so is the law.

A divorce is a complex legal process which involves state and federal governments and regulations. Attorneys and judges have even more power over the course of your life than do the state laws which govern such ungovernable things as the cause of your divorce. Your reasons for seeking to end your marital status may be irrelevant to the legal ground your state dictates you must swear to in order to obtain the legal separation you seek. The federal government has important ways of manipulating your private decisions about divorce through financial regulations; for instance, the way the Internal Revenue Service deals with your settlement decisions can substantially affect your economic freedom.

Psychotherapists cannot and do not advocate divorce, marriage, separations, or living together arrangements, but they do have experience with couples whose relationships can be complicated by unknown or misunderstood laws. For example, at least three million couples in America are living together without being married, and in many states that is illegal. In the eyes of the law, such people are criminals. In 15 states couples living together may be married without knowing it, via a common law marriage. A couple not wanting to be married may choose to live in one of our 35 states which does not regard cohabitation as evidence of a common-law marriage. However, even some of these states consider the couple married if they began their sexual relationship in a state that does recognize common-law marriages. So watch out for romantic Colorado ski trips. Colorado recognizes common-law marriages.

There are even more legal complications for those who decide to end a regular marriage. A not uncommon situation occurs when the husband decides to divorce and leaves the home. Wives have frequently been in such financial straits that they do anything to settle the divorce in order to receive desperately needed financial support. Such wives need to know that when a husband leaves, the wife can petition the courts immediately and gain support money (legally termed separation maintenance). In almost all of the 50 states, a final divorce decree is not required before obtaining reasonable funds from a separated husband.

The topics covered in this chapter are a review of the history of divorce as it affects current judicial attitudes and procedures, and the basic facts concerning officers of the court, attorneys and judges. Chapter 5 outlines each step for obtaining a divorce. Chapter 6 offers the rationale and techniques for legal and non-legal separations. Chapter 7 covers settlement matters. These legal topics all emphasize the divorce realities primarily effecting adults. Section III of the book focuses on children's legal involvements with divorce.

This manual is, of course, incapable of providing specific legal advice. The laws and definitions vary from state to state and are much too complex for any single volume to cover comprehensively. Furthermore, differences between individual divorce situations require that careful investigation be done concerning the laws that govern any particular case. But though these legal sections do not give *specific* legal instruction, they do provide essential background information and general strategies for dealing with legal issues.

For the majority of those divorcing today, the legal aspect of the experience is so powerful that their entire emotional life is effected. Expectations, goals, and identity are all influenced through dealing with attorneys and courts. People view their own behavior during the divorce crisis as strange and unpredictable. People who consider themselves reasonable develop vicious and vindictive court strategies. Loving parents find themselves deciding to flee or hurt their children through legal maneuvers or bargaining. Much of this is brought on by legal naivete '. To begin understanding how the legal process affects your emotional existance, an overview of the history of divorce is helpful.

Since the beginning of the formalization of relationships between men and women, official regulation has been managed by two institutions, the church and the state. For centuries the church dominated. It was religious doctrine that a man and a woman became one flesh upon entering the state of matrimony. Further, to end a marriage required God. The church was reluctant to take any responsibility for ending a divinely created union. Because of this, the church never granted divorce, and only very rarely permitted elaborate forms of separation or annulment. You had to have a great deal of influence in the church in order to gain any cooperation in ending a marriage. This Christian position was based on Jesus' answer when asked if it would be lawful to divorce one's wife. Jesus' answer became part of church marriage ceremonies used throughout centuries, "What therefore God has joined together, let no man put asunder."

Prior to Christianity, it was the state that ruled over the rare divorce. In 18 B.C., Roman law allowed only husbands to gain divorces. Then the Roman women won a victory, and either spouse could get a divorce on the grounds of adultery which was a serious criminal offense often punished by death.

A forerunner of the modern no-fault divorce was instituted in 536 A.D. when the Roman emperor declared that a couple could divorce without penalty if there was mutual consent. This liberal attitude only lasted about thirty years, after which divorces could be granted only under the condition of one spouse's *punishable* misconduct.

Catholic and Christian church powers eventually prevailed in the western world, and declared marriage a sacrament, a contract with God with no escape clauses. The only possibility for ending a Catholic marriage was through rare annulments, which were pronouncements from the Vatican that the marriage had never really existed in the first place.

The Protestant Reformation instituted some divorce reforms. In 17th century Europe, non-Catholic countries made divorce a matter of government. The state granted divorce on certain very limited grounds, of which the most prevalent by far was adultery.

In the 18th and 19th centuries, the number of grounds for divorce slowly increased. If your spouse engaged in the criminal activities of bigomy, desertion, or sodomy, you could obtain a divorce. During this medieval period, when the state regulated divorces, it was not much easier to get one than through the Catholic church. For example, in 18th century England, divorces could only be obtained through a decree by the King. The common man in England had very little chance of gaining the King's time, attention, or decree and so had to follow what had for centuries, and is still called, the poor man's divorce—desertion. Things have changed in merry old England and since 1969 divorce requires only proof of irretrievable breakdown in the relationship.

In the United States there is no country-wide regulatory agency administering divorce. The United States has 51 different sets of regulations, one for each state and the District of Columbia.

Appendix B lists the grounds for obtaining divorce in the United States, by state, and lists the residency requirements for each state (i.e., how long you must reside in the state before you can seek a divorce under that state's laws). There are wide variations between states. Some have a very simple "no-fault" divorce which may involve no more than a declaration of irreconcilable differences. In other states the laws still ring of older religious or moral codes such as: "buggery outside the marriage," or "gross behavior and wickedness repugnant to and in violation of the marriage covenant."

Religion has no formal role in American divorces but retains power through various attitudes towards divorce. Only the United Methodist Church has followed changing secular attitudes by providing a church divorce service. It is a pleasant ceremony usually involving all family members, in which the divorcing couple acknowledges that they can continue to exercise great care for each other.

CURRENT DIVORCE TRENDS

Statistics can be a comfort. Startling improvements in the mental health of individuals have been known to occur when they discover that their behavior was "statistically normal." Certainly no one involved in divorce in this country today should feel either like a rugged individual, or a gross abnormality. The below offered collection of statistics in that sense are comforting. The numbers also reflect an obvious point about Americans changing relationship lifestyles and attitudes toward marriage and divorce. The statistics on divorce are changing rapidly these days so you certainly can predict that divorce will be even more common tomorrow than today.

The U.S. Department of Commerce in 1978 reported that during the previous year there were 2.2 million marriages and 1.1 million divorces. From 1970 to 1977 the number of unmarried couples (1.9 million) living together increased 83%. In 1969, 70% of the people getting married were marrying for the first time. By 1976, only 59% were first marriages.

The U.S. Bureau of Census (1976) reported the average American stayed in a first marriage for seven years, then stayed single for three years before remarrying.

Twenty-nine percent of American families are single parent

homes through divorce and another 28% through separation, so not counting deaths of spouses, the majority of children today are raised for some period of time in a one-parent household.

There simply is no doubt that divorces are growing to be a more common fact of life. Each year there are more divorces and fewer marriages. From 1970 to 1978, the number of people of marriageable age who lived alone tripled to the point where a fifth of all United States households consisted of an adult living by him or herself.

However, statistics indicate that these American trends do not reflect a world-wide phenomena. For example, divorces in Eastern Europe, where they are easier to obtain than they are in America, are proportionately less. This may be due to the fact that many Eastern European countries have compulsory marriage courses in high school and mandatory counseling for couples considering marriage. The Europeans thus learn through education what Americans seem to be learning through early first marriages. Statistics indicate that in America second marriages do not end in divorce as often as first marriages.

The statistics clearly indicate that many Americans today are getting divorced, but we have few studies that tell us why. Magazine articles, novels, movies, are consistently generating theories and opinions about cultural changes which have impelled Americans toward divorce. Some aclaim it as a wave of the future in which all adults will live independent lives without hampering legal commitments. Others see it as simply one more indication of the moral decline and narcissistic trend in our culture.

This book will not wax philosophically or sociologically as to the causes of the increasing divorce rate. The purpose here is only to instruct on how to make an individual divorce serve the couple as well as possible.

ATTORNEYS, JUDGES AND COURTS

There are basically two kinds of divorce—contested (15%) and uncontested (85%). It is not only the position of this manual, but of almost every competent and ethical legal professional that regardless of your anger, resentment, or hurt, you should work to gain an uncontested divorce. There is almost nothing which can be gained or resolved through contested divorce procedures that can't be better handled outside the courts. Understand that an uncontested divorce does not mean that you and your spouse automatically agree on any of the details. It only means that your disagreements are settled *before* you enter the courtroom. That is, you use some other means—any other means—to come to a set of agreements so that the court only gives the formal stamp of approval to your worked-out arrangements. The alternative is to follow the disastrous, expensive and unfortunately often unfair court procedure in which the judge makes the crucial life decisions for you. Counseling, mediation, cooling periods, use of a friend, clergy, appeals concerning the emotional needs of children, attempts at reconciliations, giving up financial advantages, even individual psychotherapy can all help direct the course of divorce away from the court arena.

Almost all contested divorces arise out of vindictive, unreasoning angers. A contested divorce cannot be justified by a cool reasoning mind. There are three major areas in which people can arrive at amicable settlements, or become polarized into postures that necessitate the legal battle of a contested divorce: grounds for divorce, the property settlement, and custody arrangements. In this book, every step toward gaining a legal divorce decree will be described in terms of procedures for achieving an uncontested divorce.

When planning a divorce, be extremely wary of those who encourage you to battle in the courts, as opposed to encouraging you to communicate and work out as much as you can outside of legal channels. Remember that in the courts every decision is reached through a battle between hostile parties. The alienation caused by such battles can be avoided by understanding how the divorce courts operate.

Essentially the court has two tasks. The first is to determine if you have grounds for divorce that are legal in your state. If you and your spouse agree to the grounds and your attorneys help you choose the most appropriate grounds for your goals, the first court task is easily achieved. The second duty of the court is to make sure that the couple's joint affairs are fairly separated. If you and your spouse can agree on property and custody settlements, and your attorneys put the agreement in acceptable legal language, the second job of the court involves only a quickly obtained formal stamp of approval. Easy.

Courts and laws have made many positive changes over recent

years so that divorce proceedings no longer make one feel as if they are facing degrading criminal charges. The courts are basically committed to making divorce simpler and cheaper than ever and to protecting all involved parties, especially children.

An essential mechanism toward this simplification is the "no-fault" divorce. It differs from the "fault" divorce procedure in that it does not place any criminal blame and, therefore, does not penalize either party. In the past, fault divorces, in which one partner was found to be guilty of desertion, adultery, mental cruelty, or such, were used when the courts had to determine who was the injured party in the marriage. Financial and custody awards were based on whether you were the guilty or injured party. Some people have the mistaken notion that no-fault divorces mean the automatic forfeiting of rights to support payments. This is not true. Judges in no-fault divorces still use their discretion in making property and/or custody awards. The judge tends to consider all the extenuating circumstances in rendering judgments, disregarding the formal grounds used to obtain the divorce.

CHOOSING AN ATTORNEY

Choosing an attorney is one of the most important tasks faced in a divorce. You want a lawyer whose personality and methods are compatible with your needs. You need to feel able to communicate openly with your attorney. The attorney needs to agree with your personal divorce goals so that the two of you can work together as a team to have the laws in your state work for you. You also need to consider the attorney's competency in both divorce *and tax* matters. The tax requirement is relevant because, unfortunately, a divorce is not simply a matter between two spouses. There is a third party, the government. Divorcing couples require up-to-date advice concerning property settlements which give both parties the maximum tax benefits to which they are legally entitled. Although your attorney may not be an expert in tax matters, he or she must be able to obtain competent tax advice.

There are two additional requirements to consider when choosing an attorney. First, if your divorce is going to involve much legal battling, you need to engage the most knowledgeable and skillful divorce attorney you can afford. A devoted friend, who happens to be an attorney, just will not do. The attorney you choose to help you do battle must have strong, specific expertise in the divorce area where you expect problems. An attorney who has done very fine work for you in other than divorce matters will not automatically be able to serve you in a divorce proceeding. The skills of the attorney are more important than the laws themselves. Every state-licensed attorney is automatically an officer of the court, but they are far from being equally competent to make your state laws work for you. It is the skilled, educated, and experienced divorce attorney who can produce results that seem to defy the written laws.

Secondly, the attorney needs to be committed to the idea of the couple, between themselves, making as many decisions as possible. To facilitate this, it is wise for both spouses to go to all attorney meetings. If this works out correctly, the couple ends up primarily using one attorney—either his or hers—and only uses the second attorney to double check on the appropriateness of the agreements arrived at. This procedure discourages "plotting" and escalating hostilities. It encourages cooperative planning and decision making. Some attorneys are violently opposed to *any* meetings with both spouses. These attorneys claim it violates the privileged communication between attorney and client, or that they cannot serve their client's best interests while holding such meetings. Beware of such rationalizations. Ethical attorneys should encourage positive communication and welcome meetings attended by both spouses.

The best relationship between attorney and client requires equal adult participation. That means that the attorney should be able to hear and understand the client's needs and desires. Remember that the attorney's job is not to make decisions for the client, but rather to clearly communicate choices appropriate to the client's needs and desires. The client's job is to let the attorney know what he or she wants. Don't stay with an attorney with whom you do not feel you have excellent rapport.

If you are having difficulty in finding or choosing an attorney, consider using a fine service offered by the American Bar Association in all 50 states. This is a referral service in which inexpensive legal advice is offered by committed attorneys who volunteer their services. Those who are financially needy can get not only advice, but legal representation from the local Legal Aid Association (see appendix B for legal aid contacts in all states).

The wealthy can afford the sizable fees charged by top attorneys. The middle class client, who needs advice and doesn't have the financial resources to hire top attorneys, can greatly benefit from the lawyers referral service which can be contacted through your state's chapter of the American Bar Association. You may have to go through some minor bureaucratic difficulties, but you will be able to talk to a skilled attorney who will help you find appropriate attorneys to consider as your legal respresentative.

Do you actually need an attorney at all in order to get a divorce? Yes. Certain states do give residents the right to represent themselves in court. It is almost always better to spend time finding the best professional legal advice you can rather than trying to deal with the collection of complexities surrounding divorce proceedings. There is an exception. Many states have what has been called a "Do It Yourself Divorce Kit." These kits will be described in the next section, but for now you should know that these kits are only useful in very special cases of very simple divorces. The next chapter will consider their advantages and disadvantages.

After you have chosen an attorney, you can plan your initial meeting. At that very first face-to-face contact, you may well be able to decide whether you have sufficient rapport with them to allow you to work together. To make the first meeting go as smoothly as possible, write down all the things you expect the lawyer will need to know. Always retain a copy of anything you give to your attorney. Misplaced or lost documents are a source of much frustration and expense.

Below is a list of things you might take to your first meeting:
1. Place and date of both spouses birth.
2. Place and date of current marriage and any previous marriages of either party.
3. If there were former divorces; dates, places, and circumstances of these divorces.
4. Names and birth dates and place of all natural and adopted children.
5. Where each spouse currently lives and how long these residences have been maintained.
6. A brief accounting of income, assets, and liabilities of each spouse.

Other information that the attorney will probably be interested in at the first meeting is an idea of what you want from the divorce, as well as what you feel is in favor and not in favor of your getting what you want from the divorce. It is crucial that you be very open and honest with your attorney. Lawyers can best serve when they know all facts. If you don't feel you can be open with a particular attorney, consider changing attorneys. If you do, for any reason, at any time, decide to change attorneys, you must be ready to pay for all work done up to the point of dismissal. Lawyers have the right to keep all documents in their possession until they have been paid for their services.

There are other questions you should be ready to openly discuss with your attorney. These matters concern the following:

1. What is the nature of your present marital relationship? That is, how friendly or unfriendly are you with your spouse and what conflicts or issues exist between you?
2. The attitudes of both spouses towards a divorce.
3. How cooperative can the spouse be expected to be in terms of agreeing with your point of view on support, property, and custody matters?
4. Whether any involved party (spouse or children) have any health, emotional, or legal problems.
5. Whether either spouse has other important romantic relationships or plans.
6. Details of the present marriage regarding separations (legal or non-legal), details of any mental health counseling of either spouse.
7. Employment information and history of both spouses.
8. How much time pressure exists for either spouse to gain a legal separation or a divorce?
9. Any future plans of either spouse.

All of the above matters, whether prepared in written form or through forethought, should be matters you feel ready to openly discuss with your attorney at early meetings.

There is another matter that should be taken up at the very first meeting: his fee. You should ask for an estimate of fees for the entire divorce procedure and find out what that includes. Fees are frequently negotiable. Furthermore, fees for legal services vary widely.

To say that many attorneys overcharge is to grossly understate the case. The simplest divorce can cost the attorney about two dollars in forms, perhaps twenty dollars for typing, and perhaps one hour of professional time. A three hundred and fifty dollar statement for services would be common for this type of case in which the attorney never has to leave his or her office. It is not uncommon for an attorney to ask for a retainer of five thousand dollars before beginning to work on a *contested* divorce.

The number of fee horror stories can only be matched by the horror stories attorneys hear about their clients' spouses. Avoid the horrors. Frankly discuss *all* aspects and charges with your attorney. Do more than ask for the hourly rate. Discuss fee schedules and determine who will pay for the services. In some states, under certain circumstances, husbands pay for the wife's legal counsel. In other states, judges decide if your spouse is legally responsible for paying your attorney's fees. Regardless of whether the fees will be paid by you or someone else, you need to find out how the attorney expects to be paid. Are retainers required? What if the spouse doesn't meet the legal obligations? Judges rarely jail a spouse for non-payment of attorney's fees. How does your attorney handle collection of fees?

In addition to fees, a client should determine whether the attorney is genuinely supportive of the client's approach to the divorce. If you feel you can talk to, afford, and have a common goal with the attorney you've chosen to interview in early meetings, then you can feel relatively safe in retaining them. Even with all those positive aspects, you may frequently find yourself at odds with your attorney. Some disagreements are to be expected and should be worked out rather than switch lawyers when the first conflict occurs.

Divorce attorneys are in a difficult position. It is very natural for the attorney to become part of the unpleasant experience. Lawyers, therefore, are in danger of being disliked for reasons not actually deserved. Clients often feel they did not end up with the financial settlements or custody arrangements they really wanted. The feeling of being short changed leads to targeting attorneys, judges, and courts for undeserved dissatisfactions. Beware of confusing the negative aspects of the divorce situation with the person helping you deal with it.

There are, however, times and situations where you should question the behavior of your attorney. Knowing when to question requires some knowledge of certain tactics which unsatisfactory or less than ethical attorneys employ. Be alert to the following as reasons for considering seeking more suitable counsel:

1. An attorney who advises against direct communication with your spouse. It does, of course, make sense for your attorney to advise you not to write anything without legal counsel, but reasons for non-written, non-binding communications between spouses should be suspected. Be aware that many attorneys prefer to bargain between themselves for less than ethical or practical reasons. Bargaining between lawyers which is done outside the direct monitoring by you and your spouse can turn out to be very expensive and frequently not in your best interest.

2. An attorney who does not communicate each step being taken may be taking you. You have the right to expect to be able to reach your attorney easily and have calls promptly returned. Attorneys who claim they cannot reach other attorneys may just be making excuses. Some communication difficulties can be expected, but a habit of non-communication should not be tolerated.

3. Be hesitant in dealing with an attorney who is very paternalistic and wants to make decisions for you. They should offer you expert advice. They should give you optional plans for dealing with your problems. They should present you with the advantages and disadvantages of each offered option. You should be encouraged to decide on your own plan of action.

4. Be wary of attorneys who ask you to do paperwork which takes up your or their time which you cannot logically justify. The attorney may be making excuses for delays or may be providing justifications for charging higher fees. The simple rule is that everything your attorney does should make sense to you. If it does not, be suspicious.

It comes down to the fact that in seeking a divorce decree you need to use the laws and the courts. In order to make best use of the laws of your state, you will need legal counsel. Spend the time and effort to find and work with an attorney you consider the best you can employ.

To summarize the steps in getting the legal advice required, consider getting as much inexpensive legal advice as you can through the domestic court of your county, a community social service agency, the legal aid society, or the lawyers' referral service. The information you can get from these sources could provide the majority of the legal help you will need. When you get to the stage of hiring a personal attorney, you should go with as much written information as possible. Be honest about all details and get from the attorney a clear picture of all costs that might be expected if the whole divorce goes as simply or with as much difficulty as might reasonably be expected. Make sure the attorney has the necessary divorce law, court and tax expertise you need. Determine if you share goals and an easy flow of communication with your attorney.

The more you know about the divorce procedures, the more effectively you can use your attorney, the better decisions you can make, and the more helpfully you can deal with your spouse. The following chapter provides the basic information as to how one goes about getting a divorce.

CHAPTER 5

Divorce Methodology

Five steps that must be taken to obtain a valid divorce in America:

1) *Meet the residency requirements in the state in which you intend to get the divorce.*

Each state has rules governing whether one or both spouses need to live in the state in order to use their courts for divorce. Appendix B lists those residency requirements for each state.

2) *Select the grounds (legal reasons) under which you will be seeking the divorce.*

Each state has its own collection of grounds. You need to select those grounds which will meet your legal needs. Appendix B lists the grounds used in each of the fifty states and the District of Columbia.

3) *File with the county clerk all required legal forms.*

These forms also vary from state to state. The information required is usually limited to a few basic facts. In certain rare cases, the forms require details on: a) separation agreements (agreements on the division of property), b) spousal support (agreement on the financial aid one spouse will give the other), c) child custody (arrangements for primary custody of children and visitation rights of non-custodial parent), and d) child support (the arrangements for the financial support of children).

4) *Get a court date when the divorce case will be heard and decided upon by a judge.*

5) *Have the court date.*

The purpose of the court hearing is for the judge to review the divorce. If the judge determines you have legal grounds for divorce and that your plans for financial, property, and child affairs are satisfactorily worked out, he awards a decree (legal decision) that you are no longer married.

Those are the five steps. The courts tend to be accomodating, and the more you learn, the less you'll fear the whole situation. For instance, a divorce can sometimes be awarded before the property, support, and custody arrangements are finalized at a later hearing. Although an uncommon procedure, separating the divorce from the financial arrangements is sometimes done when there is a need for a divorce *now* and when complications about the settlements are expected to take more time than the spouses want to wait before being legally single.

The following five sections offer the most important details about the five basic steps. The details do three things. First, they tell you how to find the specifics that apply in your particular state. Second, they answer the most common questions that arise. Third, and most important, the details describe methods for accomplishing the steps in ways designed to increase the quality of communication between the spouses. There are pitfalls at each step which can alienate the couple and push them toward the anger which is so counterproductive to the goal of an uncontested divorce. Revengeful anger is the emotional justification for a majority of contested divorces.

One final general fact about obtaining a divorce is that although each state has its own laws controlling divorce, individual judges decisions (the way they choose to interpret the state laws or procedures) is much more important than the law itself. In part, this discretionary power of the judges is because our society's attitudes change faster than do written laws. Judges' decisions reflect the current attitudes or trends of the society and so can appear to conflict with the law as written.

Divorce Residency Requirements:

Each state has laws governing how long and under what conditions a person or couple needs to be residing (living in) or having a domicile (a home) in the state prior to being able to legally file for a divorce. The trend among all states is simplification of residency requirements. But, as in all the matters concerning the divorce, states do vary in what they require. Appendix B offers the specific residency requirements for all fifty states and the District of Columbia.

Some states have a very short time of residency prior to filing for divorce. Arizona, for example, requires only 90 days residency by either spouse. Nevada, home of the once famous quickie Reno divorce, requires about half the residency time (six weeks) needed in Arizona. If you desire an even faster divorce, you can obtain an entire divorce in one day in Haiti or the Dominican Republic. There are, however, some problems with the "foreign divorce," which legally is defined as divorce obtained in any other than the place in which you normally reside. Appendix C is a glossary of relevant legal terms in divorce. If offers some help, but is insufficient to allow laymen to believe they can competently understand an important legal document. If decisions are involved, it is best to have the document translated and explained by an attorney.

Most states require six months of residency by one or both spouses before filing. Some states have extremely complicated residency requirements, including whether you were married in that particular state, how long you lived in the specific county in which you are filing, and so on. Fortunately, the majority of the states have lenient residency requirements, and most people do not have to leave their home state in order to obtain a divorce.

Traveling to another state or county to get a quicker or simpler divorce gets tricky despite the fact that states generally recognize divorces granted in other states. The constitutional principle of "Full Faith and Credit" means that states accept the good sense and good will of another state's court decisions. But sometimes jurisdiction disputes can lead to a "Divisible Divorce" in which one state terminates the marriage and grants the divorce, but the spouse in another state can bring their own legal suit to deal with property settlement, support and/or custody matters.

With the tendencies towards more uniform divorce actions, it is usually unnecessary to get a "foreign divorce." If your residency situation seems more complex than can be clarified through the general information offered in Appendix B, you should gain more complete legal advice through an attorney, the nearest Legal Aid contact (also listed by state in Appendix B) or your state's Lawyers Referral Service (reached by calling your State Bar Association).

Selection of Grounds:

Each state has a number of grounds (the range being one to about fifteen) which are legal reasons the state recognizes as valid for terminating a marriage. The clear trend is towards the no-fault divorce. Not long ago divorces were granted only if someone was found to be the guilty party. Chivalry usually dictated that the husband take the rap and be the villain, because if a lady was found guilty of any of the crimes necessary to divorce, her reputation was tarnished and her place in society damaged.

For instance, in New York, a few years ago the most feasible of the few legal grounds for divorce was adultery. New Yorkers, then, had to pretend that the husband was "caught" in an adulterous act, a degrading and dishonest procedure. The only alternative was to go to a state with more lenient or acceptable divorce grounds and establish residency. New York has now joined some forty other states in adding a no-fault divorce ground to their laws.

New York also uses a Separation Ground no-fault approach used by about twenty other states, in which a couple gets a legal separation which later evolves into a no-fault divorce. In New York the law requires that the couple obtain either a decree of legal separation granted by the courts or a written separation agreement and then live apart for one year. With the Separation Ground no-fault system, the court takes the position that when a couple sets up separate residences for extended periods of time, typically a year, the marriage is irretrievably broken, so a divorce is granted. Incidentally, New York, like most all states, has retained fault grounds for gaining divorces. Adultery, abandonment for one year, imprisonment for three years, or cruel and inhuman treatment are still grounds for divorce in New York.

The most common form of the no-fault divorce is just a straightforward statement signed by both parties that there has been a breakdown of the marriage. Terms such as "marriage irretrievably broken" or "irreconcilable differences causing irredeemable breakdown of marriage" are examples of the language used for no-fault divorces.

There are definite advantages and disadvantages associated with the use of either fault or no-fault grounds. No-fault grounds are simpler. The court does not have to review evidence, listen to conflicting testimony, and decide where the fault lies. All of these take time, money, and can result in decisions which severely penalize or unfairly treat one or both parties. No fault judgments are quicker, cheaper, and altogether simpler than the fault system which demands that the courts find a guilty party.

Another major advantage of the no-fault divorce is that it embraces the spirit of non-alienation and cooperation between the divorcing spouses. Accusing someone of adultery, desertion, addictions, cruel and inhuman treatment, sexual inadequacies, or insanity does not tend to enhance or maintain a friendship with that person. As soon as one litigant (person involved in a legal action) legally attacks another's character by charging them in court, the usual defense in divorce actions is to show that the accuser is worse. A countersuit based on the poor moral behavior of the original plaintiff is a common ploy.

However, there are cases when the use of fault grounds are very appropriate to one's needs and desires. One might genuinely believe his or her spouse to be an inappropriate parental figure. By proving to the court that the person is morally irresponsible, he or she could protect children from a damaging parent by gaining full child custody. In such cases, the courts are involved in criminal proceedings. The court penalizes one spouse for actions which were injurous to another party—the other spouse or the children. It is possible that the criminal grounds approach could best meet certain legal needs. The fault divorce grounds available in your state may, in fact, be your actual reason for seeking a divorce. Desertion, nonsupport for a number of years, institutionalization for criminal or mental reasons are grounds for divorce in many states and in some situations are clearly the most appropriate grounds for a particular divorce action.

Even if you do have legitimate fault grounds, you still might be better off using the no-fault approach. You can achieve the same legal result, a divorce, and have the additional benefit of less emotional strain, ugliness, expensive court time, and exposure of your private life. A very important bonus for not using fault grounds can be a better after-divorce relationship with your former spouse. Furthermore, no-fault divorces are, by definition, uncontested, so you can easily subtract at least one and maybe two zeros from the financial costs of the usual contested divorce. There is no way to put a dollar value on all that is gained by a cooperative divorce because major benefits involve the quality of one's life.

One essential consideration in choosing particular grounds for the divorce involves rights that are gained or lost with certain grounds. The no-fault grounds do not, as is commonly thought, mean the giving up of property or other rights. However, the advantages and disadvantages of each divorce ground should be discussed with legal counsel qualified to interpret your state's laws.

Filing for Divorce:

Filing for divorce can be done by either spouse individually or it can be done jointly. Filing does not refer to the physical act of taking the papers to the county clerk's office but to stating in legal form who is asking (or petitioning the courts) for a divorce. Traditionally it was the wife who, as a social courtesy, was allowed to file for the divorce decree.

Joint filing, in which both parties ask for the divorce, is usually most desirable. It stresses the cooperative nature and spirit of the divorce. Many states require joint filing as a condition for either a no-fault divorce or for a legal separation which later can evolve into a no-fault divorce.

If one party files for a divorce, the other party will be "served," that is, legally notified of the pending divorce action.

Filing for a divorce is very simple. If there are attorneys involved, they usually gather the necessary information, fill out the appropriate forms, and register these forms (file them) with the county clerk. However, filing does not require the services of a lawyer. The do-it-yourself divorce is a definite trend in this country and, despite objections from some attorneys, there is little doubt that it is becoming more popular.

Do-it-yourself divorces are generally limited to non-contested divorces. Courts support them because of the simplification, reduced court time, and reduced financial expense to all concerned. They are *much* less expensive. In the simplest case of an uncontested divorce, you would probably have expenses of $50 or less, compared to a minimum amount of $350 once attorneys are involved.

Some states have made the do-it-yourself divorce procedure very easy. In Oregon it is possible to get a divorce by mailing in a notarized form. In many states, enterprising publishers have produced do-it-yourself divorce kits. These kits contain all the necessary legal forms for your state, along with plain English instructions for filling them out, filing, and obtaining a legal divorce decree. The kits range in price from about $25 to $135. The forms alone cost about five dollars, so if you don't need the instructions, you might be able to obtain an attorney-free divorce with just the forms and a little help from a legally knowledgeable friend. The Legal Aid and Lawyers Referral Services are two sources for finding the right friend. A third good source is the county family or domestic court facility. As the name implies this recent addition to our judicial system is a court which deals with family matters. You can call your county's domestic court and arrange for an appointment with a counselor or case worker whose services are free. Case workers from family relations court have the expertise to, for instance, work out a legal separation agreement which involves the basic, if not all the legal, documents required for a full-fledged divorce in many states.

The do-it-yourself divorce procedures vary from state to state, but they always involve the following steps:
1. Notification of both spouses that a divorce action is being taken.
2. Determination of valid grounds under which you will be seeking the divorce.
3. Providing a mutual agreement covering the division of all property, any support matters, and child custodial arrangements.
4. Filling out the proper forms in the proper language and filing them properly.

Sometimes you can get immense help with each of these steps from a friendly county clerk.

The do-it-yourself divorce can, at this time, be advised for only the simplest of marital partings. The attorneyless divorce is most useful in cases of short marriages among young people where there are no children and few assets to either divide or spend on legal counsel.

Filing for divorce is usually easy. Unless the forms need to include all the information required to establish a legal separation, they are very simply a formal notice of intent to divorce. It is rare for a state to require that complete separation or custody arrangements be included in the filing documents.

Gaining a Court Date:

A court date is the date at which the court hears the details of the divorce, and if all is well, the judge grants the divorce decree. In order for the judge to declare the marriage ended, he or she must meet on a scheduled date with all the essential parties or their legal representatives and formally approve the way the couple will divide their assets, liabilities, and responsibilities. Until the judge grants the divorce, the couple remains legally married and can be held accountable for all their actions as are other married people. The fact that you have filed for a divorce does not legally relieve you of any of your marital responsibilities.

The court date is usually assigned at the time of the filing. Some states have a specified length of time which must pass between the filing and the court date. In Colorado, there is a ninty-day wait after the filing before a court date can be assigned. But states differ widely, and in many states, the court date is the next available spot on the court's docket (schedule).

In a contested divorce, a very common device used to frustrate and wear down the opposition involves delays and delays and delays and intolerably long delays and last minute delays. There are seemingly an unending number of delaying tactics. For example, the divorce case may be assigned to the member of a law firm with business at the state legislature. It is mandatory for judges to grant a delay if that attorney, however suddenly, is required for the state's business. It's one of the hundreds of delaying tactics regularly used and provides one more reason for seeking a cooperative divorce.

The advantages of a cooperative divorce are so great that when a couple seeks marital counseling, the possibility of divorce counseling is discussed. The couple is told that the counseling techniques are designed to promote a quality of communications which will be invaluable to them in the present, as well as in later relationships or *in case they eventually decide on a separation or divorce.* Mentioning divorce at the beginning of marital counseling could set up negative expectations, but this risk is more than offset by the the advantages of planting the seed for cooperative communication in case the couple eventually wants to set up a court date.

Day in Court:

The day in court can involve minutes or years. If the action only requires that the judge note that the legal separation has continued the stipulated length of time, then a final decree can be awarded in minutes and neither spouse need be present. In such cases, you are notified by mail of the divorce decree. Legal separations that evolve into full divorces are called "convertible divorces" and are one of the more popular no-fault divorce trends.

In uncontested, no-fault divorces the judge reviews the evidence of legal grounds, such as a jointly signed statement that the marriage has been irretrievably broken. If, as is usually the case, the property settlement, support agreement, and custody arrangements are part of the divorce, the judge reviews these, and if he agrees that they are fair and that both parties have carefully considered the agreements (usually by having adequate legal counsel), the judge grants the divorce. It takes about an hour, and both parties presence is not required. Attorneys can represent clients and/or the client's notarized statements may be sufficient. The only requirement is that it must be verified that both spouses were notified of the court date.

Serving notice is a very formal procedure. The legal requirement of "having papers served" involves proving that the formal notices of divorce action were received by the non-filing spouse. The spouse who receives the notice can choose to do nothing: not hire counsel, nor participate in deciding any of the arrangements, nor even show up in court. The consequences of doing nothing are that the divorce will most probably be granted to the spouse who initiated and continued the process. Further, the divorce will most probably be granted under all the conditions that the filing person desires. In other words, if you were served with notice of a divorce action and do nothing, you could lose many important rights—to property, tax advantages, financial support, and your children.

If you leave the state, you can retain your rights in any divorce action by having a lawyer represent you. However, you cannot, in divorce actions, give your attorney "power of attorney" which is the power to act in your behalf by making binding decisions for you.

What the attorney can do by staying active in the case is to protect the client's rights.

Brief minutes or a few hours in court can be expected with uncontested divorce situations. The hours stretch into days, weeks, and months and in a fair amount of cases even decades, when there is a contested divorce. A divorce can be contested on grounds, property settlements, support payments, or child custody matters.

Later chapters discuss specifics as to how to amicably agree on financial (Chapter 7) and custody (Chapter 8) matters. Even if you feel you have a cooperative spouse, it is wise to review those chapters to learn the techniques that improve your chances of maintaining your cooperative relationship.

What happens when the settlement or support or custody matters are not agreed upon ahead of time? Then the adversary system of courts goes into full swing. The plaintiff and defendent challenge each other as to facts. Testimony is heard, witnesses are called in, the attorneys examine and re-examine witnesses, motions are made, accepted and denied. Both parties must defend their statements, their beliefs, and frequently their character. These are challenged by experts committed to convincing the judge that husband or wife is immoral or a liar or mentally incapable, perhaps, of seeing his or her own children. It is difficult to describe the anguish felt by those who have gone through contested divorce procedures.

Less dramatically, in a contested divorce the two sides attempt to establish the facts that will convince the judge to make a ruling or decision in their favor. It is a cumbersome system that often fails to reach decisions nearly as satisfactory as those made by two people honestly and informally working together. Good counseling can produce cooperativeness even between angry combatants. Some form of divorce counseling or divorce mediation should always be attempted before subjecting one's own future and that of one's children to the adversarial judicial system. Eighty-five percent of couples manage to have uncontested divorces. They have been able to work very hard outside the courtroom and overcome biases, angers and stresses in order to go into the courtroom with an agreed-upon plan for the divorce. It is worth the work to achieve this goal.

CHAPTER 6

Separations: Legal and Non-Legal

Separations—spouses living apart—can be helpful for both emotional and legal reasons. Separation means the *planned* setting up of two households. Desertion, on the other hand, is when one spouse leaves, usually without prior knowledge and/or consent of the other. Usually desertion also implies a lack of financial or emotional support for the deserted spouse. Frequently, the deserting spouse's whereabouts are known. Abandonment is desertion with no intent of returning and without leaving a forwarding address, i.e., disappearing.

The two forms of separations are legal and non-legal. Non-legal does not mean illegal but rather less formal, in that it does not require any court proceedings either to initiate or maintain. There are grey areas between legal and non-legal separations. In states without laws covering legal separations a more formal separation may be initiated by drawing up a mutually signed agreement which is notarized. This kind of semi-legal separation can safeguard against later difficulties in a contested divorce. For example, one spouse bringing suit for divorce under desertion or adultery grounds would be impossible if there existed a notarized agreement prior to the separation which specified the terms agreed to by both parties.

Be aware that separations, legal or non-legal, are not divorces and that the parties remain responsible to all the commitments of marriage. Unless a formal agreement states otherwise, spouses can be held legally responsible for actions which violate marital commitments during the separation. It pays to be very careful and not risk property, support, or custodial rights through a sloppy separation. Before separating, be aprised of the following details:

Non-legal Separations: Every separation has legal implications. In many states there is the recognition of voluntary separations for some statutory passage of time (legal amount of time) as grounds for a no-fault divorce. *Involuntary* separations, even if funds are regularly given and contact maintained, are, in many states, grounds for a fault divorce because of desertion.

Set aside the legal ramifications for a moment to consider the psychological aspects of a married couple establishing two households. As a part of marital counseling, it is frequently useful to experiment with limited physical separations. Understanding how a separation serves a therapeutic purpose as part of marital counseling increases one's understanding of some benefits that can be derived from "trial" separations.

The term *trial* separation means exactly that. Under therapeutic supervision, a trial separation is an experiment in living apart. Separated people have the opportunity to experience what living without the other spouse is like. People learn to what extent the other person is missed. The trial separation educates as to how living alone effects life in terms of friendships, children, recreational, financial and sexual needs. The therapist determines to what degree each person has a sense of freedom or loss as a result of separation. The problems of living together are regularly clarified through a separation. The amount of sadness, joy, loneliness, feelings of failure, relief, panic or some combination of these are important grist for the marital therapy mill.

The two most important things to be learned from trial separations are how the separation effects motivation to work on the marital relationships, and what each person wants to change about themselves.

Reaping the possible benefits from a trial separation involves much more than just setting up two households. Marital counselors plan separations with a careful set of agreements which prevent most of the alienating or painful aspects of separation.

Before a couple separates, they should agree on the form and extent of outside socialization and romantic explorations. Where there are not significant romantic partners waiting in the wings, most counselors encourage the couple to initially agree to various kinds of friendly socialization, but not dating. The jealousy, envy, anger, and hurt which can come from either real or imagined romantic attachments do not help ailing relationships. There are, of course, cases where investigation of other relationships is a prime purpose of the trial separation. Even here, agreements about details of what can be expected should be carefully articulated and clarified for both partners.

It is also very important for the couple to have a firm understanding of what will be the nature, extent, and times of their continued contact during the separation. There should be regular opportunities for communication between the couple. Marital counseling appointments are not enough. A typical plan might be for one dinner out each week. Two hours together in a public place over a meal encourages basic civil communication, even between a couple going through an uncomfortable, incompatible period.

Other agreements which help trial separations to proceed on a therapeutically smooth course are about financial support (it's best if set amounts are given at regular intervals), and all matters concerning any children. When there are children, adults usually understand how carefully they need to plan for them. The three most important aspects to be planned are informing them of the separation, explaining to them the reasons for the separation, and explaining what contact they will have with both the custodial and non-custodial parent. Advice on handling these matters is essentially the same as handling them during a formal divorce. Chapter 9 on children dealing with divorce should be helpful.

If the couple is engaged in counseling at the time of the trial separation, a variety of formal therapeutic strategies are employed to investigate the viability of the marriage. If the trial separation is carried out without counseling, the couple should still work out ways to share the thoughts and feelings they experience with their spouse. The time spent apart allows for cooling angers, the opportunity to reflect on the situation without the pressure of the other's presence, and the opportunity to experience one's self in a new way. The limited time that is spent with each other should involve a commitment from each to be as friendly and cooperative as possible. Work toward sending and receiving messages with a minimum of hostility. If you cannot usefully and peacefully talk between yourselves and are not in a counseling situation, try communication in the presence of a third party, such as a friend you both respect. The goal should be to allow for the exchange of information between spouses.

It is helpful, during separations, to read about relationships and their problems and solutions. There are books which have a pro-marriage bias and contain techniques for preserving the marital union (e.g., Stewart's 1980 book, "Helping Couples Change," Masters and Johnsons, "Pair Bonding"). Then there are books which advocate the joys of singledom ("Single Blessedness," Adams and "First Person Singular: Living the Good Life Alone," Johnson) and those which present middle grounds ("The Challenge of Being Single," Edwards & Hoover, and "The World of the Formerly Married," Hunt). Appendix D lists a selection of the more stimulating and thoughtful readings from hundreds available.

A final bit of advice for gaining the most from trial separation is to agree at the outset as to the length of the separation. This does not mean agreeing upon some calendar date at which time you must either move back together or file for divorce. It means deciding how long the trial separation should be before having a discussion to decide what you will agree to do next, such as: continue the separation as is, change certain rules governing the separation, apply for a legal separation, file for divorce, obtain legal advice, obtain counseling, decide to move back together, or whatever.

Two days is not a long enough separation to permit making such decisions. Two years is too long. Experience with many couples experimenting with separations has indicated that a well planned trial separation requires roughly six to eight weeks for the couple to gain sufficient information to allow for thoughtful options to be discussed. A particular situation might require some other length of time. Job required separations are often used as unofficial trial separations. Regardless of how long the separation lasts, it is still best to schedule some specific time to get together as a couple, or with an agreed-upon third party in order to make your next decisions.

Legal Separations:

There are a number of good reasons for getting a separation which is sanctioned (approved of) or decreed (legally valid) by a court. One example is when a couple prefers not to live together, but is unwilling to divorce, as in the case of many Roman Catholics, or a divorce may be a disadvantage for financial reasons. Marriages have certain tax advantages. There are circumstances in which the major source of income is destroyed if split, as in the case of a business where dividing the equity would necessitate terminating the business. *Forced* sales of almost anything (homes, businesses, securities) generally produce substantial financial losses sometimes too devastating to sustain.

Legal separations have certain social advantages over divorces. The procedures for gaining a legal separation are less publically embarrassing than those involved in a divorce. Some people want to be able to have new relationships with the understanding that marriage would be impossible because they are already married.

A currently popular reason for legal separations is that it can be designed to produce a clean financial separation between people who want to live separate lives for some period of time, but wish to retain easy options for reconciliation. In these cases the clearest legal form of disengagement is the legally sanctioned separation.

When a separation becomes a legal entity and, therefore, is governed by state law, it, as with all aspects of divorce, varies from state to state. Table 1 (pages 116-119) presents major facts concerning each state's regulations for legal separations. First, the table indicates whether the state has legal separation regulations. The table's second column notes if legal separations in the state are convertible to a full divorce. Many states use legal separations as a form of no-fault divorce. In these states you can obtain a legal separation, live in separate households under terms defining the legal separation for a specified length of time, and then ask the courts to convert the separation into a divorce decree. Table 1 also reviews important details of the separation laws of each state, such as the length of time required to convert to a full divorce and particular separation factors required in order to convert to valid divorce grounds. As with all information in the book, the data must be considered as a guide. Before making life-changing decisions, specifics are needed that require the legal research and expertise of state licensed attorneys.

The hallmark of the legal separation is the formal separation agreement. Legal separations require formally prepared and stated agreements concerning a collection of matters only a few of which are the classic support, custody, and property arrangements. No one without extensive legal expertise in the divorce law field should attempt to prepare legal separation documents. To appreciate the complexities involved, review the following list of articles which are required for most legal separation agreements. The titles of each article are followed by a brief description of matters covered in that particular article. Although the everyday language may make more sense to the lay person, it is of no use to courts, while the legal phrases and terms which may seem like unnecessary gibberish are, in reality, time-tested ways of making statements which legally safeguard the parties involved. This need to use the legally accepted terminology is one important reason why today's legal separations and divorces require competent legal counsel.

Recitals: an article which gives all the facts about the marriage, children, home, and purposes of the separation agreement.

Separate Residences: an article which makes it lawful for the couple to have separate residences free from control or interference by the other spouse.

Molestation: an article which acts like a court restraining order. It makes it illegal for one person to bother the other in ways described in the article. It allows for legal disciplining of the party who violates the restraining order.

Separate Ownership: this article states what will be owned by each person after the separation. It is not the property settlement which is the topic of the next chapter in this manual.

Responsibility for Debts: this article states when each spouse will no longer be responsible for the other's debts and that they are giving up rights to each other's estates (all assets) if the other dies. This latter point concerning death may be in a separate article dealing with releases of claims on all aspects of the other's estates. The property settlement will be the place where the agreements of *past* debts (e.g.'s, installment payments, dental bills) are made.

Mutual Release and Discharge of General Claims: this article states that subject to the provisions of this agreement, each party has released, remissed, and forever discharged, and by these presence does for himself or herself, and his or her heirs, legal representatives, executors, administors, and assigns, release, remiss and forever discharge the other of and from all cause or causes of action, claims, demands or rights whatsoever, in law or in equity which either of the parties hereto ever had, presently has, against the other except any and all cause or causes of action for divorce or separation action now pending, or brought hereafter by the other for those specifically exempted herein.

The above article has obviously not been translated into everyday English. It is offered as an example of an article in a separation agreement written in legal language. It has been included in its entirety as the shortest and simplest of the articles listed. Surely you understand what it's saying. There is usually another article similar to it which releases all claims to the other's property.

Implementation: an article which guarantees the relevant documents, such as tax materials, will be given to the other party automatically.

Custody and Visitation: this is the article which determines who will be the primary custodial parent and who will be the visiting parent for which children and for how long. All the rights of the custodial and visiting parents are spelled out. Child support is usually the subject of a separate article. These matters are also the subject of Chapter 8 in this book.

Support and Maintenance: this article deals with all details about how much spousal support will be given by whom, to whom, for how long, and under what conditions.

Waiver of Other Provision for Support: an article which states that claims for support other than that covered in the preceeding paragraph will not be made, ever.

Independent Income: this article states which income of the husband and wife are to be theirs alone and not subject to claims by the other.

Personal Property: usually division of personal property is accomplished by a private agreement between the spouses. Sometimes a very detailed article is needed to either list it all (every dish) or more typically major articles (furniture).

There are many possible additional articles the most frequent of which are those which 1) guarantee that the parties will let each other know new addresses; 2) states that both parties had legal counsel, who counsel was and how they were to be paid; 3) that both spouses have been made aware of the meanings and consequences of everything in the document; 4) state the legal meanings of gifts to each other or to children; 5) say which will interpret the terms of the document; 6) state what happens if all or part of the separation document is later found to be legally invalid; 7) state how reconciliations and remarriages will be handled.

Legal separation agreements are every bit as carefully constructed as divorce agreements. In the case of the convertible divorce, the legal separation document, in fact, becomes the divorce document. Whether a legal separation is the basis for an eventual divorce or just a very specific set of agreements for a trial separation, it involves sufficient complications to justify legal counsel. Legal Aid or the Lawyer's Referral Service previously described offer two economically reasonable alternatives to hiring a private attorney. There is also the Domestic Relations Court which may specialize in legal separations and offers free legal counsel. The best help will come from the source that is most knowledgeable about your state's legal separation laws and practices.

Legal separations are like divorce in that they are the least complicated when the major decisions and agreements are worked out ahead of time between the spouses. If the couple requires the court to arrive at the major decisions there is little doubt that the adversarial system will escalate the differences between the spouses, fire up all animosities, increase ten to fifty fold the financial expenses and prolong the entire process. Furthermore, the negative relationship between the spouses will be escalated, fired up, increased ten to fifty fold and prolonged. A key to avoiding the entire court mess is the settlement agreement. If the settlement can be somehow agreed upon outside the legal establishment, the couple has taken a most important step towards achieving the desired non-contested divorce or legal separation. The next chapter deals with that key issue; Settlement Agreements.

Table 1—Separation Laws by State

State	State has Legal Separation	Separations Can Convert to Divorce Grounds	Details
Alabama	Yes	Yes	Separate maintenance for 2 years.
Alaska	No	No	Desertion for 1 year is one divorce ground.
Arizona	Yes	Yes	Requires the same grounds as for divorce.

State	State has Legal Separation	Separations Can Convert to Divorce Grounds	Details
Arkansas	No	No	Desertion for 1 year is one divorce ground.
California	Yes	Yes	Requires the same grounds as for divorce where both consent.
Colorado	Yes	Yes	Requires the same grounds as for divorce. Converted after six months by either spouse.
Connecticut	Yes	Yes	Any time after legal separation a conversion to divorce can be made by either spouse.
Delaware	No	No	Voluntary separation is a divorce ground.
District of Columbia	Yes	Yes	Voluntary separation is a divorce ground.
Florida	No	No	Legal separation not recognized.
Georgia	Yes	No	Desertion for 1 year is divorce ground.
Hawaii	Yes	Yes	Separation for 2 years is divorce ground.
Idaho	No	No	State recognizes right to separate maintenance.
Illinois	Yes	No	Legal separation is at judge's discretion.
Indiana	No	No	No-fault divorces available.
Iowa	Yes	Yes	Divorce after legal separation is considered no-fault marriage breakdown.
Kansas	Yes	Yes	Divorce after legal separation is considered no-fault due to incompatibility.
Kentucky	Yes	Yes	Converted to divorce after 1 year by one person's motion.
Louisiana	Yes	Yes	Voluntary living apart is divorce ground.
Maine	Yes	No	Separation grounds involve living apart one year.
Maryland	Yes	No	Voluntary separation for one year is a no-fault divorce ground.
Massachusetts	Yes	Yes	Six months after court approval if both file, 12 months if one files.
Michigan	Yes	Yes	Breakdown of marriage is a no-fault divorce ground.
Minnesota	Yes	No	Irretrievable breakdown is a no-fault divorce ground.
Mississippi	No	No	Court can provide for separate maintenance.
Missouri	Yes	Yes	Grounds for divorce or legal separation are irretrievable marriage breakdown (no-fault).
Montana	Yes	No	Ground for divorce or legal separation are no-fault marital problems.

State	State has Legal Separation	Separations Can Convert to Divorce Grounds	Details
Nebraska	Yes	No	Separation grounds at court's discretion; divorce grounds, no-fault marriage problems.
Nevada	No	No	Living apart 1 year is no-fault divorce ground.
New Hampshire	Yes	No	Marriage problems are no-fault divorce grounds.
New Jersey	Yes	No	Separate living 18 months is no-fault divorce ground.
New Mexico	Yes	Yes-No	Legal separation ground if permanent separation (incompatibility is no-fault divorce ground).
New York	Yes	Yes	Divorce after 1 year of legal separation.
North Carolina	Yes	No	Separation for 1 year is divorce ground.
North Dakota	Yes	Yes	Divorce granted after 1 year of legal separation.
Ohio	No	No	Can have separation agreement.
Oklahoma	Yes	No	Incompatibility is no-fault divorce ground.
Oregon	Yes	No	Irreconcilable marriage problems are no-fault grounds.
Pennsylvania	No	No	Living separately 3 years or marriage irretrievably broken are no-fault divorce grounds.
Rhode Island	Yes	No	Living separately 3 years or irreconcilable differences are no-fault divorce grounds.
South Carolina	No	No	Separation continuous for 1 year is no-fault divorce ground.
South Dakota	Yes	No	Willful desertion or neglect for 1 year are fault divorce grounds.
Tennessee	Yes	No	Irreconcilable differences are no-fault divorce grounds.
Texas	No	No	Living apart 3 years or irreconcilable differences are no-fault divorce grounds.
Utah	Yes	Yes	3 years after legal separation granted is divorce ground.
Vermont	Yes	Yes-No	Living apart 6 months is no-fault divorce ground.
Virginia	Yes	Yes	Legal separations convert to divorce after 1 year if either party applies.
Washington	Yes	No	Irretrievable broken marriage is no-fault divorce ground.

State	State has Legal Separation	Separations Can Convert to Divorce Grounds	Details
West Virginia	No	No	Financial support may be ordered if there is failure to provide funds.
Wisconsin	Yes	Yes	Converts to divorce with request of either spouse after 1 year.
Wyoming	Yes	No	Irreconcilable differences are grounds for no-fault divorce.

CHAPTER 7

Settlements: Painful and Painless

It used to be very simple. Until the 19th century, all marital property was turned over to the husband. The wife's personal property automatically became the husband's at the time of the marriage. In those days even the wife herself was considered the husband's property. A few holdouts might like to maintain that pre-19th century stance. The American courts have not.

The 1970's were, and the 1980's will continue to be, a time of radical change in the legislation of rights that both men and women have in various forms of formal and informal relationships. Marriages, divorces, and the variety of ways people live together have drastically altered in recent years.

This modern cultural revolution has produced new problems between people which have eventually required the courts to intervene with new laws. One very fine authoritative guide has been compiled to help "homemates" understand the laws that govern their live-in love (Sonenblick & Sowerwine, "The Legality of Love," 1981). The book instructs for both ends of the stick: how to protect one's self from palimony suits, and the legal rights of a lover. The state by state guide in Appendix B outlines certain laws that govern unwed couples, straight or gay. Our parents would have had a hard time believing such topics could even be discussed in a book, and they certainly couldn't have imagined how many thousands of people would need to know their legal rights as lovers.

Like the establishment of financial rights for live-in lovers, there have been changes in divorce property settlements. They have become much more complicated as courts, like society in general, are regarding marriages less as sanctified sexual unions and more like dissolvable partnerships with a basic economic base. The newer laws attempt to completely and cleanly dissolve the financial connections between the partners so that they can continue their lives unencumbered by old financial ties. Thus courts are leaning towards lump settlements at the time of the divorce rather than complicated long-term payment plans. Such arrangements have the additional benefit of preventing later court battles which arise from delayed or unmet payments. Though initially most ex-spouses feel keen responsibilities to comply with court-ordered settlement payments, as the years go by court ordered payments tend to seem like obligatory impositions. Non-compliance with such payments does represent contempt of court, but very few people are taken to court and are even more rarely jailed for late or skipped payments.

It is much easier to have a good divorce settlement when it is all over with the divorce decree. A "good" settlement is one in which the two people are concerned about each other's financial and mental security, with the shared goal that each should be able to form new relationships. If the settlement causes continuing anger or hatred, you can end up with an "unconsummated divorce" in which financial resentments and bonds to a former spouse can perpetuate an emotional energy toward a former spouse and actually handicap one from forming new, significant relationships.

Some of the newer trends in settlements started about a decade ago when the legal profession constructed what was felt to be a model law. Called the Uniform Marriage and Divorce Act, this statute called not only for the lump-sum settlements but also temporary financial aid lasting only long enough to support a dependent spouse until they could arrange to be self-supporting. This attempt at an ideal statute recognized the modern reality that marriages no longer lasted entire lifetimes and that women no longer needed or wanted lifetime financial dependence on a male. About 20% of our states have legislated versions of the Uniform Divorce Act.

There are now 47 states (all but Mississippi, Virginia, and West Virginia) whose laws divide property either "equally" (assets appraised and split down the middle) or "equitably" (the judge decides what is fair distribution of assets). Because judges using either the equal or equitable rules have still regularly produced unfair and unpredictible outcomes, it makes no sense to allow the courts to divide your property. The anger between a couple which prevents them from designing their own settlement is a luxury very few can afford.

Extremely profitable businesses have sprung up to help judges make property decisions. Even lawyers, who would love to tap the income potential from the money-splitting aspects of divorce, cannot claim to have the complex financial expertise demanded by the new math of divorce. Appraisers, accountants and economists all have become expensive professional witnesses that evaluate pension plans, cost of living projections, stock market fluctuations, real estate trends and financial instruments, art collection values, etc. For $600 per day, R. J. & Smythe & Company's "equitable-distribution" division evaluated the financial worth of any business or object. One Dallas attorney specializes in appraising corporations for divorce settlements with fees up to $10,000. A university professor of economics from Cleveland charges $1,000 per report to project the amount of money necessary to maintain a particular standard of living.

Though couples should be able to do without most of these new expensive divorce craftsmen, one type of expert that is necessary and that most laymen and even lawyers and judges are apt to overlook is the tax expert. The tax implications of any settlement must be examined so that Uncle Sam, the third party in all divorces, doesn't end up with a sizable and avoidable share that could substantially effect the quality of life available to divorced people or their children. It is nice to know that expenses incurred gaining tax advice are deductible under the tax code.

Even the term divorce is being changed and in many states today is officially referred to as "dissolution of marriage." This less harsh term reinforces the direction of legal trends in dealing with the division of marital property. Alimony, a major aspect of the financial settlement associated with divorce, has undergone much change in terms of both cultural attitudes and the courts' current practices. Only a short while ago alimony was considered the wife's legal compensation for some wrong done to her by her husband. Alimony then carried the connotation of punitive damages (punishment payments) like a legal sentence imposed on the husband for having criminally victimized his wife. The changed attitude of today's courts is reflected in the use of the term maintenance instead of alimony. Even more impressive is the fact that it is now awarded to husbands as well as to wives.

The most accurate label for what used to be called alimony is "spousal support." Classically, alimony was a kind of permanent punishment which could only end with death or perhaps with the wife's remarriage. The trend today is to have *limited* maintenance or spousal support. Financial aid in the form of *limited* support or *limited* maintenance is awarded to either spouse at the court's discretion, based on factors such as financial need, physical capabilities, employability, and when any economic realities may change for either spouse. For example, a court might decide that the wife needs financial support for a five year period to allow young children to become old enough for her to have a full time job or attend school to train for her profession. When the wife's income exceeds the husband's, or his income is reduced by factors such as health problems or having primary custody of children, the wife may be ordered to provide financial support to the husband. Courts are liable to award long-term payments only to those who are aged or disabled. Recent figures show that today only 14% of divorced women are receiving alimony (support payments for life) and the percentage is steadily declining.

The above paragraphs review recent trends. The legal realities are that individual states may or may not have incorporated these trends into law or practice. The United States Supreme Court has found that state laws which grant alimony only to wives are unconstitutional violations of equal protection laws. Yet, in certain states, alimony still cannot legally be awarded to men. Table 2 (pages 124-127) is a guide to the current statutes (laws) of each state. What individual state courts have jurisdiction (the right) to do varies all the way from having the power to divide all property and order maintenance to having no power to divide any property. Table 2 also gives information as to each state's laws regarding ending alimony payments. In some states alimony ends as soon as the recipient (the one who gets the alimony or spousal support) remarries or cohabitates. Some state laws prevent any alimony if adultery was the fault ground on which the divorce was granted. There are even states which have laws against *any* alimony. Most states do have laws which determine how spousal support payments can be modified.

Table 2—State by State Alimony (Spousal Support) Highlights

State	Highlights
Alabama	May be granted if the wife needs financial support beyond the property settlement or if the husband is found at fault in the divorce. Alimony may be terminated if the wife remarries or cohabitates.
Alaska	May be ganted to either spouse according to need. Marital misconduct is not considered in the awarding of alimony.
Arizona	May be granted to either spouse on the basis of health, financial capability, length of marriage, need.
Arkansas	The judge may order alimony and fees for the enforcement of alimony and take property or securities to gain payment. Marital conduct may be considered in making the awards. Post-marital conduct can cause termination of alimony.
California	May be granted either spouse for "relevant" circumstances. Alimony terminates on the death of either spouse or remarriage of the recipient.
Colorado	May be granted either spouse if they lack the ability for self-support or child custodianship prevents employment. Alimony terminates upon remarriage of the recipient.
Connecticut	May be granted either spouse. Fault is considered. Alimony may be modified if the recipient is cohabitating.
Delaware	May be awarded dependent on divorce grounds.
District of Columbia	May be awarded either spouse. No termination provisions in the law.
Florida	May be awarded either spouse as rehabilitative or permanent, may be modified. Fault and financial factors are considered.
Georgia	May be awarded either spouse according to need. Adultery or desertion bars any alimony. Post-divorce behavior is grounds for modification or termination of alimony.
Hawaii	May be awarded either spouse at the court's discretion. Alimony can be either modified or terminated with remarriage of recipient.
Idaho	May be awarded wife for fault of husband. Post-divorce cohabitation by recipient may terminate alimony.
Illinois	May be awarded to either spouse if financial need or employment handicaps require.
Indiana	May be granted to either spouse.
Iowa	May be awarded to either spouse as the court deems fair.

State	Highlights
Kansas	May be awarded either spouse.
Kentucky	May be awarded either spouse as court deems fair, or on grounds of insufficient property, or inability to self-support. Fault may be considered. Always terminates on death of either or remarriage of recipient.
Louisiana	Alimony may be granted either spouse lacking sufficient support means. Fault is considered. Alimony terminates when unnecessary or when recipient remarries.
Maine	Can be awarded either spouse in the form of specific sums instead of regular payments. Court may assign property profits as alimony for life or for shorter periods.
Maryland	Granted to either spouse. Terminates on the death of the payer or the remarriage of the recipient. May be terminated by recipient's post-divorce sexual behavior.
Massachusetts	Alimony can be granted to either spouse on the basis of marital behavior, length of marriage, age, health, employability, financial future possibilities, income, need, contributions as housewife, and other reasons. Remarriage of recipient is a cause for modification.
Michigan	Alimony may be granted to either spouse. The conduct of each spouse is relevant. Remarriage of recipient may cause termination of alimony.
Minnesota	Alimony granted a financially dependent spouse, unable to self-support and lacking sufficient funds.
Mississippi	Alimony may be granted to either, but if both are capable of self-support, none "should" be granted.
Missouri	Alimony is granted to either spouse and is modifiable, terminatable on the death of either or remarriage of the recipient.
Montana	Alimony can be granted to either spouse regardless of marital conduct according to financial needs and ability to self-support. Terminates on the death of either or remarriage of the recipient.
Nebraska	Alimony grantable to either spouse if the court finds reasonable. It can be modified, but must be in the original divorce decree. Alimony terminates on death of either or remarriage of recipient unless a lump sum alimony was awarded. Post-divorce cohabitation is *not* a modification ground.
Nevada	Alimony can be awarded to either spouse. It terminates on the death of either or remarriage of the recipient. It may be later modified.
New Hampshire	Alimony may be granted to either spouse as the court finds proper. It may be modified every three years. The state does not allow permanent alimony.
New Jersey	Alimony may be granted to either on the basis of need, duration of marriage. Fault is considered. Alimony terminates on remarriage of recipient. Cohabitation after divorce is insufficient reason for modification.
New Mexico	Alimony may be granted to either spouse from the other spouse's separate property.

State	Highlights
New York	The court may require support for either spouse on the basis of the length of the marriage, ability to self-support, situational circumstances. Any fault ground for divorce disallows gaining spousal support.
North Carolina	Alimony may be given to either spouse if dependent, unless adultery of the dependent spouse was the divorce grounds, or the dependent spouse used separation grounds to gain the divorce. Fault is considered in alimony matters.
North Dakota	Alimony can be granted to either spouse as the court deems fair. Remarriage does not automatically terminate alimony.
Ohio	Alimony may be granted to either spouse. The court may divide property to provide alimony as a lump sum or periodic payments may be ordered in forms of cash, real estate or personal property.
Oklahoma	Alimony may be granted to either spouse. The divorce order must differentiate between alimony and property settlement. The latter is irrevocable. Alimony terminates when either spouse dies or the recipient remarries.
Oregon	Alimony can be granted to either spouse as a lump sum or periodic payments. The amounts and details are based on the judge's discretion. Neither remarriage nor later cohabitation of the recipient can automatically terminate alimony.
Pennsylvania	Alimony can be awarded to either spouse.
Rhode Island	Alimony can be granted to either spouse. It is automatically terminated by remarriage of the recipient.
South Carolina	Alimony may be granted to either spouse as a lump sum or in installment payments. Adultery bars alimony.
South Dakota	Alimony can be granted to either spouse for life or any shorter period.
Tennessee	Alimony can be granted to either spouse (filing for a divorce) at the court's discretion. Alimony payments automatically end for marital misconduct. After the divorce is final, alimony may be modified.
Texas	The court can not award alimony, but the couple may agree to some form of payments as part of the property settlements.
Utah	Alimony can be awarded to either spouse at the court's discretion. Alimony is terminated by cohabitation or remarriage of the recipient.
Vermont	Alimony can be granted to either spouse according to circumstances. No automatic reductions occur to recipient for cohabitation.
Virginia	Alimony may be granted to either spouse in payments or in lump sum. It ceases upon remarriage or death of the recipient. No permanent alimony if the payor was granted the divorce on any fault ground. Any other divorce procedure allows for alimony.
Washington	Granted to either without regard to marital misconduct, but on the court's consideration of each's financial resources and prospects for income, as well as the duration of the marriage.

State	Highlights
West Virginia	Granted to either spouse. If a no-fault divorce, alimony is only granted if some fault can be shown. Cohabitation may be grounds for modifying alimony.
Wisconsin	Granted to either spouse with consideration of all relavent factors. Remarriage of recipient terminates alimony. Cohabitation is grounds for termination.
Wyoming	Alimony is granted to the wife only. Can be a specific sum or profits from husband's real estate.

Although Table 2 does highlight state laws governing alimony, it is essential to remember that the attitude and practice of the judge who rules on alimony is more important than the law. This is testified to by the almost universal use of the term "may," which introduces the statement by laws for all the states. Judge's discretion allows them to interpret laws so broadly that almost anything can be decided and, therefore, be legally binding. Even more powerful than the laws and/or the judge, however, is the couple. State laws or even the judges can only govern formal court decisions. A cooperative couple can easily override almost anything their state laws or courts dictate. For instance, in Texas, the court cannot award alimony—it's against state law—but the couple could agree to payments made by one to another as part of their decision about the property settlement. That illustrates only one formal way to legalize maintenance payments in a state which prohibits spousal support. If the couple doesn't need legal sanctions or controls for their lives, they can privately agree to any financial deal they want.

The rest of this chapter will focus on property settlements. Property settlements here will deal mainly with the division of all assets owned by either or both spouses and not with spousal support, maintenance, or custody matters, even though these may, in many situations, be relevant and even part of the settlement agreement. Custody and child support, which represent major financial matters in marriages with children, have been reserved for a later chapter.

There are very potent emotions as well as legal consequences which arise in the process and outcome of property settlements. Because each person will end up with fewer worldly goods (about half) than they formerly had. Furthermore, this loss comes at the very time and with the very person with whom they are ending a very emotional relationship. Such a set of circumstances, which crucially involves one's psychological and economic status, is a very loaded situation indeed.

The most basic tenet is not to allow emotional positions to dominate settlement agreements. A spouse feeling guilty for being the person who "caused" the divorce may want to assuage guilt by being overly generous in the settlement. Similarly, a rejected spouse may be willing to agree to any settlement because they hope that by being a victim or by being so cooperative, they will effect a reconciliation. Such attitudes, especially if they result in unfair settlements, cause a dangerous amount of post-settlement resentment. The most common hinderance to reasonable settlements is the use of the financial settlement as an instrument of revenge or punishment. There is also the case where dependent spouses still look to the other for all decision making and, thus, allow the other to decide on what is a proper settlement, which may well be inappropriate to either person's needs. Other handicapping psychological situations occur when one or both parties are too depressed or too upset to realistically estimate current or future financial needs. In other words, highly emotional times are rotten times to make any decisions, certainly those as important as the financially binding property settlement agreements.

Yet it is common for a divorcing couple to attempt to make economic decisions at an emotional time. What well may happen then is that when the couple's lawyer(s) hear the revengeful, overgenerous, or somehow inappropriate settlement ideas the couple has generated, he or she can realistically point out how unfair the ideas are, that the judge will disallow the inequitable split, and all the things the couple's present plan ignores, such as the extremely important tax aspects. Shocked by the inadequacy of their own attempt, the couple may turn the entire settlement over to attorneys. This step is one that should almost always be avoided since it might cost you all hopes for an amicable relationship with your spouse, as well as all of your savings.

For a couple to accomplish a reasonable settlement plan, the procedure first of all must take into account the danger of making decisions hastily or during highly emotional times. The most useful settlement agreement procedure involves the following five goals:

1) Awareness: Both parties need to be fully knowledgeable about the value of all current and future assets and liabilities. Gaining this information provides a necessary starting place from which the couple can hopefully establish a cooperative stance.

2) Seek competent advice: Others have been through the process of arranging settlements. There are professionals who specialize in tax and divorce settlements. There are non-professionals, friends and relatives who have acquired practical knowledge through personal experience. Don't re-invent the wheel by ignoring other settlement experiences or expertise, but at the same time don't allow others to make decisions that are yours. Seeking advice and guidance should be seen as a step designed to permit you to do an educated job of exercising your options.

3) Equitable Division: Equitable division very rarely means 50/50 splits. Usually factors in the two people's lives (e.g.'s, earning power, responsibilities for children, other dependents, tax brackets, financial needs on a long and short term basis) determine different financial needs for each spouse. Equitable should be translated to mean fair when all circumstances are taken into account. Avoid forced sales. Allow funds for career preparation. Don't be a martyr or a fool. Aim to be generous.

4) Subjective Fairness: A fair property settlement unfortunately is usually only received by those who get 80% or more of the common property. In other words, it is very difficult for the division of the property to be perceived as fair by both parties. Both are losing so much of what has been theirs that perceptions of fairness are significantly distorted. A great rule of thumb is that when you get to a point where both people believe they are giving about 60%, thus feeling they are being generous but not robbed, you have achieved subjective fairness. When one member of the couple truly feels they are giving as much as 75% in the settlement, the resentments that evolve tend to be troublesome and long-lasting.

5) Team Mate Approach: Any attitude of one upmanship, opponents winning through intimidations, emotional blackmail, winning at all, is detrimental. The goal should be to achieve a spirit of working together. "If we could have accomplished that, we never would have gone for a divorce in the first place." Don't let that be your quote. You have decided on a divorce. You are arranging for

single lives. Making settlement agreements is one perfect time to end battling and begin a peaceful relationship. Work as a team.

If the couple can agree that the above five are reasonable goals, then you are in an ideal position to begin the actual process of working on the settlement agreement. The next step is to set up a time when you will begin the process.

All meetings should be held when both people are in the proper mood. Divorcing people regularly go through mood cycles which include depressions, angers, and other negative mental states. Even if a particular time has been set aside to work on agreements, remember that the emotional climate should be right for the teamwork, fairness goal to be realized. Both parties should assume the responsibility for judging if they are in the right mood. Don't start, or continue once started, working on the settlement in a negative emotional environment.

The first task to be handled is typically the easiest and so can serve to set the cooperative atmosphere for later, more difficult sessions. This first task is the clerical listing of assets and liabilities. Together the couple should produce a list of real estate, income instruments, cash, personal property, cars, furniture, mortgages, current bills, installment loans, tax bills, individual debts. The personal property need not be listed down to the last handkerchief, only that property which one or both feel should be part of the property settlement. There needs to be sufficient discussion of all items so that both understand what is involved. For example, knowledge of that year's tax liability should be understood by husband and wife. No decision about divisions should be made at the time of the property listing. The basic aim for initial meetings is to establish a cooperative working relationship. Producing the list is a secondary aim.

In arriving at complicated agreements, it is best to work out the easiest parts first. Success breeds success. Making some agreements where there is little or no conflict sets the stage for later productive bargaining. For these reasons, it is typically best to work out property items first, spousal support matters second, and custody last. However, if the couple feels that custody arrangements will be the least troublesome matter between them, then it might well be handled first. This same principle of easiest first is applicable within a settlement area. For instance, if a disagreement about the sound system ownership develops early in your discussion of property division, put aside discussion of the stereo until other easily arrived at property agreements are made.

These meetings might well start with each person producing a list of things that they particularly love and want. This list should not include major items, such as the family home or savings account, but rather items like a favorite painting or piece of furniture. This session can then proceed like a gift giving event and, of course, is designed to establish an atmosphere of good will. When you come to an item both people want, put that item aside until the list of mutually desired items is sufficiently long to allow for trades. "OK, you can have the antique clock if I can have the little TV and copper pans." It may resemble a monopoly game ("trade for all four railroads for Vermont Avenue and Park Place"), but it is not. It is a way to build up skills at meeting goals for an amicable settlement.

It is unwise to try to complete a draft of the entire settlement agreement in one or two meetings. A series of short meetings permits thinking time between meetings, the gaining of outside advice, and most importantly prevents the fatigue factor of long sessions that leads to short tempers. About 6 to 12 meetings usually provides most couples with a set of agreements about the property settlement which can be reviewed by an appropriate legal advisor.

If you can't seem to accomplish any of the advised steps for any reasons, do not rush to turn it over to attorneys or the courts. If the couple is unable to draft a settlement agreement by themselves. they should consider finding a mediator. A third party whom both respect and trust may well be able to save them from the prospect of a legally determined set of decisions. Friends, relatives, a clergyman have all served as mediators. There are also professionals who can help, such as a case worker from the Domestic Relations Court, available at no or minimal cost. A counselor or therapist with mediation skills might work if both parties have enough confidence to invest the time and effort to see if it is useful. It often is the case that one or two mediated sessions are all that are needed to get the couple past trouble spots and allow them to proceed by themselves.

After the couple has worked out what they consider a good property settlement, it should be presented in written form to an attorney. Even if you can't reach total agreement, be aware that the more you are able to work out, the more you both benefit from less lawyer involvement. However, some legal expertise will always be needed to fashion the property settlements into forms which will most effectively serve the couple.

Work on financial support (maintenance, alimony, spousal support) usually proceeds after the property settlement has been *tentatively* worked out. All agreements should be considered tentative until all aspects of the divorce are worked out. You may go back and give up Park Place in a previous property agreement in order to gain a higher regular income through spousal support.

Here are the more important things to keep in mind when you are considering spousal support. Judges certainly consider most of these factors.

1) Living singularly rather than as a couple raises the cost of living at least 15%.

2) Parenting takes time and energy and reduces the primary parent's income producing abilities.

3) Factors which influence the length of time the supported spouse will have special financial needs. Time for this person's job, education, or training. Time for the custodial parent to parent while children are growing. Time to find a reasonable job. Time before money is inherited. Time and expense of relocations.

4) Other means of support need to be considered, such as help from a divorcing person's parents, independent income sources, income from property such as rents, or financial status of new mates.

5) Skills with handling money.

6) Child custody provisions.

7) A need for education or vocational training.

8) State laws concerning how alimony is modified or terminated.

9) Income potential in the near and distant future. The Internal Revenue Service ceases to consider alimony as a deduction when the supported spouse remarries.

10) Tax benefits, e.g., the payer deducts spousal support and the dependent spouse pays taxes on the support as income. An ideal financial settlement will produce a minimum of taxes for both.

If the couple does not agree on spousal support, the court will do the deciding. The dangers of having the court decide have been mentioned repeatedly, but if you remain unimpressed with the potential severity of court imposed settlements, simply talk with some people who have experienced them. Reading about court battles pales in comparison to the impact gained from hearing from friends who have suffered the inequities, financial consequences, and cruelties imposed by the legal system.

Spousal support can be modified. If a court makes a decision on spousal support which is considered unfair, wrong, or inappropriate, it is possible to appeal to a higher court. Most appeals regarding support are lost. Higher courts generally trust and uphold lower courts' judgments. One reason lower courts' decisions are upheld is that judges appreciate the lower court advantages of hearing and seeing the parties involved. Higher courts typically review judgment via papers. Appeals have their best chance when they are based on points of law rather than on the wisdom of the decisions.

The most feasible way to modify settlements is by returning to the same court that made the original settlement. Later modifications (change in spousal support) are most often granted on the basis of a change in circumstances. The circumstances that can qualify for modification of support are new or changed financial needs, cost of living changes, and new marriages. The likely possibility of such changes again argues in favor of the couple deciding and agreeing on spousal support before going to court. Any outlandish mistakes will certainly be discovered by your attorney, who has the responsibility of looking over your tentative agreement prior to court time. If the couple's agreement is found by attorneys to be somehow inappropriate, the couple should simply return to their own meetings for further direct discussions. Do not consider poor decisions proof that the two attorneys should work it out between themselves in or outside a courtroom. That can be every bit as deadly as a full fledged courtroom battle.

There are many situations, however, when you want to get help from your legal counsel after arriving at your settlement agreement. It is best if both parties attend all important attorney meetings since there is less chance for devisive plots or fears of plots. The attorney who is interested in doing the job of helping you understand your rights and explaining state laws and procedures will have little problem with meetings which include both spouses. Conscientious, ethical attorneys are not interested in having couples pursue their marital battles in court as a means of padding their own income or perpetuating the hostility that can so easily flair up between a divorcing couple.

Unless children are involved, reaching agreements concerning property settlements and spousal support is the majority of work that needs to be done for a non-contested divorce. The entire matter of custody and child support is the topic of a later chapter, but you should realize that strong court trends in all states and the federal government favor tougher child support.

Most post divorce litigation is over alimony. You may be able to avoid painful court procedures by avoiding alimony altogether. That is, it is wise for couples to consider the advantages of working out a property settlement which negates the need for *any* spousal support. This is accomplished by giving the party who would normally receive support a share of current or future assets which is approximately equal to the total of support payments the court might award. Failure to pay alimony ordered by the court can lead to jail for the payer, though it is rare, complicated and does little for either party financially or for their continuing relationship.

Another settlement factor is relevant if you live in one of the minority of states which currently has communal property laws. These laws recognize property gained during the marriage as belonging equally to husband and wife, regardless of the relative contributions of either toward the acquisition of that property. Household labor is equated with career labor, and property tends to be divided exactly equally or according to the judge's discretion. The settlement complications in community property states, again, are only considerations that require attention if the couple fails to arrive at mutually acceptable agreements.

While planning the divorce settlement, it is a very wise step for any non-wage earning member of the family (most traditionally, the wife) to make sure a credit identity is established *before the divorce.* Credit cards are almost a necessity in today's society, and most married women do not have credit in their own names. Having a credit card as Mrs. Anybody will not allow you to have a credit card after the divorce. One way to deal with this is to have current credit cards listed in your own name while you are still married. Under the Equal Credit Opportunity Act you may have cards issued under any name you like, for instance your maiden name. Obtaining a credit card is just one step in establishing necessary credit. In order to have a good credit rating one must first gain credit, then use it, then establish a record of making prompt and regular payments. Very helpful details on how ex-wives or ex-wives-to-be can deal with the credit problem are available in, ''The Credit Handbook for Women'' and ''Establishing Credit 101,'' free publications available from Public Affairs, American Express Company, Sixth Floor, American Express Plaza, New York, NY, 10004.

Here is an interesting fact that might help when wrestling with settlement agreements. There is a fad for ''boomerang divorces'' which are divorces gone through by loving married couples who plan to continue living together, but choose to divorce. These couples have voluntarily decided to go through the problems of arriving at property settlements in exchange for the legal advantages they feel a live-in arrangement has over marriage. The book, ''The Legality of Love,'' lists twelve financial advantages to be derived from boomerang divorces. The authors who oppose boomerang divorces list the problems of such arrangements.

Whether or not you are a voluntary or reluctant participant, if you are divorcing, you will have to be a party to a settlement agreement. With effort you can make the law work for you rather than against you. Grit your teeth, pour a drink, get an arbitrator, but somehow do the work it takes to reach an agreed-upon property settlement between you and your spouse.

Part III
Children and Divorce

CHAPTER 8

Child Custody

Seventy percent of divorcing couples have minor children. Today there are about ten million children of divorced American couples who live with one parent. Children's custody and their financial support creates the majority of divorce-related litigation disputes, both at the time of the original divorce decree and later.

Quantitative statements are powerless to describe the immense impact custody matters have on those involved. Children, unlike property, cannot be equitably divided. The joys, responsibilities, and emotional involvements which exist between parents and children are clearly much too complex to be either handled or contained within a courtroom. Yet when parents divorce, these issues about children, do, in fact, become legal matters. Courts must, and do make decisions about where children will live and with whom, how they will be supported, and how much time parents can spend with their own children.

It is not difficult to understand why custody battles can be so damaging for families. Winning a court custody battle essentially involves one parent trying to prove the other unfit to parent. The hideous task of consciously trying to conjure up and gather proof of some kind of moral degeneracy about a person one chose to wed and have children with is as dehumanizing as contending with the charges that that person has conjured up and is attempting to prove about you. Try to imagine friends, neighbors, and relatives being brought into court to publicly declare your inadequacy as a human being fit to raise your own children. Without going through such an experience, it is unlikely that you can accurately project the hurt and alienation that results from such a trauma.

All of the above reflects on the affects of such proceedings on the adults involved. For children, the affects are even more profound. Where will they live? What parent will they "lose"? How much residual animosity between the parents will filter down to them in terms of being taught to do without a parent or even expected to disrespect or hate their own father or mother? The biggest problem is that while children may be able to be realistically reassured that they are *not* the cause of parental battles that led to the divorce, in custody disputes they are, in reality, the center of the conflict. They are the cause of their parents' frightening battles, and most of them know it.

This chamber of horrors introduces this chapter in order to impress readers with the need to avoid legal custody battles. Fortunately, full-fledged court custody fights are rare. Most divorcing couples agree on the major facets of custody so easily that such agreements can serve as the first easy steps that set a positive stage for later, tougher negotiations between divorcing adults. In fact, the agreements are so easily arrived at that in many cases they end up being somewhat naively constructed. Children and parents can suffer the consequences of ill-thought-out custodial and/or child support arrangements which, while certainly not as disastrous as custody fights, are still sufficiently difficult to merit careful planning.

THE CUSTODY TREND—CONCURRENT CUSTODY

Before getting into the details of the typical current custody precidents, practices and suggestions, the wave of the future—concurrent custody, will be reviewed. The courts as well as the culture are slowly realizing that children do best with two parents and that it is damaging and inhuman to take away a parent's parental responsibilities and joys. These beliefs are awkwardly infiltrating our laws at a snail's pace. As of this writing, less than 10% of the states have statutes which permit any form of joint custody. California, Iowa, North Carolina, Oregon, and Wisconsin have been the first to inact legislation defining joint custody.

In 1980, California wrote into its laws the following: "...it is the public policy of this state to assure minor children frequent and continuing contact with both parents after the parents have separated or dissolved their marriage and in order to effect such policy, it is necessary to encourage parents to share the rights and responsibilities of childrearing...."

The way this law works is that the courts tend to award joint custody when both *or either* parent requests it. This California law is very tough. If the judge decides, for any reason, that joint custody cannot work, then he must state in the decision exactly why it was denied. The law further states, "the court shall consider which parent is more likely to allow the child frequent and continuing contact with the non-custodial parent...", so that if one parent wants joint custody and the other parent wants sole (primary custody with the other parent having visitation rights) the California judge may well award sole custody to the parent who wanted joint custody because they have displayed the better attitude about sharing parenting.

There are definite problems with the trend for concurrent custody. These are implied in the following excerpts from a draft for a joint custody statute in Colorado.

"The court upon application of either parent or person seeking custody may enter an order of joint custody.

The court prior to entering an order awarding joint custody shall make a finding that an award of joint custody would be advantageous to the child and in his or her best interest.

In making an award of joint custody the court should consider the following factors:

1. The ability of the parties to cooperate and to make decisions jointly.

2. The past pattern of involvement of the parties with the child that reflects a system of values and mutual support that by such joint custody award they would act in a manner to provide a positive and nourishing relationship with the child.

3. The physical proximity of the parties to each other and the practicality of the award of joint custody in relation to where the child is to reside.

4. Whether such an award of joint custody is likely to allow the child more frequent or continuing contact with both parents.

For purposes of this section "Joint Custody" means an order

awarding legal custody of the minor child to both parents, providing that decisions as to health, education and general welfare shall be made jointly, which may or may not provide that physical custody shall be shared by both parents.

Any award of joint custody may be modified or terminated on the petition of one or both parents or on the court's own motion if it is shown the best interest of the child requires modification or termination of the order.

In a request for modification of joint custody, the burden of proof is upon the party seeking a change and the evidence must be clear and convincing that such a change is in the best interest of the child.''

Thus, joint custody requires cooperative parents who live close to each other and generally respect each other's parenting abilities.

The major problem with joint custody involves the difficulties that arise when the parents disagree on some important aspect of a child's life. Repeated trips to court to solve parental differences is clearly impractical. Some states have agencies of various kinds which handle such problems. I frequently write into formal custody recommendations that disputes will be mediated by a child mental health professional that both parents have agreed upon beforehand. If they are unwilling to use a mediator or to agree to follow the child expert's advice, if mediation fails, then I do not consider them appropriate parents for joint custody. Other professionals insist that joint custody is so necessary that they will plan for disagreements that cannot be mediated to be submitted for binding arbitration (a way of forcing parties to agree to the decision of an arbitration).

This trend for *some* form of joint custody has come about through raised consciousness about the injustices suffered through the traditional sole custody arrangements. Two recent psychological studies typify influential data that is slowly impelling courts toward the newer custody modes. Wallerstein and Kelly in *Surviving the Break Up* and Lora Tessman in *Children of Parting Parents* evaluated children who lived under the traditional sole custody pattern.

Wallerstein & Kelly's study found that children in sole custody divorced situations expressed much less positive feelings about the divorce than did the parents. Five years after the separation, 80% of the parents, but only 22% of the children, thought the divorce had been a good idea. Even the 34% of the children who were regarded by the researchers as doing especially well still felt unhappy, lonely and sorrowful in regard to the divorce. The authors concluded that, "There is considerable evidence in this study that divorce was highly beneficial for many adults. There is, however, no comparable evidence regarding the experience of the children...." Remember that these conclusions related to children who were under sole custody arrangements.

Tessmen's study provides convincing evidence that children bond with both parents and that there is a depression which children suffer when they lose either parent, not just the mother. Of the children Tessman studied who had the mother as their primary custodian, the most angry or depressed were the children who were visited infrequently or not at all by their fathers.

It seems clear that for a child to resolve the loss of a father, children need to go through some genuine mourning procedure. Tessman described that the young children who were able to grieve did so because they were around some close adult who shared their feeling of loss.

When a parent dies, an important part of the healing process is for the child to talk much about the departed parent. The more positive memories when repeated and, perhaps, even embellished provide the child with a secure belief that he/she was valued and loved by the dead parent. Only after a substantial time has passed will anger about "desertion" by death be useful to the child.

At the time of divorce when the child first loses a parent and needs positive input about the missing parent is exactly the time when most typically, the mother's need is for a negative view of her former spouse. Furthermore, those mothers who do share the feeling of mourning with their children may well be seriously depressed and not available to their children in any important way. Thus, the needs of the mother and child are usually diametrically opposite at the time of the divorce. In addition, at the time of the divorce, children who are fearful at having been "abandoned" by one parent cannot risk alienation from the remaining parent and will typically hide the need to mourn and all positive feelings about the absent parent in order to preserve the emotional bond with the parent they still have around.

Not being able to openly mourn a missing parent is the primary cause for the extended depression observed in children some 5 years after the divorce.

It is clear that a custody arrangement where the child has both parents on a real basis prevents the events described in the research. For instance, in the Wallerstein and Kelly study it was found that the primary factor among those children who had a good post-divorce adjustment was a continuity of relationship with both parents, where visiting was regular and dependable and encouraged by the custodial parent. Good father-child relationships were found to produce high self-esteem and the absence of depression in children of both sexes and all ages.

A direct evaluation of children actually living in joint custody arrangements was begun by Susan Steinman in 1978. She concluded, "Overall, these children did not suffer the feelings of rejection and abandonment frequently seen when one divorced parent did not remain in regular contact." The limitation of the Steinman study is that the conclusions cannot be extended to situations where both parents do not want joint custody as her subjects were all from parents who strongly wanted and chose a joint custody arrangement. There is not good data yet available on the effect of California-like laws which are designed to impose joint custody on less willing parents.

"SPIRIT" VERSUS "LETTER" OF CUSTODY ARRANGEMENTS

Whether contemplating a fierce battle or an amicable settlement about children, divorcing couples need to learn about the emotional and legal consequences of custody and child support matters.

Legal authorities regularly deal with the concepts of "the letter of the law" and "the spirit of the law." The idea expressed by the two terms is that laws cannot be blindly applied to any individual case (letter of the law) without considering the underlying intent of the law (spirit of the law). One major purpose of this book is to inform about letters of law. The present chapter presents a formal review of the basic types of custody employed by the courts, as well as offers insight into the basic custody-related terms, such as "best interest of the child." However, before the "letter," it is essential to impart the essential spirit of quality custody arrangements as it has been revealed through some 20 years of helping parents and children deal with the legally complex and emotionally crucial problems of custody matters.

This "spirit" is presented in the form of an abbreviated set of specific custody recommendations as they might have evolved from a comprehensive custody study. The recommendations will, however, be amplified by including some philosophical and practical justifications which underlie each recommendation. It is within the explanatory justifications that the "spirit" of quality custody arrangements can be found. The particular recommendations serve only to present solutions to one hypothetical family's custody dilemmas. Every family situation is different because of its unique combination of individual personalities, life patterns, financial circumstances, and emotional bonds between family members. Therefore, custody solutions must be custom-designed to meet the unique needs for any individual family. The following recommendations, therefore, cannot be considered as ideal or to be used intact to fit any real family.

Custody Recommendation Example

1. Mrs. Z should be appointed primary custodian of both children with Mr. Z having specific visitation as detailed below.

(The majority of the children's time is spent living with the custodial parent. The visiting parent can, however, have *any amount* of time with the children that the custody document states, from one supervised (in someone else's presence) hour every decade to 10 or 50 or 80 or whatever percent of time is stated in the custody document. Who should serve as the custodial parent and what should be the specific visitation for the non-custodial parent are the basic decisions to be made in the majority of today's custody cases.)

2. Mr. Z's visitation rights under the condition that both parents homes are in the same geographical region so that appreciable travel time between homes or school is not a factor.

a) Visitation during the school year shall be from after school on the first Friday of each month until after school on the second Monday following the first Friday of the month.

(This particular visitation approach during the school year provides the children extended periods of time with both parents.

It's design is to discourage the "responsibility-burdened mother" versus the "recreation-director father" routine. The school time visitation plan here meets the desires and needs of one family. The point is to construct a plan for the special needs of each family. One father, for example, who was a ski instructor, had one visitation schedule during the ski season school year and another during the non-ski season school year. People with seasonal or home-based or traveling occupations should arrange the children's visitations to accommodate their occupations as well as their parental value systems. Don't accept some legal hack phrase such as "reasonable visitation" to define your contact with your children. Certainly if you and your children's other parent are and remain reasonable there will be no problem with visitation no matter what the custody document states, but the work of carefully constructing a thought-out document serves to clarify many issues between the parents and avoid all kinds of later problems in and out of courts. The custody document is something that *potentially* can be ignored by two parents who creatively plan for their own and their children's lives as each current situation develops. The custody document serves as the authority of each parent's rights and responsibilities only under those circumstances when the parents are not able to agree.)

b) Special occasions which modify the school year schedule are: Christmas (winter) and Easter (spring) school holidays in which the parents will equally split the time with both children with the father deciding on how the winter vacation will be split during even numbered years (e.g., 1984, 1986, 1988) and the spring vacation during the odd numbered years (e.g., 1985, 1987, 1989). The mother will make the choices on the years it is not the father's option. Whichever parent is not with the children on Christmas evening and morning will have the children for the Thanksgiving school holiday. Each parent's birthday can be celebrated with the children visiting that day and overnight. The son's birthday will be with the father on odd numbered years and the mother on even numbered years. The daughter's birthday will be with her mother on odd numbered years and her father on even numbered years.

(These particular custody plans would be most applicable for children of elementary school age. A nursing infant or an older teenager would have very different needs and would require different arrangements. The infant could not spend a week away from its mother, while older teenagers may want to have some say in these decisions themselves.

Again, parents can, with cooperative work, come up with creative and mutually satisfactory agreements not likely to be produced in the courtroom. One set of parents had been completely at odds because they disagreed as to whether the father could competently care for the health and safety of a two-year-old during extended vacations. The enraged father was willing to fight in court to determine if he could or could not have extended vacations with his own son. One quick mediation session was all that was necessary for both parents to agree that the vacation schedule would permit extended trips for the father and son once he had reached six years old. The chance for such an easy solution to have been reached in a court of law after extended court arguments and delays would be very slim. It has been a rare court-drafted custody arrangement that builds in changes with time, yet time factors are frequently very relevant. For instance, it is often wise for children to have some input as to where and with whom they will live once they become about sixteen.)

c) Summer vacations, defined as public school summer recess, shall be split between the parents with the father deciding on his time with the children on even numbered summers. The mother shall have the option on how the time is divided on odd numbered summers. The parent making the choices about the summer must inform all parties eight weeks before the school summber vacation begins or the other parent has the right to plan the summer. The time spent with each parent shall be continuous unless both parents agree to some other pattern.

(Summers provide special times when both parents can be the real time and vacation parent. It can also be a time for longer periods with the non-custodial parent and offer relief time for the custodial parent who typically shoulders the major child-rearing responsibilities. The children's freedom from regular school obligations can also allow opportunities for an extremely crucial aspect of the parent-child relationship—one-on-one time. Too often children of divorce are always with their siblings when they are with their parents. The summer provides flexibility so that arrangements for one-on-one time is most easily possible. This individual time is so important that provision for it is regularly included in the during-school year custody recommendations and is comprised of some form of the classical alternating weekend visitation plan. When a non-custodial parent has only overnight visits with children on weekends, a weekday evening dinner with each child individually is often included to provide for that crucial one-on-one time.

The part of the summer custody recommendation which notes that the summer times with parents should be continuous unless otherwise agreed to by both parents exemplifies two points. First, it addresses the problem of one parent consciously or unconsciously harrassing the other. A vindictive parent could make the other parent's summer difficult by using their "power" to plan the summer to have the children traveling back and forth every 3 to 5 days. Second, it shows how anything either parent can predict as difficult can be written into the custody agreement. Some agreements may end up rather lengthy, but like financial settlements, thought and care prior to the court date can avoid later lengthy and expensive problems.)

3. Custody arrangements under the condition that parents reside in separate geographic locations.

a) If either parent moves more than 50 miles from the other parent then it is recommended that Mrs. Z maintain primary custodianship of the children but that Mr. Z's visitation is altered as follows. Mr. Z would have the children for ¾ths of the summer vacations and of the school-defined Christmas and Easter vacations. In addition, Mr. Z can have visitation with his children any one weekend a month during the school year if he offers Mrs. Z four weeks advance notice and pays all associated travel expenses for either him to come to the children or for the children to travel to him.

(Certain circumstances should alter the custody plans while others should not. In general you can go back to court to alter custody under any significant change of circumstances. This is intended for major changes such as serious illness or criminal activities. Going back to court is usually a tremendous imposition, expense, and pain for one or both parties, and so an original well-thought-out custody plan can again serve. Parents can agree and state in the original custody plan under what conditions custody plans will or will not change and what are reasons for going back to court. Geographical moves are such a common occurrence in our society and have such important implications for custody arrangements that it is wise to cover this possibility within the original custody agreement. Other common occurrences that the parents should consider in the original agreement are whether either parent remarrying or co-habitating constitutes a reason for any custody revision.

In the example recommendation the idea behind the increased time for the father under the geographical separation is simply to make up for time together that was lost because of the move. Again each family's unique circumstances should lead to unique custody arrangements. It is possible to construct good custody arrangements (i.e., those which maximize the children gaining the best parenting possible from both parents under the circumstances) even where there is distrust and bad faith between the parents. It may require carefully worked out and complicated arrangements, such as how the children's clothes will be readied for each parental exchange or how the children can be protected from being with both parents at the same time, but there are those cases where such arrangements are necessary for the children's welfare. There have been, in many cases, custody documents which include definite disincentives for parents who are suspected of wanting to disenfranchise the other parent by, for instance, moving so far away it would make impossible genuine contact between the children and that parent. Custody documents can include the stipulation that if the custodial parent moves more than 100 miles away, primary custodianship reverses to the other parent. A more common safeguard for the children of battling parents comes with the built-in use of a Child Mental Health Professional. Here the custodial agreement uses a clause which states that when parents disagree on some aspect of custody, they must abide by the decision of a child psychologist or child psychiatrist. When such experts are employed it is wise to have prior parental agreement as to the particular professional or agency to be used.

Custody arrangements can include many parental and child rights not included in the brief example offered but listed in this chapter. There are also certain things that cannot be legislated. Some are obvious. No document can mandate a child's long-term love or respect. Only time and experience with parents can fashion the child's bond with any parent. One mistaken notion commonly held by parents is that they can control the other parent's child-rearing practices with the custody document. While a parent can protect a child from criminal abuse or neglect from the other parent, they cannot dictate things like bedtimes, menus, recreational activities, or even discipline techniques. The courts recognize that there are a wide range of acceptable parenting styles and each parent has the right to raise their own children according to their own beliefs. It may be very painful to see your child exposed to things or treated in ways that violate your deep convictions, but unless laws are being violated either parent has the right to raise their children as they see fit.

What the court does respect in custody arrangements are details which are designed to implement the rights of both parents and children to maximize a continuing good relationship. Most parents, for instance, never question that they can have regular telephone or mail communications with their children, so such details are not usually part of the custody arrangements, but if there is a doubt, such privileges can be included in the custody document and they will be permitted by most courts.)

The point to be made about the all imporant "spirit" of custody arrangements is that they can and should be designed to fit your individual family's needs. You and your spouse have the information which allows you to do it much better than the courts. You may require the help of some mediator and you certainly will require the help of legal counsel to place the agreement in the proper legal language and form, but it will still be the agreement you reached rather than a set of decisions made for you by the courts. This is an alternative to be avoided at almost any cost. This chapter may offer some ideas on creative solutions to problems. A rich source of ideas is a 1982 book, "Mom's House, Dad's House," by Isolina Rice. Get ideas from whatever source you can to allow you to work out your future with your children.

TYPES OF CUSTODY

There are four basic custodial plans for children of divorce. Today the vast majority of children still have one "custodial" and one "visiting" parent. The child resides with the custodial parent who is the primary decision maker, for instance, in regards to health, financial, religious, educational and disciplinary matters. The visiting parent has the child(ren) for short periods of time, such as some weekends, vacations, and holidays. All of the most important features of this custodial-visitation type arrangement are things that can be negotiated between the couple. The couple can agree as to who will be the custodial and who will be the visiting parent. The parents can also set up the visitation rights of the visiting parent (frequency, times and length of visits). The couple can also agree on how the child will be financially supported. They may even formally arrange for certain childrearing decisions to be shared. The couple can further agree under what conditions all of these visitations, financial and childrearing decisions, including the primary custodialship may change. In other words, it is possible for the divorcing couple to agree on every major aspect of how their children will be raised. The court only intervenes if it finds the arrangements detrimental to the child's welfare. Two legal trends which are influencing court judgments on custody matters today are: 1) that the agreement demonstrates that *both* parents are assuming responsibilities for their offspring in accordance with their abilities and 2) that the children are guaranteed adequate financial support.

A second custodial arrangement, which has already been described as clearly appearing to be the future direction of child custody, is most correctly termed joint custody (it is sometimes referred to as con-current, alternating, or divided custody). With joint custody the parents share *legal* custody. Sharing legal custody means the mother and the father equally share the authority and responsibility for the decision making regarding all major aspects of their children's lives, i.e., the health, welfare, education, religion, socialization and discipline. They also share responsibility for the provision of food, shelter, clothing and other essentials for the security and safety of the children although these financial responsibilities are typically specifically outlined in those parts of the custody agreement which deal with child support matters.

Joint custody does *not* mean parents will have equal physical custody of the child(ren). Joint custody plans will include stipulations as to how the physical custody of the child(ren) will be handled and it, similar to sole custody arrangements, can vary from each parent having anything from zero to 100% of the child(ren)'s physical custody.

Physical custody (or residential care) of the child in joint custody arrangements usually involves specific day-to-day rights and responsibilities associated with maintaining children's homelife. For instance, it is usually agreed for obvious practical reasons that emergency medical decisions and/or daily discipline matters will be decided upon solely by the parent having the physical custody at any particular time.

Joint custody works when the relationship between the parents is good enough to allow for continued positive communication, cooperative attitudes, and mutual respect for each other's parenting practices. The following excerpts from a sample joint custody arrangement offers an example of the kind of custodial contract parents would agree to in order to allow for an effective joint custody arrangement.

Joint Custody Agreement Excerpts

"We, Gerald Alpern, here referred to as Jerry, and Carol Alpern, here referred to as Carol, are husband and wife seeking a dissolution of our marriage. We have two children of our marriage: Tyler Jon, age 14 and Thomas Eric, age 13.

We believe each of us to be fit parents and recognize the unique contribution each of us has to offer our children. We wish to continue to share responsibility for the care of the children and each fully participate in all major decisions affecting their health, education and welfare, while disrupting their life patterns as little as possible. We intend to have joint custody of our children and propose only the most minimal necessary formality in scheduling time with them, subject to consideration of schedules and the necessity of reasonable notice, in order to retain a flexible opportunity for each of us to be with the children and help raise them. Our primary concern has been and shall be the best interests of our children within the reality of our marital dissolution.

We have reached this mutual agreement voluntarily by the process of mediation through a neutral attorney, Lisa Mark. We understand that the mediator was not representing either or both of us.

In consideration of the promises made by each of us to the other, it is agreed between us as follows:

1. Jerry and Carol shall share joint legal custody of Tyler and Tom.

2. Tyler and Tom shall reside with Jerry as further set forth below.

3. Should any change of circumstances occur materially effecting the care of the children or Carol's access to them, the residence of the children shall be reconsidered in light of then existing circumstances. Should either Jerry or Carol move from the Aspen area, every effort shall be made to facilitate the continued exercise of joint custody so that the children shall continue to enjoy the benefit of both parents. In considering future living arrangements for the children, both parents shall have regard for the children's preference and the environment and care which each can provide.

4. It is anticipated that Carol, as well as Jerry, shall spend regular and considerable time with the children. Carol shall be with the children and responsible for their care at least seven days and seven nights per month, which shall include one weekend, the time and arrangements for which shall be agreed upon no later than the 25th day of the preceeding month. Carol shall also spend time with the children, when possible, on their birthdays and during major holidays.

5. It is expressly understood that the above enumerated times that Carol shall be with the children and responsible for their immediate care are minimums. Both parents' changing career obligations require flexibility in child care responsibilities and parental involvement. The terms of this agreement are to be liberally interpreted to allow the children the maximum benefit to be derived from the love, concern and care of both parents.

6. The parties will attempt to work together to avoid any future disputes. Should any dispute arise which we cannot resolve, we wish to avoid the expense and acrimony of formal court proceedings. Therefore, any controversy arising out of or relating to this agreement or the breach thereof, shall be settled by first attempting mediation with Dr. Kenneth J. Tutt, psychologist. If mediation fails and either parent chooses not to abide by the psychologist's judgment as to how to resolve the parental difference then the matter will be settled by arbitration through the services of Lisa Mark, attorney, or

anyone else on whom we mutually agree. Both parties agree to abide by any such arbitration decision.''

Courts have traditionally held a bias against joint custody especially when it involves frequent changes of physical custody where it is suspected to produce too unstable an environment for children. Repeated alternation of home, supervising parents and sometimes even schools and friends, have been viewed by judges as potential sources of insecurity and stress for children. However, in cases where the parents are geographically and tempermentally close and themselves seek some workable form of joint custody as desirable *and* their joint custody plan includes some feasible method for resolving disputes, then, judges can be expected to be most disposed toward joint custody.

Courts and child experts will not approve of joint custody plans when they are used to split the children to satisfy the parents' sense of equitable division of children. Solomon's gambit of threatening to cut a child in two provided a wise end for a biblical quarrel over custody, but dividing children has until recently not been often employed by modern day courts. If cooperative parents truly feel that joint (divided) custody is best for their child(ren), it would be prudent for them to seek the advice, counsel, and testimony of professional child experts to convince the court of the advisability of such an agreement.

A third custodial form is split custody where each parent becomes the custodial parent for one or more of the children. (Johnny lives with his father and Tilly with her mother). The father has primary custody of Johnny and is the visiting parent to Tilly, while the mother is the custodial parent of Tilly and the visiting parent of Johnny. Again, the court's tendency has been to disapprove of such arrangements. The courts' rationale is that divorce already fractures a family and further splintering through division of the children only increases the children's trauma. So again, the couple seeking this rarer type of custody will be pressured to prove the arrangement will be beneficial to the children, not the parents.

There are situations where split custody is psychologically advantageous to children. One commonly accepted situation is where the divorce occurs between adults with children from previous marriages, and the children are split in order to live with their natural biological parents. Deep-seated negative feelings between siblings or between a particular parent and a particular child could also psychologically justify a split custody arrangement. As with joint or divided custody, it will be rare that the court will be prone towards split custody without the expert approval of some knowledgeable child expert, in addition to cooperative and positive attitudes on the part of the involved children and adults.

The last form of custodial arrangement, and the rarest of all, occurs when the court decides that neither parent is adequate or able to provide for the children's well being and awards custody to a third party. Relatives or childcaring institutions are the two most usual recipients of a child's custody in such cases. Physical or mental health of the parents or child can influence either the court or family to seek third party custodial arrangements. Usually professional case studies will be ordered by the court before making third party placements. As in all child custody matters, the judge is responsible for acting on what is termed and considered "the best interest of the child."

BEST INTERESTS OF CHILDREN

Historically, the emphasis on children's welfare is not of long standing. English common law, the source of much early American law, decreed that children were the property of the father and, as such, were automatically his when there was a divorce. Only a short time ago, women's "proper" role in society was narrowly defined as dealing with home and children. During that era, women were expected to provide the primary care and nurturance for children, while men were expected to provide the financial support. As a result, courts awarded all children to mothers and all financial responsibilities to fathers.

Even though our culture is drastically changing in regards to women's and men's roles and the courts have begun to change their language and laws, there still remains a strong bias that leads courts to believe that the child's best interests are served by awarding all children to mothers and all financial responsibilities to fathers. There have been important legal reforms. The Supreme Court has judged it unconstitutional for states to sexually discriminate in spousal support matters. For example, states now must permit "alimony" to be paid or received by spouses of either sex. Another reform has been in the appreciation of a child's psychological, as well as physical wellbeing.

This trend is reflected in Michigan's Child Custody Act of 1976, wherein the judge is required in disputed custody cases to consider the mental health of the competing parties, as well as their capacity to give the child(ren) love and affection. The same law compels the judge to consider the "love, affection, and other emotional ties" between the child and each parent. This is a vast improvement over decisions which considered only the financial status of each parent.

The biases of laws and judges aside, the best interest of children are, as everyone realizes, immensely complex. It may be simple when only one of the parents demonstrates gross inadequacies. In the real world of contested custody cases, however, judges are regularly presented with evidence suggesting important inadequacies on the part of both parents, in addition to very complicated emotional ties between parents and children.

It is advisable to start dealing with the complexities that need to be addressed for the child's best interest by outlining items which should be included in typical custodial agreements where parents are cooperatively trying to provide the best for their children.

The following list may appear too detailed for amicable parents. It is not. Legal custody arrangements outline each parent's rights which means it is a legal contract stating what each parent can do, not what they must do. If the parent and children agree, they can easily ignore the written custodial document. With both parents agreement, the visiting parent may have the children twice or twenty times as long as is called for in the custodial document. Who would object? It is only where there is disagreement that the document becomes important, and thus, a detailed contract can be an essential way to prevent disputes either in or out of court. Furthermore, a formal agreement that anticipates future events provides a kind of clarity and justice for all that aids the on-going relationship between the parents. These considerations justify the spelling out of visitation rights with more than just the quick phrase "reasonable visitation," so often used as the only statement concerning visitation. Similarly, child support arrangements need to consider much more than simply what monthly amount is to be paid to maintain the children financially.

Custody Matters to be Considered:

   1. Who is to be the primary custodian?

2. How are the major childrearing decisions to be made, such as medical, religious, and educational decisions?

3. What are the non-custodial parent's visiting rights to be on a weekly, monthly, vacational basis? How will each special occasion, such as holidays and birthdays, be divided between the parents?

4. Under what conditions can any of the above be changed? What if a parent or a child marries, joins the armed forces, dies, enters a new religious group, moves a substantial distance away, becomes emotionally or physically incapacitated?

5. How will disputes on visitation be resolved? Any approach, such as agreement to mediation or arbitration by a clergyman, child expert, or friend is better than the slow, expensive, often unfair judicial method.

Child Support Matters to be Considered:

1. What will be the regular day-to-day financial contributions of *both* parents? When will financial contributions start and under what conditions will they end (e.g., parent or child marries, child becomes self-supporting)?

2. What are the circumstances under which the regular financial support will be increased (e.g., inflation, special educational or medical needs), or decreased (e.g., financial problems of contributing parent, less need for financial aid by custodial parent or child because of inheritances, or such)?

3. How will emergency or unforeseen financial needs be met? Whe pays for medical insurance? Who pays for, *and who owns* and holds life insurance policies where the children are beneficiaries? What is to be done about medical needs not covered by medical insurance, such as dental or mental health needs?

4. What are the tax consequences of all financial arrangements? Who declares the children as dependents?

5. How will visitation travel expenses be paid if the geographical distance between child and visiting parent changes? Who pays for the children's daily expenses while with a visiting parent?

A reasonable approach for working through the child custody and support lists is essentially the same as the approach suggested earlier for arriving at mutually acceptable property settlements. The couple schedules non-emotional times to discuss the easiest terms first in order to provide a cooperative atmosphere. Whether they are able to do this alone or with arbitration or counseling, the goal is the same—to come up with a tentative agreement which is then submitted for an opinion about its legal soundness. Legal or tax feedback then provides information for further discussion, modifications, and agreements.

How can a divorcing couple be expected to so cooperatively carve out so complicated a set of agreements? More easily than might be expected. Whether or not they mutually support the idea of divorcing each other, most couples agree that they want to optimize the quality of their children's lives. I have repeatedly worked with couples who *"knew"* there was too much anger to allow them to sit in the same room, let alone discuss anything. However, after a brief explanation that their children needed them to rationally work on their future, the parents were able to sit down and cooperatively discuss their children's needs.

At first, warring couples may require a lot of help. The worst cases require that each person and their lawyers attend a formal meeting organized and run by a talented counselor who has the respect and trust of both parties. As artificial as this method of communication might at first sound, it is a thousand-fold more desirable than a contested courtroom battle. The lawyer and client, together with a counselor, aim at opening up the most direct and useful communication possible between the divorcing couple. The advantages include the fact that the meeting will be organized and monitored by a communications expert, rather than attempting such an important exchange of ideas in the midst of the formal adversarial court system. A second advantage is that only one topic is at issue (child care arrangements). This differs significantly from the court battle where complicated divorce grounds and property settlements must also be dealt with. A third advantage is that both parties share the basically non-selfserving interest in the welfare of their children. Finally, there is the advantage that the meeting can be ended and rescheduled as flexibly as the situation requires. Much more frequently than imagined, these non-litigation meetings work.

Best Interest of Parents:

The emphasized judicial principle in custody matters is that the children's interests are paramount. Parents' interests are definitely a secondary consideration. This children-centered priority has certain indisputable moral logic, but a close look at the consequences of this hierarchy of interests is necessary. First, consider the well-known phenomenon of "the fading parent." A non-custodial parent whose needs are largely ignored tends to slowly fade, that is, withdraw from their children financially, emotionally, and physically. The need to avoid the resentments that lead to fading, depressed, hate-obsessed parents is too often overlooked. Two aid stations exist for the welfare of parents locked in custodial struggles. The first is help offered through divorce counseling. The second is help offered through appropriate legal counseling.

Divorce and Legal Counseling:

For a while, some courts required that couples seeking divorce first undergo mandatory marital counseling. The goal of counseling was to investigate the possibility of a reconciliation (i.e., avoid divorce). The track record for compulsory counseling is terrible. Court-required counseling almost never leads to reversing the divorce decision. However, today the form and goals of divorce counseling are more practical than marital counseling. The goal of divorce counseling is to have the couple develop useful communication skills. Couples embarked on a clear divorce route can appreciate the advantages of learning how to talk directly to each other and reach mutual decisions. They have financial, custody, and a variety of legal problems that could certainly best be dealt with through cooperative efforts if only they engage in reasonable discussions. In some states, divorce counseling is done in two phases. In the initial phase, a counselor works with the couple in an attempt to mediate differences and arrive at mutual decisions. If the mediation fails, the couple is legally bound to abide by their attorney's arbitration of all major matters.

One important benefit of successful divorce counseling is help in avoiding guilt that the divorce is significantly damaging to their children's lives. Divorce counselors teach how divorce, in the long run, is clearly better for children than forcing them to remain in a depressed, angry or devitalized family. Parents are helped immensely by the idea that they are serving their children's mental health by divorcing rather than by "sticking it out." Once parents realize that divorce is more helpful than damaging to their chidren, then the parents are more positively motivated to extricate the children from all parental conflicts.

Divorce counseling is a growing field, and its practitioners are gaining skills and helpful strategies at a rapid rate. Certainly there is much more hope for relief from the traumas of divorce through divorce counseling than through any court procedures. This is also true of the newer forms of divorce mediation, a process whereby the couple reaches specific agreements on specific matters. The "Civilized Divorce Clinic" operated in Detroit by Drs. Walter Ambinder and Sondra Lyness specializes in divorce mediation. Dr. Ambinder is an attorney as well as a psychologist, which allows him to handle functions that some divorce mediation therapists must turn over to a legal consultant.

At this clinic once the decision for divorce is made, the therapist switches to a mediator's role in which they assume most of the responsibility for mediating the legal and financial elements of the divorce. A second therapist may function as a family counselor to one or more the parties involved. The idea is to have a coordinated effort that helps patients deal with the practical problems of divorce while at the same time defusing animosities. Divorce mediation by a psychologist should involve the use of consultant attorneys and accountants to guarantec that the mediated agreements are compatable with the legal and financial best interests of all parties. Divorce mediation typically costs between $400 and $1,000, but fees are so variable that those considering mediation should carefully establish the fee basis prior to beginning the process. However, the financial costs are usually considerably less than the costs of legal arbitration, and the potential emotional benefits are so great that most divorcing couples should seriously consider divorce counseling.

Mediation is a fast-growing trend in divorce matters. For example, in California divorce mediation is required by state law in any divorce in which child custody is involved. Lawyers, as well as social workers, psychologists, physicians, college professors, or almost anyone else can call themselves a divorce mediator, and this is a problem. The profession is new and not yet regulated by state or federal governments, so there is little to stop anyone from putting up a shingle and claiming they are a divorce mediator. It is wise to be suspicious of people who simply create a title for themselves. The fact that mediators sell their time for about half of what divorce attorneys are charging still means they earn a pretty penny. They are selling a very appealing product—settling things outside the traditional adversarial courtroom. To gain the best help and protect one's self from the unscrupulous, you need to check out the credentials, skills, ethics, and experience of the divorce mediator you choose. One of the only credential awarding bodies today for divorce mediation is the "Family Mediation Association" which has its national head-quarters in Washington, D.C. This association's policy has been to award a certificate to anyone who goes through a five day ($650) training course.

There are real dangers in mediation that is not at least monitored by a competent attorney. The mediator may not know or make each party aware of their legal rights. Negotiating parties need to be aware of their rights, and all legal ramifications of any agreement they make.

One study has shown that 55% of the couples who try mediation do, in fact, come up with agreements. The study, the Denver Custody Mediation Project, indicated that those who did gain help through divorce mediation are more satisfied with their divorces than those who relied on the courts to make decisions. One interesting finding from that study was that mediating couples were more likely to agree on a form of joint, rather than the more traditional single parent custody arrangement.

It seems clear that in the future divorce mediation will become the primary way of dealing with those human needs with which the courts are ill-equiped to deal. For now, divorcing couples will have to creatively consider the form of mediation or arbitration most appropriate to their situation. My strong advice is to use the most personal form of communicating-arbitrating-mediating possible. Two people sitting down together and hacking out agreements, later checked out by accountants and attorneys, is the most personal and, thus, the best. Next comes mediation (arbitration) where the two people work out their agreements with a third party, such as a minister or friend. The possibilities become more and more formal, to the point at which the two attorneys are given the power to work out agreements, and the parents are advised not even to discuss the matters with each other—a posture to be avoided if at all possible. The only thing worse is the prospect of a court battle deciding disputed custody.

The legal counseling most appropriate to the best interest of the parents is not that which aims at *"getting"* the other parent. Although the revenge/anger approach can offer temporary emotional relief, it, like medication for pain, does little for the underlying disease. If your attorney seems to be prodding you toward the "let's-get-the-bastard" approach, be advised that this is not good legal counseling.

Good legal counseling is that which informs the client of the ways that the courts and laws can work to best meet the long-term needs of parents and children. If the parents can agree on a basic custodial plan, then the attorney's job should be to advise you on the likelihood of it being accepted by the judge and to point out to you aspects of the agreement which you may have overlooked. Advice on how to handle the custodial arrangements in the event of geographical relocations, changing financial needs, remarriages, or tax implications are all appropriate from a good attorney.

In the case where the parents are themselves unable to agree on the custodial arrangements, the question arises as to how such decisions will be made. Again, a court battle over custody should be considered only when all other avenues have been exhausted.

There is the possibility which your lawyers may discuss with you of hiring a separate attorney to represent the children. Sometimes the court (judge) takes the initiative in doing this in contested child custody matters. An attorney designated to directly represent children is called a "guardian ad lidem." The way legal representation for children works differs between states in so many details that information about this needs to be obtained from your individual sources of legal counsel. It can be noted, however, that the use of the "guardian ad lidem" itself represents a very definite step towards the courts being the primary decision forum regarding children's custody. Before this step is taken, there are many forms of arbitration and mediation which can be used to resolve custody disagreements.

Attorneys are officers of the court who tend to function most comfortably when they are advising clients how to effectively engage in *court* matters. The custody counseling one receives from an attorney, however, is best when it leads away from court procedures in which a judge makes ultimate decisions about children's lives. Judges trained in legal matters usually do not have the psychological sophistication necessary for making child custody decisions. Some judges realize these limitations and seek mental health expertise to aid them. Prudent and caring parents who may not want to chance either the knowledge or wisdom of the judge to whom they will be assigned, have another much more satisfactory option. If the parents simply cannot make use of arbitration or mediation techniques, they may still agree to a custody case study by child experts. With this option, both parents agree to have a mental health professional (psychologist, psychiatrist, social worker) or a team of such professionals comprehensively investigate all parties involved in order to make custody recommendations. It is essential that *both* parents agree to the evaluation and that it is understood that the recommendations sought are those that are best for the child(ren). This procedure is completely different from the "hired gun" procedure where one parent hires a psychologist or psychiatrist to offer testimony in court on their behalf. "Hired gun" testimony is often of very limited value, since judges know that when an attorney allows an expert witness to testify for their client, they have made sure that the testimony will be favorable to their cause. Such testimony is quite different when both parents, before knowing the study's outcome, agree to submit to a professional assessment with the motivation of finding out what is considered best for their children.

Mental health professionals have a variety of techniques and procedures for conducting custodial studies. Both parents need to have confidence in the credentials, attitudes, and practices of the person(s) they agree to have conduct the study. The following is a handout from my office provided to parents and attorneys considering such a study. Only after both parents have consented to the format and procedures outlined in the handout, will the actual study begin.

PSYCHOLOGICAL ASSESSMENT
In Cases of
Disputed Child Custody

"Introduction:

This document has been prepared to offer an overview of the major aspects of the psychological assessment accomplished by Dr. Gerald Alpern in contested child custody cases. Although each situation involves unique features which require individualization of the techniques utilized, the typical procedures, herein described, provide a basic understanding of the major goals and features of the psychological assessment.

Dr. Alpern is a private, practicing, Colorado licensed psychologist. Formerly, he was Professor of Psychology at Indiana University Medical School where for ten years he was the Director of Research for Child Psychiatry Services. His background relevant to the accomplishing of custody evaluations includes: Senior Staff Psychologist at the Riley Child Guidance Clinic (5 years), State Certified School Psychologist (12 years), Consultant Child Psychologist at two child residential treatment centers, a corrective institution for adolescents, and an agency for handicapped children. He has published 3 books and 17 articles on various aspects of child development. Dr. Alpern has, for over 20 years, been engaged in the private practice of psychology.

Custody Dispute Evaluations Position:

The primary assumption under which the evaluations are accomplished is that all children involved in custody disputes are at high risk of significant emotional handicapping. For this reason, the evaluation must be conducted so as to:

1) Reduce the children's emotional trauma. This means that the children are examined in non-emotionally threatening ways and that all sessions are designed as a therapeutic experience which will help the children deal with on-going traumas.

2) Arrive at a set of recommendations which are in the children's best interests, both in terms of their physical and psychological wellbeing.

In order to accomplish these, it is essential that the psychologist is not acting as the agent for either parent. Only if it is understood by all parties that the assessment's primary aim is to safeguard the immediate and long-term welfare of the children, will the evaluation be done. This condition is met when both parents agree to cooperate with the evaluation (preferably by mutual consent, but sometimes through a court order). This, of course, does not commit them to an acceptance of the specific recommendations of the evaluation. It is only that the evaluation cannot be done without participation by *both* parents.

Procedures and Techniques:

Parents: Each parent is seen individually (average = 3 hours in two 1½ hour appointments). The interviews are conducted to determine their:

Mental Status: The mental status examination is a clinical evaluation of a parent's personality structure, usually accomplished during a review of life history. Objective personality tests are also utilized to gain information about the parent's mental status.

Parental Attitudes and Practices: An inquiry into parenting skills is conducted through discussions of their beliefs, plans and actions with their own and other children.

Life Plans: A discussion of parent's future plans for work, living arrangements, and relationships under the possibilities that they were either the "primary" or the "visiting" parent are used to predict aspects of children's lives with each parent.

Both parents are given opportunities to offer all information they feel would be pertinent to an effective evaluation. Although listing "negatives" about former spouses is discouraged, any information or source of information felt relevant is considered. This is done as it is imperative that both parents feel the assessment has included all significant information.

Children: The procedures for children vary drastically, depending on their chronological age and individual circumstances. Children are usually seen after both parents have been seen at least once. The children are typically seen once accompanied by each parent. From the outset, the children are guarded against believing that the custody recommendations of the study or of any future court decisions are *their responsibility.* They are encouraged to express their feelings and views, and are given complete confidentiality. Any "problems" they express and wish psychotherapeutic help with are treated within the possibilities of the situation.

Relevant Others: Any other people significant to the child's life or the assessment procedure (e.g., relatives, friends, current mates of parents, teachers, physicians, involved mental health professionals) may be contacted as a part of the procedures. No one is contacted without obtaining appropriate releases of information.

Presentation of Findings:

Two goals of the procedure are to have both parents understand

and accept the study's recommendations. Therefore, when the evaluation has been completed and a definite set of recommendations prepared, the next step is to present these to the parents, usually together, and sometimes in the presence of their legal counsel. In the initial post-study meeting, the recommendations and their rationale are presented. Further meetings, as required, are used to attempt to have the parents reach a mutual agreement. In cases where there is not a meeting of the minds, the psychological findings and recommendations are prepared in a written report for the court which can be presented with or without direct testimony from Dr. Alpern.

Fees:

The fees for the psychological assessment are based on the number of hours involved at the rate of $80 per hour. This rate is independent of the nature of services rendered. That is, whether the service is a parent conference, report preparation, or court appearance, the same hourly rate is applied. An average cost might involve 4 hours of parent interviews, 3 hours of child interviews, 2 hours of interpretation and counseling, and 2 hours of test interpretation and report preparation providing a total fee of $880 (11 hours at $80 per hour). Payment arrangements for services are determined at the time of the initial contact.

Arrangements for Psychological Assessments:

In order for adequate time to conduct the prescribed Psychological Assessment, it is desirable to schedule the initial contacts well in advance (about 8 weeks) of any legal or other required deadline. It is very important to consider the child(ren)'s psychological health in the timing not only of the assessment, but of when they will be able to enjoy the security offered by permanent placement. Arrangements for an assessment may be initiated by either party or their counsel by contacting Dr. Alpern's office (303) 925-9272. Dr. Alpern is available for telephone conferences before, during, or after evaluations to discuss with all parties any aspect of the evaluations.''

My procedures are fairly typical of the individual or custody study teams now available throughout the country. Contacting your State Psychological Association should offer you a variety of resources for conducting professional mental health custody evaluations.

CHAPTER 9

Emotional Effects of Divorce on Children

The renowned child psychologist, Louise Despert, when just beginning the study which is now considered the classic concerning the emotional effects of divorce on children, came across a startling finding. When she went through her extensive case records, she found that her clinical practice had proportionately less children from divorces than were found in the general population. This led to the hypothesis that children from divorce homes were *less* often in emotional trouble than their peers from intact families. Subsequent research has supported the original idea that the emotional trauma children suffer in a long-term troubled intact family leads to more significant emotional problems than the short-term trauma children experience with divorce.

So much for the idea that "we-must-stay-together-for-the-children's-sake." There are, nevertheless, special taumas and problems which are part of the divorce process.

Pre-Divorce Period:

Before divorce is even considered, there is a negative atmosphere within the family which is definitely experienced by children. In the pre-divorce family there is usually some form of overt and/or covert battling and unhappiness, often with a strong sense of boredom. Children past the toddling age will feel the lack of warmth between the parents. When the pre-divorce family is operating at its best, it does so by moving along by habit in a mechanical fashion which provides little joy.

At worst, the pre-divorce family blatantly displays stresses, anguish, and hatreds which poison the home atmosphere, providing a psychologically polluted environment. Regardless of whether the pre-divorce home is loud and hectic or boring and joyless, the contorted conditions prevent people from thriving. Such environments are fertile ground for the crippling of children.

Children are as psychologically resilient as they are physically resilient. Childrens' cuts, bruises and scrapes heal much faster than adults'. Likewise, they are able to recover much more quickly from divorce crises. It's like the way children respond to fever; though children's fevers go up faster and higher than adults', their fevers also drop and they recover much faster than adults. Similarly, with divorce, children's immediate reaction may be severe, but the rate at which they get over the psychological trauma is faster than adults. Knowing that children may have severe immediate responses to the initial divorce steps but will quickly recover is important information for parents considering a divorce procedure.

There are a number of things that parents can do to reduce the severe immediate responses. One important thing parents can offer their children is that their security is not dependent on the nuclear family (mother-father and siblings). Children know they need nurturance and protection in order to survive. When all their needs are met by two adults, imagine the fear generated by the possibility of death, divorce or separation of any kind from one of these all-important people. They may begin to fear the possibility of losing the rest of their security. The nightmarish fantasies of losing the other parent can cause panic or depression in children. Their feelings of vulnerability produce terrors adults have a hard time imagining.

Parents aware of these dependency fears can offer their children tremendous help by creating an extended blanket of security. The best blanket comes from making sure the children experience the love and protection of a number of extra-family adults. By encouraging children to spend time with caring relatives or friends, parents can help children to feel less panic about their need for their two parents. Special friendships with adults outside the immediate family are tremendously valuable whether or not there is a divorce or death in one's childhood. There are always times when children are troubled by things that they cannot discuss with parents, regardless of how many times parents reassure them that they are free to talk about anything. Those are ideal times for other adult friends. The prime reason for establishing the wide network of adults for children is that they will gain the wise adult guidance they need, but that they will know that there is a group of capable and protective adults in their environment. Limiting dependency on parents provides children a major defense against the imagined horrors of potential parental loss.

Another important strategy in helping children during the pre-divorce period involves letting them know that they are not responsible for the family problems. Children are much more guilt-prone than is obvious. This comes from their being so self-centered. Part of being a child is believing that they are the force behind all that happens. If, for instance, a child gets the measles, their view of reality leads them to believe they got sick because they were "bad." Likewise, if parents quarrel, children are very apt to think that somehow it was their doing. Money quarrels which might seem clearly unrelated to the child can make them feel too expensive and, thus, the cause of parental battling. Children are notoriously creative in inventing reasons why battles over moving, jobs, jealousy, anything can be their fault. Especially common is guilt over just being. "If only I wasn't around, they wouldn't be so miserable. I'm the problem. I should never have been born." Children need to be told regularly that the struggles between the parents have little to do with them. Although it is a rare parent that tells children that they are the cause of family troubles, most adults do not realize that every parental battle has the potential for creating painful guilt in children. The same childish characteristic of thinking the world should and does revolve around them renders children susceptable to believing that they are guilty whenever something goes wrong.

A third pre-divorce stress children suffer is more subtle than the previous two. It occurs when parents try to keep their difficulties a secret from the children. Such secrets cannot be kept. Children are keenly aware that something is very wrong, and if you are not open with them about it, they may really get frightened and fear some horrible disaster. This does not mean you should provide children with a front row seat to frightening scenes. Protecting children from ugly or just loud traumas is wise, but that is quite different from trying to convey the false message that everything is sunshine and roses.

Telling the child at some calm time that the parents are not getting along lets the child know that they can trust their own senses and you. It also provides an opportunity for reassuring them that they will be secure regardless of any outcome of the parental quarrels. Many children have a desertion/abandonment chamber of fantasy horrors. You needn't worry that talking to children about marital difficulties will lead them to fear divorce. Rest assured that the child over six has already heard of divorce and is fearful of it. But it's important to talk about the possibility only at a time when you feel able to calm their fears about it. If you're feeling panicky or despondent, you are too liable to infect a child with your negative view. When you feel confident that the child's life will not be disastrously affected by a divorce, then you are best able to discuss it with your children.

The Divorce Crisis:

There is no doubt that when parents separate, children are placed under stress and suffer some emotional trauma. However, some children do not overtly show their trauma. They seem perfectly at ease with all that happens. How the child shows their responses to the divorce (separation) crisis and how severely they are affected by it depends on a number of things. Age, quality of early life, amount of pre-divorce stress, number and depth of relationships with others are all important to the child's response to the actual parental separation. But the most important variable to children during the divorce is the parents' emotional stability. If the child sees that the parent is hysterical or extremely sad or hears the parent describe catastrophic changes, the child will feel and expect tragic life changes. At the very time the parent may most need support and have reduced coping abilities is when children most need the parent. No one can be expected to be a model parent during the stresses brought on by divorce. What is possible is to be alert to signs of your children's distress and to share your happier moods with them. Almost everyone has ambivilent feelings about divorce and experiences rapidly changing up and down mood swings. Children are helped by exposure to the more positive moods.

Children have certain times in their lives when they are more vulnerable to stress than at other times. Events in their own lives outside the family affect their response to the divorce crisis. School, health, or peer difficulties can cause heightened stress in children. You usually have choices about when to talk with children about parents' separating. Choose a time when a child is feeling at their best. Parents need to be aware of stress indicators in their children, and if the parent cannot give the child the positive input required, they should assume the responsibility for finding others who can. Friends, relatives, teachers, clergy, or professional mental health workers are all sources parents can use to help over-stressed children. The following are guidelines for recognizing stress in children of different ages.

Infant children (up to about age 2½) are most responsive to emotional upsets of their main caretaker which today is still usually the mother. Infants respond to stress with a disorder of eating, sleeping, or eliminating. Infants also use regression, such as reduced abilities to talk or walk as a reaction to increased levels of stress. When a young child demonstrates stress, the best therapeutic measure is reassurance given by having a calm, loving person physically hold and rock the child. A grandparent or older sibling could give an infant comfort at times when the child's mother cannot.

Pre-school aged children, roughly 2½ years to 6, are the most fearful of loss of parents. Preschoolers are very aware of their nurturance needs and are extremely fearful of separation from their parents. Divorce crisis is often expressed by the preschoolers through some form of aggression. A resurgence of tantrums about going to nursery school or about being left with the babysitter is, during the divorce crisis, frequently related to a fear of abandonment. It helps to be tolerant of these fears. Once in a while parents can respond to the child's fearfulness by allowing vacation from nursery school or by coming home early when the child is with a babysitter. Either being constantly exasperated with the preschooler's fears or giving in to the fears and never permitting a separation only increases the child's fearfulness.

The separation anxiety the child feels should be handled similarly to the way the child's first school separations are best handled. Initial school separations are best carried out slowly, calmly, and for gradually increasing periods of time. The caretaking adult might first leave the child in a school room and go into another room for a few minutes. Later, the adult goes further away for longer periods of time until the child adapts to the separation. This gradual procedure maximizes the child's comfort in what, for them, can be a rather frightening situation. The divorce crisis which produces an exaggerated fear of desertion can be coped with in the same way. The parent who will not be living with the child on a regular basis should try to have the separation occur for the child slowly and calmly. The idea is to demonstrate to the child that they will not be losing that parent. The visiting parent should have as much contact with the child through phone calls and visits as the situation allows.

Elementary school age children, from about age 6 to 12, are at the height of magical thinking age. They believe that their thoughts and wishes are the causes of most events. Someone's death can be understood by a 7 or 10 year old to have occurred because the child was bad or once imagined or wished for the death. Furthermore, elementary age children rarely talk about this kind of logic. More often, the guilt or depression is expressed in nightmares, disintegration of social or academic skills, or a psychotic-like denial of reality. Denial might be expressed by the child "forgetting" about the divorce, or by the child acting as if nothing is or will be changing. Another form of denial is the brave-little-soldier front in which the child acknowledges the divorce but acts more grown-up and supportive than they really feel. The problem with children's use of denial is that they do not grieve for their losses, though grieving is an appropriate and healing thing to do when children or adults suffer a loss.

The most helpful thing a parent can do with elementary school aged children is a lot of realistic talking about the divorce, along with other forms of reassurance. Parents should assume that the elementary school age child has both many questions and distorted views about the divorce. Regardless of whether the child verbalizes guilt about the divorce, the parent should talk with the child about how marital problems did not happen because of anything the child has thought or done. Whether or not the child talks or demonstrates feelings of loss, the parents should discuss with them how parents can divorce spouses, but not children. Do not offer false reassurances. Don't deny the realities of certain losses. Encourage the child to express their own feelings of loss. Crying should be looked upon as a healthy expression of grief. Children should not be burdened with having to hide their feelings, and it is helpful to have parents encourage open expression of anger, fear or whatever. Children of all ages are better off if they believe that while they may be disciplined for *acts,* they will never be punished for things they feel or say. Allowing children to express their feelings openly is one of the most difficult parental tasks, but it is essential to good relationships with children.

Adolescents have a unique set of mechanisms for coping with divorce. Typically, teenagers don't show signs of regression to earlier stages. Also, they do not feel as needful as younger children and so do not need to ally themselves with one parent (against the other) as a means of self-protection. To understand the most common adolescent reaction pattern to divorce, it is helpful to remember that a prime developmental goal during adolescence is to end emotional dependency on parents in order to establish individual identities. Part of a normal, healthy adolescence is achieving emotional distance from parents, so that they can feel independent and grown up. Teenagers confronted with divorce are prone to create the distance between themselves and their parents faster and, perhaps, with a bit more gusto. A divorce, strange as it may at first appear, can actually be beneficial to adolescents. The divorce process can facilitate viewing parents as individuals with strengths and weaknesses and so help the teenager break with the idealized, overdependent view of parents held by less mature children. On the other hand, divorce can present teenagers with problems that younger children don't experience. Younger children may not be aware of any sexual issues which may be a part of divorce. A teenager, however, is very aware of sexual issues and recognizes, perhaps for the first time, a parent as a sexual being, which can produce troublesome confusions.

Another divorce problem, unique to teenagers, is that it is much easier for parents to push an adolescent into premature independence or an adult-friend role. It is very confusing to teenagers to have a parent suddenly turn into a peer. Newly single parents not infrequently awkwardly express their new freedom by behaving and dressing and socializing much like the adolescent's friends. This parental regression may anger a teenager or just produce temporary distance, or it can deeply frighten and threaten them. Adolescents are not adults, and they need an adult parent much more than a new sexually active older friend.

An appreciation of the adolescent's developmental needs is necessary to dealing with teenagers during divorce. Parents need to allow teenagers some emotional space, but still be available to them at those times when the teenager needs adult parental help or support. Teenagers are not as mature as they like to act, and periodically they need tender loving care or realistic disciplining. Parents need to guard against pushing teenagers into meeting too many of the parents' new financial or emotional needs. Divorcing adults are prone, because they are forming their own new identities, to forget the pains of adolescent identity struggles. Few adults remember accurately the struggles with the first real sexual relationships, acting more grown up than one felt, or trying to figure out just who you are. The teenager who doesn't see or empty an overflowing wastebasket, is not quite as irresponsible as it appears. Try to remember how many wastebaskets you saw when you were 15 and completely preoccupied with whether you were sufficiently attractive or popular or were acting in ways that others saw as crazy. While adults may feel upset about a teenager's messed-up room, their adolescent may feel their lives are not worthwhile because of a messed up social evening. Adolescents do commit suicide because of anguish over sexual anxieties or peer disapproval. Of all the developmental phases humans go through, the adolescent period tends to be the most stormy and traumatic in spite of the facade of it being a time of fun-filled freedom.

Post-Divorce Period:

After the crisis is over, that is, the physical separation has occurred, and the legal circumstances are resolved, come the problems associated with the post-divorce period.

A study by Westman states that in half of all divorces involving children, legal battles continued after the divorce. Half of the litigations dealt with money matters and half with custody problems. A major finding was that for as many as 30% of today's families, the on-going post-divorce traumas were "*intense* for about two years." Divorce decrees do not automatically end the legal battles and certainly do not prevent the aftershocks.

Even without further legal complications, there are a series of post-divorce problems children face. First, the child must adjust to a custodial parent who is not the same person as before the divorce. The custodial parent often changes in less than positive ways because they have more tasks to do, less money to spend, and a whole array of emotional and social readjustments to make. There is a fair chance that the custodial parent's coping skills will be reduced while their emotional inconsistencies will be increased.

The non-custodial parent problem is their absence and, in addition, all the possible personality complications which make them less psychologically available to their children. The relationship between the divorcing parents which, of course, continues to be of prime importance to children, is usually characterized by a confused combination of wanting to be close to, forget, or punish the former spouse.

There are also post-divorce matters that are relatively independent of the parents. Children may (1) maintain the fantasy of a reconciliation, (2) feel ashamed of the divorce-broken family status, (3) have to deal with insecurities born of lost faith in family unity. The more extreme symptoms of ticks, school phobias, fears of sleep, preoccupation with death, fear of being alone, blatant hostilities, or prolonged silences may abate after the period of the divorce crisis. The post-divorce period tends to give rise to longer lasting reactions.

In describing the more common post-divorce problems, there will certainly be reactions which every child or parent exhibits to some degree. It would be almost impossible for any parent to completely avoid any negative statements about one's ex-spouse. All children of divorce will sometimes find themselves in the middle of a parental battle. This section should be read with the knowledge that post-divorce problems produce significant dangers for children *only* when suffered strongly and repeatedly. Furthermore, do not lose sight of the fact that there are a large number of children, like parents, who joyfully greet a marital separation as immense relief, celebrate the end of the bad marriage and immediately begin to thrive.

The following are the most typical problem-causing reactions of separated or divorced parents toward their children.

Being Over-Generous or Over-Solicitous of Children:

Guilt over depriving children of their other parent too frequently leads parents to abdicate their role as disciplinarians. All children need appropriate discipline from parents. The guilt ridden parent is in danger of needing to have their children see them as a giver, a parental Santa Claus, or a doting grandparent. This particular parenting error is more commonly made by the non-custodial parent, although many custodial parents also over-indulge their "suffering" children.

Over-taxing the Child's Maturity:

There are a number of direct and indirect pressures with which divorced parents may burden their children. Asking the child to do more of the housework or earn more of the family income than they can comfortably accomplish while adequately maintaining school and social lives represents only a minor form of this error. The primary mistake occurs when the parent uses children to meet their needs to discuss their adult problems. The child is at high risk of having their maturity overestimated by parents who need to talk about situations their children can neither adequately understand nor, more importantly, do much about. It takes a great deal of maturity to realize that most people presenting problems are only seeking an understanding listener, rather than a problem solving machine. Children who hear, but can't solve a parent's problems, can be deeply troubled. Again, it is generally a good thing to be open and discuss things with children. As a matter of fact, the usual error adults make in talking to children is the tendency to be condescending. However, repeatedly telling a pre-adolescent or even most adolescent children about financial or sexual matters is clearly ill-advised. Adults must use careful judgment in walking that fine line between having conversations that are either over-simplified or over-burdening. A parent talking to their children as adults can generally be good as long as it does not require the child to become a peer of the parent.

Vilifying the Other Spouse:

One prime difference for children between losing a parent through death as opposed to divorce is that children tend to idealize the former and devalue the latter. The tendency to devalue the non-custodial parent occurs because of the children's needs to shore up their threatened security by forming a strong alliance with the custodial parent. In instances in which the parent(s) intensify this tendency by involving the child(ren) in post-divorce conflicts, it can be significantly damaging. Both parents should share the important goal of promoting in the child a good image of both their mother and father. Although there are situations in which the child(ren) need face certain facts about their parents, the usual error is that parents blurt out at a highly emotional time, the "truth" about their ex-spouse. If a parent rationally decides to inform their children of some facts about the other parent, it should be accomplished during a calm, pre-planned time. An emotional outburst listing the crimes of a mother or father to the child can damage children's relationship with their mother or father and in the long run hurt their ability to relate to men or women.

There are other inappropriate positions imposed on children of divorce. Children are sometimes used by one parent to spy on the other. Children can be scapegoats and are exposed to statements of the "you're-just-like-your-father/mother" type. Children are very often used as inappropriate message passers between parents. "Tell your mother I would like to be with you three extra days on Thanksgiving." Changing visitation agreements are frequently difficult tasks for professional attorneys and are usually too complex and emotionally loaded for involved children. In hundreds of ways, children are put in the middle of parental conflict. They are asked to take sides. It is a difficult job for children to cope with the over-tired, over-emotional, and over-self-centered people parents can easily become because of the stress of ending a marriage.

Divorces are very confusing, and it is not only the explosive, angry, hate-filled divorce that produces confusion. In cases where the parents maintain friendly relations throughout the divorce process, children are confronted with the apparently inexplicable fact that even good relationships are in danger of ending. Parents in the so-called "amicable" divorces have the very difficult task of explaining a separateness between the parents that may be essentially invisible to children.

Regardless of whether the divorce is a so-called "good" or "bad" divorce for children, all divorces, at first, generate guilt and later, shame and resentment. The child's view of parents ending a relationship stimulates what is labeled by child experts as child's neurosis of abandonment. The expression of this neurosis is most classically demonstrated by school phobia in which the child seems to be terrified of something at school when in reality the underlying fear is of leaving (losing) their home.

Perhaps these fears will be lessened in general as children see more and more of their peers survive the ending of marriages. *The 1979 Journal of Social Issues* describes how current trends indicate that by 1990, 33% of America's children will experience their parent's divorce before they reach the age of eighteen. This statistic may seem terrifying until you remember that the research clearly shows that children consistantly come out of divorces emotionally healthy and, in fact, tend to be less troubled than children forced to live in the middle of unhappy marriages.

In the August, 1981 *American Psychologist,* Lawrence Kurdek integrated and summarized the major research on what determines how well or poorly American children go through divorces. His first accomplishment was to group 116 separate studies of children under the four areas that determine how well children deal with divorce.

The first factor called the "macro-system" refers to the beliefs and attitudes surrounding family life in the child's culture. The degrees to which a child's culture tends to reject, accept, condone, ignore, approve or disapprove of divorce and of single parent families are a major factor in the quality of a child's divorce adjustment.

The child's "exosystem," the second relevant area, refers to the stability of the child's individual post-divorce environment including the amount of financial stress, home and school changes, parents' emotional stability and availability.

The nature of the intra-family interaction during both the pre-and post-separation periods is called the "micro-system," and is the third area which determines the child's adjustment.

The child's own individual psychological competencies for dealing with stress, the "ontogenic system" is the final, critical factor to understanding the degree to which a child will be emotionally handicapped by divorce.

This chapter concludes with a summary of the most interesting findings about each of the four areas:

Macro-System:

American society has drastically changed its attitude toward divorce. The single-parent family is no longer viewed as an aberration. Ostracizing of children from divorced families could rarely occur these days for the simple reason that children from divorces comprise a substantial percentage of their school population. If divorcing parents expect their children to be subjected to ridicule, shame, or rejection, then there is a danger that their children will also expect it. In other words, children may be led to expect responses from others and make their expectations a reality by withdrawing from peers which, in fact, leads to peer alienation.

This same power parents have to negatively affect their children's adjustment can, of course, also be used positively. Parents can help their children by engineering contact with other children from divorced families. Studies suggest that the most helpful support available to divorcing children is contact with children who have come out of the other side of divorce.

A variety of ways for parents to help their children's fears about divorce are available through the primary organization that serves the divorced. *Parents without Partners* has over 500 local chapters with well over 100,000 members. This club is too often looked upon as existing only to provide single parents with a way to meet eligible partners. Although this is certainly one of the organization's purposes, one should not overlook the club's ability to provide child guidance help.

Whatever other techniques are used to convince children of their continuing positive social status, though from a divorced family, the most important factor is the parents' own beliefs. The parents need confidence that their children will not be handicapped by divorce.

One fear custodial parents frequently have is that the child will be damaged by the loss of a live-in adult of the opposite sex; that the child will not have a sex role model, or that they will not learn how to be close to one sex. These fears are archaic. Today, sex role typing is much less rigid than only a few years ago. Our culture is leaning more and more toward androgynous sex roles in which, for instance, housework and careers are not exclusively delegated to one sex or another. Furthermore, children are less limited to immediate family relationships. Teachers, relatives, coaches, parents' friends, parents of friends, in short, many adults of both sexes are readily available to children as role models, heroes, examples, and love objects.

Divorcing parents have little to fear that the current and future cultural macro-system will negatively affect their children. Parents can help their children by clearly communicating this to them through their own conviction and behavior.

Exosystem:

Any child who suddenly was moved to a new home and had to adjust to a new environment, friends, and, perhaps, less favorable financial situations, could be expected to suffer some emotional consequences. Add to this the possibility of instabilities caused by new parental divorce stresses, and it is easy to understand how the post-divorce environment could hinder children's life adjustments.

Exactly because such problems are so predictable, they are amenable to control. The trick is to look at the child's environment from the child's point of view. This view needs to be wider and wiser than the child might employ. For example, a trip to Disneyland might at first be thought of as a great treat. However, it could easily represent a change which, in fact, would increase the child's instability. If the trip involved missing school, separation from important peer activities, or any important existing routines, then the trip could be detrimental. Timing is important in a child's world; regular schedules provide an order which is a strong basis for their security. Delaying the journey to Disneyland until a regular school vacation could make the trip less disruptive.

In addition to the stability that comes from maintaining established patterns, a stability born out of new patterns can also be helpful to children during the post-divorce period. The prime example of this concerns the regularity and predictability of time with the visiting parent. The child will be immensely comforted by knowing exactly when he or she will have visits with the non-custodial parent. The ability to circle a particular date on the calendar when mother or father will be seen quiets fears of parental abandonment. A regular schedule of visits also offers proof to the child that the absent parent has enough interest in maintaining the relationship that they are willing to commit themselves to definite future times.

One realistic aspect of the post-divorce environment is the stability based on financial resources. The regularity of child support payments is of paramount psychological importance. Children over 8 almost always become keenly aware of whether support payments are made, are adequate, and are on time. Whether the custodial parent means to or not, their attitudes towards the support paying visiting parent is conveyed to the children. Children's feeling of being loved by the financially supporting parent can easily become connected to support payments. Regularity of the payments adds to the post-divorce home stability in at least three different ways: the prevention of financial stresses because of erratic income; the lack of financial stress and emotional consequences for the custodial parent and the avoidance of the desertion fears of children who worry about unstable financial support from the supporting parent.

The government is taking an increasingly active role in ensuring regular support payments. All states now subscribe to the *Uniform Reciprocal Enforcement of Support Act*. This federal legislation provides clout to trace support-obligated parents across state lines and enforce payments. Not only are the state courts requiring more support for children, but federal laws now provide a variety of services and techniques for guaranteeing the court-ordered support payments. There is a parent locator service run through the Department of Health, Education, and Welfare. The Internal Revenue Service is now authorized to collect support. Garnishing federal payrolls is allowed. New legislation has made bankruptcy no longer a viable technique for avoiding child support payments. To find out specifics of how these laws and services function, check with the family or domestic relationship court; every county has one.

A very basic contributor to children's post-divorce adjustment is the mimizing of radical life changes. There is a strong tendency to confuse the awkwardness of changed habit patterns with the loss of a former member of the household. The child may think they're missing mother or father when they are actually missing their own bed or old friends or usual morning routine. Children do get upset by the change of room, routines, and other habitual patterns. When they attribute such upsets to the loss of a parent, their misdirected grieving can both amplify and prolong the divorce trauma. This is another reason why the fewer changes, the better. Parents who do not have to make home, job and other routine changes as a result of divorce should try to delay the changes long enough to permit the child freedom from too much jarring.

Micro-System:

If children's total life adjustment was completely dependent upon the quality of the family's interaction, children of divorce would probably be extremely damaged psychologically. Immediately before and after the parents' separation is when adults typically exhibit their lowest levels of parental competencies because they are embroiled in their own emotional struggles. This is also the time when the children are the most confused and panic-prone since it is when the actual family splintering occurs. Luckily, children are extremely resilient, both physically and emotionally. They may show initial dramatic responses but recover very quickly.

Even though it is true that children do generally recover from the more intense initial responses to separation, knowing how to minimize the trauma serves them not only through the difficult separation step but paves the way for a smoother post-divorce period.

A constructive step can be taken when the children are told about the separation. An ideal description of how to inform children is offered knowing that circumstances frequently prevent parents from acting ideally. However, knowledge about the ideal may help with designing the best adaptation possible in the "real world."

Ideally, both parents sit down with the children prior to the separation, and together calmly present the forthcoming event in a way that first and foremost reassures the children about the lack of any dramatic or traumatic changes in their lives and that they will continue to receive much love and attention from both parents. The children should be given reasons for the separation which they can understand. It is most important that the reasons can in no way be interpreted as being the fault of the children. Children need to know that the parents separating is not their responsibility and that they are not guilty of causing the split. The ideal atmosphere lets the children know that they can get answers to any questions, then or at any time in the future. Finally, it should be made clear that any reactions, questions, or opinions they have can be freely expressed without fear of anger or rejection by either parent.

There are very good and obvious reasons for each aspect of this ideal formula. Concerned parents can almost always work out ways to have the essential aspects of the ideal fit their own situation. Take the time to work out the best way to inform your children of the separation. The first time one hears about something sets the basic tone, so it is crucial that the children first hear about the separation from you.

There are other predictable pre- and post-separation difficulties that can be minimized with careful thought. A major area are issues concerned with parental dating. For many reasons, such as hopes for reconciliation between the parents, jealousy of parent's time and attention, fear of losing the parent and just plain difficulty in adapting to a new lifestyle, children typically do not have positive responses to their parents having romantic relationships. Children need to be informed about the "dating" needs and plans of both the custodial and visiting parent.

Again, it is far better to present the idea well in advance of the reality. It also helps if when new adults come into the parents' lives, the children are included. New adults are much less threatening if they make themselves known, trustworthy, and possibly even enjoyable to the children. Children will vary in their response to parental post-separation dating. Some encourage their parents to date. Other children hide their fears or jealousies. Some children are truly oblivious to the whole thing. Likely reactions are not very predictable for any sex, age, or particular child. Parents should just be aware of the potential emotional response their dating is liable to have on their children and be ready to honestly face the situation if it arises.

Not unexpectedly, dating has a tremendous effect on former spouses, and for them the subject can be as sensitive an issue as with the children. A negative emotional response from a separated or divorced mate can easily produce a secondary emotional effect on children, and even a major legal effect. The prime example is post-divorce cohabitation. Custodial mothers have been shocked to discover that having a live-in boyfriend caused their children to be taken away from them and custody awarded to a vengeful, or, perhaps, even legitimately concerned father. This has happened even when the live-in situation was judged by mental health experts to be psychologically beneficial and healthy for the children. Courts have a moral bias which can judge *any* cohabitation arrangements to be antithetical to the child's best interests. Custody changes have been based on the sole fact of cohabitation, so it is wise to agree in a formal document about questions concerning post-divorce dating and cohabitation. It can avoid later major stresses, strains, and disasters.

On the other hand, it is counter-productive to work out in advance certain post-divorce matters, such as future adoption of children or visitation procedures ten years down the line. Only matters which can predictably have a reasonable chance of occurance within a few years of the divorce should be worked through as a kind of emotional insurance for children.

The single most essential ingredient for an emotionally healthy trip through the pre-post-separation-crisis period is the establishment of candid, calm, and reassuring communication from both parents to the children. Open communication allows children to feel that their parents accept and understand them. All the issues such as dating, visitation, loyalties are handled best when children can honestly discuss or feel free to display their rational and irrational feelings.

Ontogenic System:

Of all the factors influencing children's emotional reaction to divorce, their own individual personalities are the most mysterious variables. The fact is that two identically aged and sexed children can be exposed to the same divorce situation in the same way, and one will apparently thrive while the other has a catastrophic reaction. Why the difference? Surely the answer lies in some complex interaction between the unique genetic and environmental factors that renders each of us individuals.

These complexities do not mean the task of helping children deal with divorce is so hopeless that parents might as well abdicate responsibility for their children's responses. Parents should heed, consider, and act on all the issues discussed. But the complexity of the ontogenic system does mean that parents cannot take all the credit or all the blame for their children's responses. Parents sometimes feel so much self-guilt that they are emotionally unavailable to their children. If the children are going through a rough time, there are definite steps a parent can productively take; wallowing in self-blame is not one of them.

Incidentally, if the children display positive attitudes and behaviors, it doesn't hurt to take credit for having done a wonderful job. Of course, in reality, you may realize that people have much less ability to effect changes in others than we often times imagine, but feeling we are a potent force for good nourishes the soul.

The first real task in dealing with children's ontogenic responses to divorce is to assess when children are, in fact, suffering to the point where there is significant handicap. Parents have a very subjective view of their children to begin with and the additional stresses of divorce further hamper objectivity. Therefore, the task of evaluating the emotional status of the children may best be assigned to others.

Parents' guilt or other emotional responses can lead them to conclude that every nightmare, nail bite, outburst, or tear confirms their fears that they have emotionally incapacitated their children. Sometimes the error is in the opposite direction and the parents do not see major signs of their children's significant stresses. Either mistake can lead to unfortunate consequences. Parents, during the divorce crisis period and even afterward, should take the time to check with others about their children's emotional status.

If the children are school age, free professional opinions concerning the child's functioning are available. Children's teachers are usually able to offer objective opinions as to whether the children's social, academic, or behavior functioning indicates serious problems.

Another good source for checking on children's emotional well-being is from their friends. If the child is 12 or older, talking with their peers can guide parents. When the children are pre-adolescent, the friends behavior responses tell the story. If the child is much more socially isolated than before the divorce for as long as six weeks, then the problem may be considered potentially significant. Again, remember that the immediate response to the separation can be very dramatic. It is only when the response is dangerous or continues for a protracted period that parents should be alarmed. Generally four to six weeks may be considered a protracted period.

The ultimate, objective outside opinion, of course, would come from a child expert, such as a child psychologist or psychiatrist. If parents feel that there is a problem, they should seek the opinion of a professional child mental health worker. The professional helps in two ways. First, there is the assessment or diagnosis. The child expert can judge whether the symptoms being seen are, in fact, indicative of some problem that should be addressed. Second, if a serious problem is found, the professional can determine an appropriate treatment strategy. Just as parents can over- or under-estimate the existence of a problem, their subjectivity and emotional stresses may also lead to errors in judgment as to what the child needs. Trips to Disneyland, increased allowance, increased contact with parents can either be advantageous or disadvantageous strategies for dealing with a child stricken with a form of continuing grief about a parental conflict.

The warnings offered earlier in the book concerning the dangers of engaging appropriate legal help are just as important when considering hiring a mental health professional. There are great differences in the ethics, humanitarianism, and especially the skills among mental health professionals. Some people with excellent credentials will find justification for long, extensive, and expensive therapy. Others claim expertise in areas outside their training and competency. Such dangers mean that titles alone are insufficient to guide you in choosing a therapist or counselor. Rather than titles, consider using a recommendation from some other professional whose opinion you trust. For example, a trusted physician, attorney, or academnician *who knows* the abilities of other professionals is one good referral source. Another useful procedure is to listen to friends or acquaintances who have actually utilized the services of the person you're considering.

The most important thing, however, is to use your own judgment once you have begun working with someone. If after two or three visits you do not feel comfortable and confident about what is happening, you should seriously consider finding someone else. It is usually helpful to discuss such concerns with the professional rather than abruptly terminating treatment, but do not continue to work with someone whom your common sense tells you is not being helpful. Excellent mental health help is available; when you need the help, take the time to find it.

A complication is how much to trust children's sense about a mental health professional. Children who are having trouble dealing with the stress of divorce may not be in touch with either their need for help or the competency of the person offering it. In spite of these complications, their judgment should be respected, and if after a few visits the child feels negatively about the mental health worker, termination should be seriously considered. Any child mental health expert worth their fees should be able to establish good rapport with a troubled child within two or three visits or offer you *very* convincing reasons why not.

In summary, children can be expected to go through difficult times during the divorce crisis period. The behavior can be dramatic, but it is usually of a relatively short duration. Whether the parent suspects the child adjustment to be appropriate or inappropriate, some outside objective opinion (such as teachers) should be sought. When parents or others consider the children in emotional turmoil that lasts more than a four- to six-week period, then carefully chosen mental health expertise should be sought to evaluate the situation.

Part IV
Appendices

Appendix A

MY RELATIONSHIP WITH CAROL

An appendix describing my own divorce and primary relationship is considered a relevant addendum to the book, as it provides readers with an important source of my beliefs and biases about relationships. Carol is my closest friend. She has consistently been the most intellectually and physically stimulating person I have known. As of this writing, we have been divorced for three years. We had been married for 15. At the time we separated, we were enjoying a much more satisfying marriage than 95% of the "intact" marriages I knew about. We were intense lovers, stimulating companions, supportive of each other's individuality, and we shared a common set of beliefs.

Since the divorce, we have retained those features, and have also gotten rid of lots of crap, meaning a collection of things which hindered individuality but which most people consider inherent to committed coupling. "You have to be mature enough to give up certain freedoms to enjoy the advantages of a meaningful relationship." That quote embodies the belief of most people; Carol and I have challenged it. Very few people believe the high quality of our post-divorce relationship. Those who do know how close we are are confused as to why we ever got a divorce in the first place. They believe all the changes necessary to reduce the crap could have been accomplished without a legal divorce. Carol and I know that is not true.

This appendix involves ideas that many will consider impossible, impractical, or just unpalatable. Carol's and my relationship is not presented as a model for anyone else. Our present state is not ideal for the two of us; many imperfections remain. I am chronicalling it because I've lived it, know it, and it serves as the major source and, perhaps, most convincing testimonial to ideas presented in this book. Having lived through a positive divorce experience gave me an emotional bias which immeasurably increased the rational bias I'd had from over 20 years of professionally viewing others' relationships.

Ten years ago I read *How I Found Freedom In An Unfree World,* by Harry Brown. The book presents an approach for shedding various financial, marital, friendship, governmental, and family traps that limit an individual's freedom. I became a believer in Mr. Brown's proposals for: 1) deciding on which of life's tasks could be characterized as obligatory and nonjoyful; 2) imagining exactly what "dues" must be paid to get out of the burdensome "shoulds" and then, 3) mustering up the guts to pay the dues and enjoy a freer life.

Consider the commonly experienced "trap" of feeling a strong obligation to visit relatives while vacationing in one's home town. This, like all traps, is an imposition on one's freedom. You are hampered from fully enjoying the visit because you "should" spend part of your valued limited time visiting people you would not choose as friends. The dues to be paid may be that the relatives will think less of you if you don't visit and may even complain about you to others. Brown suggests paying the dues and enjoying the freedom.

I found his ideas extremely valuable except for the section on marriage which I read with genuine horror. In this section, Mr. Brown briskly reported that in order to preserve a good marital relationship, the first and most essential step was to get a divorce. I considered the idea ludicrous and began to hypothesize about the neurotic psychopathology which prevented Mr. Brown's otherwise creative mind from being able to maintain an emotionally close, growing and fruitful relationship with a spouse. With pride, based on my splendid eight year marriage at the time, I magnanimously forgave Mr. Brown his flaw.

In the same way, you, gentle reader, may find this book useful and yet, gleen from this appendix a broad hint of Alpern's neurosis. If so, be generous, and wait a few years.

Seven years after I initially read Mr. Brown's book, I did seek a divorce for the explicit purpose of enhancing my relationship with Carol. I am very aware of the possibility that seven years from now I may well be a strong proponant of Master's and Johnson's view expressed in their volume, "Pair Bonding," that the most fulfilling relationships come through committed, monogomous marriages. It is also possible that some years after that, I'll believe it important to have some form of open marriage. Knowing that I could decide to adopt any of these relationship styles brought me to the sobering fact that all changes can not be dignified with the label "growth." Nevertheless, to implement well thought out changes is a fulfilling way to live. That may be because it's opposite, dread fear of change, seems clearly a form of death.

Carol and I were married in the early 1960s. She was a 21-year-old nurse, I was a 31-year-old assistant professor of psychology. Our romantic love was strong. I ended a three year personal psychoanalysis and married a Catholic girl, no minor feat for a man with a standard Woody Allen Jewish background. Carol happily ended the nursing career which had failed to satisfy her creative needs and in rapid succession gave birth to our two sons. We derived much pleasure from our fairly stereotypical sex-typed roles in those early years of marriage. Over the next five or so years, I happily pursued my professional life at the university. Carol seemed a bit tired, but taking care of a home, two young children and a professionally-oriented husband seemed, then, to be standard, normal, and what was to be done. We felt content. We had a close monogomous relationship in which we continued to enjoy each other's company above all others. The needs of others for extra-marital romantic encounters did not seem relevant to our lives. We felt no moral condemnation of people who lived other sexual styles; we simply felt complete within our relationship.

In the early 1970s, Carol began art school. The children were in elementary school. It seemed very appropriate to both of us that she pursue a career in a field that would tap her considerable creative talent.

The changes that began with Carol's metriculation into art school were, however, much more meaningful than they seemed at the time. The reduction of the time she devoted to homemaking provided only the slightest disruptions. After all, I was no chauvenist. Having been an independent bachelor for years I could, not too unhappily, resurrect my minimal homemaking skills. Since I had been lecturing for years on the expanding role of fathers in our changing culture, I could easily justify assuming added parental and household responsibilities. It seemed appropriate and consistent with our raised consciousness about women's rights. Traditional wives are wonderful things, and everyone should enjoy the benefits of having one—even women.

The changes which were most relevant were more subtle. Carol now had friends at school which we did not share. Also, the schooling required her to spend some evenings away from home. These things stirred up vague anxieties in me. Although I was completely confident and secure about the high quality of our relationship, I inexipcably felt something was amiss when Carol wasn't around or was with people I didn't know. Both feelings were, on a rational basis, nonsensical. I certainly had friends at the university whom Carol didn't know and were in no way a threat to our relationship. And I had no idea of why I should feel strange when she was gone during evenings when I had so many projects and activities that were completely involving. Even when Carol talked about friends I didn't know or activities she engaged in independently, it caused me some discomfort. It wasn't discussed. It was barely conscious. It was ignored.

In 1974, we began planning a six month sabbatical leave from the university. We had always loved traveling together. Being unplugged from our usual tasks and responsibilities had always provided us with our closest times. Now we were planning a trip of six months. We had never had anything near that amount of free time.

Our high expectations were more than met. We loved the travel. We were together practically 24 hours of each day. We discovered unexpected ability for mutual stimulation.

One thing had jolted me as we drove down the street within five minutes of beginning our trip. An interesting fantasy occurred to me, and I asked Carol, "Do you think there's a chance we won't come back to this life (place, job, way of being)?" In my own mind, I felt the odds were 50 to 1 that we would return. After all, we both had satisfying occupations, good friends, lived in what we considered the most beautiful spot within 30 miles of work, the kids were happy, etc., etc.

Knowing Carol to be a stubborn, wonderful innovator, I fully expected her estimate to be drastically different. Perhaps she would claim the chances for a new life to be as high as 50-50. In my mental scenario, I planned to smile and wisely be quiet; I didn't want our trip to begin with a silly argument. Carol thought for a brief time and then announced, "One in a hundred that we'll return." I did remain quiet.

During that six months of traveling we spoke often of how we believed life should ideally be lived. By the end of the sabbatical, we had come to a collection of decisions. The easy ones were those we felt emotionally ready to handle. We would move to the most appealing place we had ever seen, and we would share, as equally as possible, the financial and home responsibilities involved in the relocation.

The difficult decisions we made about what comprised the ideal life were made easier because we both agreed we were not emotionally ready to implement them. We agreed that "ideally" two people should be able to live together in a committed love relationship with almost no restrictions on the other's independence. The fullest expression of the development of friends, careers, infatuations, sports, and such should be the right and responsibility of each individual which should be supported by the other. We were not deciding to be irresponsibly self-indulgent, but rather to be devoted to promoting individual development through a supportive love relationship. We decided these were ideals, and that though we could implement many facets of them, we were emotionally unprepared to deal with separate sexual lives, financial fortunes, or separate goals at that particular time.

During the next two years, we successfully achieved the relocation. Carol began producing and selling art, and I began a psychology practice. The replanting of our children, home, careers, and community involvement went surprisingly smoothly. Sometime during those two years, we experimented with outside sexual relationships. That, too, seemed somewhat easier to deal with than we had originally imagined. It's not that it was painless. There were long silences and looks of hurt, disappointment and guilt feelings; but it was bearable, in part, because it was an honest experimentation with what we had labeled as ideal and, thus, worth trying. It certainly helped that we worked to keep the outside sexual encounters relatively equal, relatively infrequent, and that we were honest with each other. Psychic pain can be treated much like physical pain. Athletes regularly endure physical pain to achieve athletic accomplishments. Learning any new skill requires the student to stretch the mind, which is usually experienced as discomfort. Carol and I applied this same concept in order to achieve our sexual freedom ideal. Both of us exercised consideration of the other by doing all we could to prevent the other from feeling threatened, unloved, unwanted, or unprimary.

An unexpected and more difficult problem came after we had reached a level of social, sexual, and financial security in our new lives. We both began to suffer feelings of inequities.

Carol wanted to produce art full time, and we agreed that she should. My career was more financially rewarding, so I shouldered the major financial burdens. Carol felt she was then expected to do most of the housework which prevented her from spending the time needed to develop her career. This seemed unfair to her since she reasoned that she had done all of the housework while I was learning my profession. I felt she wanted too many freedoms and was assuming too few responsibilities. The resentments were not gigantic. They were discussed. However, they seemed to be resolved inadequately. The mutual affection and support remained.

One morning I came back from a meditative jog and came up with the outlandish suggestion that a divorce, as a positive step to ending the resentments, could enhance our relationship and our lives.

In rapid succession, Carol went through resistance, anger, sadness, and finally thoughtfulness. We backpacked into the mountains, cried, laughed, planned and finally agreed that we wanted to try it. If the divorce didn't work out, we could always remarry. To us, it was pioneering an idea in a form we had never heard of.

Currently, we live in two places. I live in our former house in which she has maintained a partial financial investment. That solved equal division of equity without having to sell our home or disrupt our children's physical lives and offered her the easiest long-term investment she could have. I have legal custody of the children only because we agreed that my larger income and larger home makes it easier for me to physically provide for the children. A live-in housekeeper performs the chores the boys and I choose not to do.

Carol has her own apartment. It provides us with the isolated hideaway for our intimate times about three times a week. Her small apartment is an affordable, easily cared-for space. She is free from obligatory family responsibilities. She invites our boys over one at a time and maintains high quality relationships with each of them. She can eat, sleep, work, read, put the lights on and off, and be with whatever friends she wants whenever she wants. So can I.

Both of us have other relationships which are more important than they were when we first experimented with other relationships. Carol has had a two year relationship with a man she cares for and with whom she has traveled extensively. After the separation, I began with a variety of casual, moderately involved relationships with women. The first draft of this book, however, is being written on a five week island stay with a woman who is a close, important, and stimulating friend.

Carol and I carefully worked out a formal legal agreement designed to be fair and to eliminate as much as possible from the divorce the third party (the government). It was a fine agreement in August of 1978. We ignore it all the time. Money is dispensed according to need, rather than the terms of the settlement. The custody agreements are essentially irrelevant. We make any necessary decisions about our children with our children. Carol and I now are with each other primarily at those times when we want to be with each other. We can easily separate at times when that's desirable. We have both learned that we can independently manage our laundry needs, as well as other relationships. We are very close. We have fewer quarrels. It seems very good.

There were many tough times during the two years when we were unsuccessful in limiting the pain. I remember one period of about six weeks when we were totally alienated. That had *never* happened in our fifteen years of marriage. I remember tears, doubts and terrible feelings of having somehow thrown away the best part of my life. Those times, however, were less frequent than those when both of us revelled in the glory bought with our guts.

Some problems have remained problems. We never did get through the strange pain involved with having our children spend time with each other's romantic friends. The first time my boys enjoyed an airplane ride piloted by Carol's friend was very painful. Although I rationally didn't believe it possible that I could lose my children's affections because they could also enjoy the company of another man, I was unable to feel comfortable with that situation. Carol and I simply do not include our children when we are with romantic friends.

Another problem that remains is that other people are very troubled by Carol's and my on-going relationship. Even though we work hard to be completely truthful with others and explain our continuing relationship, we have consistently had them deny our relationship, be hurt by it, or try to undermine it. Others do not share our belief that being totally with the person you are with at that moment is satisfactory. They are bothered by the fact that many other moments are shared between Carol and I. They are bothered by this even if they clearly state that they, themselves, are not looking for a constant, committed relationship.

Carol and I have reached a belief that it really doesn't make a lot of difference what a person does when they are not with you. Most adults need a variety of involvements in business, social, athletic, spiritual, and vocational spheres. Unless your needs are for an exclusive, monogomous, constant relationship, it theoretically shouldn't matter if, when the partner is not with you, they are playing tennis or making love with someone else. Most people feel that's an outrageous concept. We don't. Many people indicate that they understand, and even agree with our style of relationship, but with time, find themselves very uncomfortable about it. It is a problem as yet unsolved.

Many people claim to appreciate the advantages of separate living spaces and separate finances. People also see our children as very secure and even better off because of our present way of being with them. What seems hardest for others to accept is the sexual freedom, or more specifically, that the other important relationships which include sexuality are not a terrifying threat: "they will meet someone they love more." The other challenge made to our relationship is that if it works, it must be that Carol and I really don't care that deeply for each other.

Allowing each other to enjoy romantic relationships *in addition* to the one that we shared is just another risk we believe has to be taken to allow life to be lived in the way that makes the most sense to us. It is possible that one of us could find someone who will win them away emotionally and physically. It seems very unlikely that our history and our mutual ability to stimulate our growth, our shared interest, and our love could ever be replaced. But if it could, I believe we would genuinely wish it for each other. Both Carol and I know that we could survive the loss of the other's primary attention and go on to find other fine relationships. Certainly, we would mourn for the loss. We would certainly remain each others' very special friend. I do not think of it as a realistic enough possibility to contemplate it as much as other people seem to. Perhaps we are brave pioneers. Perhaps we are incredibly naive. We are enjoying our relationship.

That provides an overview of my divorce and my relationship. Again, it is offered to add credence to my bias that divorce can not only be amicable, but can allow for improved relationships between former spouses. Few divorcing couples will want to even consider having a primary, on-going relationship with their former spouse, but perhaps the knowledge that this is a possibility will serve to allow consideration of a genuine friendship with the person once chosen to love "till death do you part."

P.S. The third draft of this book is being finished 15 months after the above was written. For the last year, Carol and I have lived together, at first, in an open divorce and more recently, in a monogamous divorce. Both of these have been good. And so it goes . . .

Appendix B

STATE BY STATE

A. Divorce—Dissolution Grounds
B. Divorce Residency Requirements
C. Legal Aid Contacts

ALABAMA:
- A. Divorce—Dissolution Grounds
  - a) No Fault:
    1. Final decree of legal separation in effect for two years.
    2. Incompatability (of temperament)
    3. Irretrievable Breakdown of Marriage
  - b) Fault:
    1. Abandonment and/or Desertion (2 years)
    2. Adultery
    3. Alcohol or Drug Addiction
    4. Crime Against Nature
    5. Imprisonment (2 years)
    6. Insanity or Mental Illness (5 years)
    7. Non-support (2 years)
    8. Physical Violence
    9. Pregnancy (pregnancy by another man before marriage unknown to husband)
    10. Sexual Incapacity
- B. Divorce Residency Requirements
  - a) Six months if other spouse is non-resident.
- C. Legal Aid Contact
  - a) Birmingham: Legal Assistant Corp. of Birmingham
  - b) Mobil: Committee on Legal Aid, New Court House Building (205-438-4381)

ALASKA:
- A. Divorce—Dissolution Grounds
  - a) No Fault:

1. Incompatability (if both agree on settlement and custody)
2. Incompatability (when one spouse can't be found)
  b) Fault:
    1. Abandonment and/or Desertion (1 year)
    2. Adultery
    3. Alcohol Addiction (1 year)
    4. Cruelty
    5. Drug Addiction
    6. Imprisonment (felony conviction)
    7. Incompatability (of temperment)
    8. Insanity or Mental Illness (institution 18 months)
B. Divorce Residency Requirements
  a) None, if spouses agree to Alaska jurisdiction and file together.
C. Legal Aid Contact
  a) Anchorage: Alaska Legal Services Corporation, 524 West 6th Avenue, 95510 (907) 272-9431

ARIZONA:
A. Divorce—Dissolution Grounds
  a) No Fault:
    1. Irretrievable Breakdown of Marriage
  b) Fault: (none)
B. Divorce Residency Requirements
  a) 90 days by either spouse.
C. Legal Aid Contact
  a) Phoenix: District of Arizona, U.S. District Court, 85025 (602) 261-3561
  b) Tucson: County Bar Assn., 55 West Congress, 85701 (602-623-6260)

ARKANSAS:
A. Divorce—Dissolution Grounds
  a) No Fault:
    1. Separation without Support (No Fault after 3 years)
  b) Fault:
    1. Abandonment and/or Desertion (1 year)
    2. Alcohol or Drug Addiction (1 year)

       3. Bigamy
       4. Cruelty
       5. Impotence
       6. Imprisonment (felony conviction)
       7. Indignities to Innocent Party
       8. Non-support

B. Divorce Residency Requirements
    a) One spouse's residence 60 days before filing and 3 months before decree is obtained.

C. Legal Aid Contact
    a) Little Rock: Public Defender, Pulaski County Court House, 72201 (501-374-9203)

CALIFORNIA:

A. Divorce—Dissolution Grounds
    a) No Fault:
        1. Irretrievable Breakdown of Marriage
    b) Fault:
        1. Insanity or Mental Illness (incurable)

B. Divorce Residency Requirements
    a) One spouse's residence for six months.

C. Legal Aid Contact
    a) Los Angeles: ACLU Foundation of Southern California, 633 So. Shatto Place, 90005 (213-487-1720)
    b) Sacramento: 1900 K. Street, Suite 203, 95814 (916-446-7901)
    c) San Diego: 400 Granger Building, 964 5th Avenue, 92101 (714-232-2214)
    d) San Francisco: Mission Community Legal Defense, 2922 Mission Street, 94110 (415-826-5333)

COLORADO:

A. Divorce—Dissolution Grounds
    a) No Fault:
        1. Irretrievable Breakdown of Marriage
    b) Fault: (none)

B. Divorce Residency Requirements
    a) One spouse resident for 90 days before filing: decree 90 days after filing.

C. Legal Aid Contact
  a) Denver: Colorado Legal Aid Society Service, 912 Broadway Street, 80205

CONNECTICUT:
  A. Divorce—Dissolution Grounds
  a) No Fault:
    1. Irretrievable Breakdown of Marriage
    2. Separation without Support (18 months)
  b) Fault:
    1. Abandonment and/or Desertion (1 year)
    2. Adultery
    3. Alcoholic
    4. Cruelty
    5. Fraudulent Contract
    6. Imprisonment (sentance for life or more than one year for infamous crime)
    7. Insanity or Mental Illness (5 years hospitalization)
    8. Seven Years Absence
  B. Divorce Residency Requirements
  a) One spouse resident for one year before filing.
  b) One spouse resident at time of marriage with intent to remain resident of state.
  c) Cause of divorce occurred after one spouse resided in state.
  C. Legal Aid Contact
  a) Hartford: Public Defender, 750 Main St., 06103

DELAWARE:
  A. Divorce—Dissolution Grounds
  a) No Fault:
    1. Irretrievable Breakdown of Marriage
    2. Voluntary Separation
    3. Separation by Incompatability
  b) Fault:
    1. Irretrievable Breakdown of Marriage (separation by mental illness)
    2. Irretrievable Breakdown of Marriage (separation caused by misconduct)

B. Divorce Residency Requirements
   a) One spouse resident six months before filing.
   b) Judgment of divorce final after three months.
C. Legal Aid Contact
   a) Wilmington: 204 West 7th Street, 19801 (302) 665-7351

DISTRICT OF COLUMBIA:
A. Divorce—Dissolution Grounds
   a) No Fault:
      1. Voluntarily living apart for 6 months without cohabitation.
      2. Living apart for one year without cohabitation within same domicile, but living separate lives.
   b) Fault: (none)
B. Divorce Residency Requirements
   a) One spouse resident for six months before filing.
C. Legal Aid Contact
   a) Washington: Suite 300, 666 11th Street, N.W., 20001 (202) 628-1161

FLORIDA:
A. Divorce—Dissolution Grounds
   a) No Fault:
      1. Irretrievable Breakdown of Marriage
   b) Fault:
      1. Mental Incompetence (3 years)
B. Divorce Residency Requirements
   a) One spouse (plaintiff) resident for six months. No delay for final decree.
C. Legal Aid Contact
   a) Tallahassee: Leon County Legal Aid Society, 103 B, Leon County Courthouse, 32301

GEORGIA:
A. Divorce—Dissolution Grounds
   a) No Fault:
      1. Irretrievable Breakdown of Marriage
   b) Fault:
      1. Abandonment and/or Desertion (1 year)

    2. Adultery
    3. Alcoholic
    4. Conviction of Turpitude
    5. Cruelty
    6. Drug Addiction
    7. Force, Duress or Fraud in Obtaining Marriage
    8. Impotence
    9. Imprisonment (2 years)
   10. Incest
   11. Insanity or Mental Illness
   12. Mental Incapacity
   13. Pregnancy (pregnancy by another man before marriage unknown to husband)

B. Divorce Residency Requirements
    a) One spouse resident 6 months before filing.

C. Legal Aid Contact
    a) Atlanta: 153 Pryor Street, S.W., 30303 (404) 524-5811

HAWAII:

A. Divorce—Dissolution Grounds
    a) No Fault:
        1. Irretrievable Breakdown of Marriage
        2. Final decree of legal separation in effect for more than 2 years.
        3. Voluntarily living apart for two years.
    b) Fault: (none)

B. Divorce Residency Requirements
    a) One spouse resident six months before filing.

C. Legal Aid Contact
    a) Honolulu: Suite 404, North Vineyard Blvd., 96817 (808) 536-4302

IDAHO:

A. Divorce—Dissolution Grounds
    a) No Fault:
        1. Irretrievable Breakdown of Marriage
        2. Separation without Support (5 years)
    b) Fault:
        1. Abandonment and/or Desertion

        2. Adultery
        3. Alcoholic
        4. Conviction of Felony
        5. Cruelty
        6. Insanity or Mental Illness (3 years confinement)
        7. Willfull Neglect
  B. Divorce Residency Requirements
    a) Six weeks with spouse before legal action is filed.
  C. Legal Aid Contact
    a) Boise: 104½ So. Capital Blvd., 83701 (208) 345-0106

ILLINOIS:
  A. Divorce—Dissolution Grounds
    a) No Fault: (none)
    b) Fault:
        1. Abandonment and/or Desertion (1 year)
        2. Adultery
        3. Alcoholic (2 years)
        4. Attempt on Life of Spouse
        5. Bigamy
        6. Conviction of Felony or Infamous Crime
        7. Drug Addiction
        8. Impotence
        9. Infection of Spouse with Venereal Disease
  B. Divorce Residency Requirements
    a) One spouse domiciled in state at time of filing. Domicile maintained for 90 days preceding gain of final divorce decree.
  C. Legal Aid Contact
    a) Chicago: Suite 1225, 180 N. LaSalle St., 60601 (312) 263-0982
    b) Springfield: 516 East Monroe St., 62701 (217) 544-7492

INDIANA:
  A. Divorce—Dissolution Grounds
    a) No Fault:
        1. Irretrievable Breakdown of Marriage
    b) Fault:
        1. Conviction of Infamous Crime during Marriage

    2. Impotence (at time of marriage)

    3. Insanity or Mental Illness (2 years)

B. Divorce Residency Requirements

    a) One spouse resident six months before filing.

C. Legal Aid Contact

    a) Indianapolis: Room 112, 615 N. Alabama, 46204 (317) 635-9538

IOWA:

A. Divorce—Dissolution Grounds

    a) No Fault:

        1. Irretrievable Breakdown of Marriage

    b) Fault:

        1. Mental Illness

B. Divorce Residency Requirements

    a) One spouse resident for one year prior to filing and non-filing spouse must be a resident when divorce is filed.

C. Legal Aid Contact

    a) Des Moines: 102 East Grand Avenue, 50309 (515) 282-8375

KANSAS:

A. Divorce—Dissolution Grounds

    a) No Fault:

        1. Incompatability

    b) Fault:

        1. Abandonment and/or Desertion (1 year)

        2. Adultery

        3. Alcoholic

        4. Cruelty

        5. Gross Neglect of Duty

        6. Imprisonment (and conviction of felony)

        7. Insanity or Mental Illness (3 years confinement)

B. Divorce Residency Requirements

    a) Plaintiff resident 60 days before filing.

C. Legal Aid Contact

    a) Kansas City: 909 Huron Building, 907 N. 7th, 66101 (913) 621-0200

KENTUCKY:
- A. Divorce—Dissolution Grounds
    - a) No Fault:
        1. Irretrievable Breakdown of Marriage (and living apart without sexual contact for 60 days)
- B. Divorce Residency Requirements
    - a) One spouse resident 180 days before filing.
- C. Legal Aid Contact
    - a) Lexington: 180 Market Street, 40507 (606) 255-8025
    - b) Louisville: 307 South 5th Street, 40402

LOUISIANA:
- A. Divorce—Dissolution Grounds
    - a) No Fault:
        1. Final Decree of Legal Separation in Effect for more than One Year
        2. Living Apart for Two Years
    - b) Fault:
        1. Abandonment and/or Desertion
        2. Adultery
        3. Alcoholic
        4. Attempt to Kill Spouse
        5. Conviction of Felony
        6. Cruelty
        7. Imprisonment
        8. Non-Support
        9. Proof of Felony by Spouse
        10. Public Defamation
        11. Voluntary Separation (1 year)
        12. Voluntary Separation (6 months and affidavit showing irreconcilable differences)
- B. Divorce Residency Requirements
    - a) None
- C. Legal Aid Contact
    - a) New Orleans: Room 511, 211 Camp St., 70130 (504) 523-2597

MAINE:
- A. Divorce—Dissolution Grounds
  - a) No Fault:
    - 1. Irretrievable Breakdown of Marriage
  - b) Fault:
    - 1. Abandonment and/or Desertion (3 years)
    - 2. Adultery
    - 3. Alcohol or Drug Addiction
    - 4. Cruelty
    - 5. Impotence
    - 6. Non-Support
- B. Divorce Residency Requirements
  - a) Parties married or lived in State.
  - b) Plaintiff resident of State when grounds arose.
  - c) Plaintiff a resident for six months.
  - d) Defendant resident of State.
- C. Legal Aid Contact
  - a) Portland: 178 Middle Street, (207) 774-8211

MARYLAND:
- A. Divorce—Dissolution Grounds
  - a) No Fault:
    - 1. Involuntary Separation without Cohabitation for Three Years.
    - 2. Voluntary Separation without Cohabitation for One Year.
  - b) Fault:
    - 1. Abandonment and/or Desertion (1 year)
    - 2. Adultery
    - 3. Conviction of Felony
    - 4. Impotence (at time of marriage)
    - 5. Imprisonment (3 years)
    - 6. Insanity or Mental Illness (3 year confinement)
- B. Divorce Residency Requirements
  - a) None, if grounds arose within state.
  - b) One year for one spouse if grounds arose out of state.
  - c) Two years if grounds are insanity.
- C. Legal Aid Contact
  - a) Baltimore: 341 North Calvert St., 21202 (301) 539-5340

MASSACHUSETTS:
A. Divorce—Dissolution Grounds
- a) No Fault:
  1. Irretrievable Breakdown of Marriage: if both file joint separation agreement, divorce final 6 months after court approval of agreement.
  2. Irretrievable Breakdown of Marriage: if one files, divorce final 12 months after filing.
- b) Fault:
  1. Abandonment and/or Desertion (1 year)
  2. Adultery
  3. Alcohol or Drug Addiction
  4. Cruelty
  5. Impotence
  6. Imprisonment
  7. Non-Support

B. Divorce Residency Requirements
- a) Lived together, married in state and one resident of state when filing.
- b) Plaintiff living in state if ground occurred in state.
- c) Plaintiff living in state one year if ground occurred outside of state.

C. Legal Aid Contact
- a) Boston: 15 State Street, 02109
- b) Salem: 189 Jefferson Avenue, 01970 (617) 744-4500

MICHIGAN:
A. Divorce—Dissolution Grounds
- a) No Fault:
  1. Irretrievable Breakdown of Marriage
- b) Fault: (none)

B. Divorce Residency Requirements
- a) One spouse 180 days before filing if grounds occurred within state.
- b) One spouse one year before filing if grounds occurred outside state.

C. Legal Aid Contact
- a) Detroit: 600 Woodward Avenue, 48226
- b) Lansing: P.O. Box 1071, 48933 (517) 484-7773

MINNESOTA:
- A. Divorce—Dissolution Grounds
    - a) No Fault:
        1. Irretrievable Breakdown of Marriage
    - b) Fault: (none)
- B. Divorce Residency Requirements
    - a) One spouse 180 days before filing.
- C. Legal Aid Contact
    - a) Minneapolis: 501 Park Avenue, 55415 (612) 332-1441

MISSISSIPPI:
- A. Divorce—Dissolution Grounds
    - a) No Fault:
        1. Irretrievable Breakdown of Marriage: if non-contested and agrees on property settlement and custody.
    - b) Fault:
        1. Abandonment and/or Desertion (1 year)
        2. Adultery
        3. Alcoholic
        4. Bigamy
        5. Close Blood Relationship with Spouse
        6. Cruelty
        7. Drug Addiction
        8. Impotence
        9. Imprisonment (penitentiary)
        10. Insanity or Mental Illness (at time of marriage)
        11. Insanity or Mental Illness (confinement of 3 years)
        12. Pregnancy (pregnancy by another man before marriage unknown to husband)
- B. Divorce Residency Requirements
    - a) One spouse resident for six months before filing.
- C. Legal Aid Contact
    - a) Jackson: P.O. Box 8777, 39204 (601) 373-1120

MISSOURI:
- A. Divorce—Dissolution Grounds
    - a) No Fault:
        1. Irretrievable Breakdown of Marriage

    b) Fault:
        1. Abandonment and/or Desertion (1 year)
        2. Adultery
        3. Alcoholic
        4. Conviction of Felony
        5. Cruelty
        6. Impotence
        7. Personal Indignities
        8. Pregnancy (pregnancy by another man before marriage unknown to husband)
        9. Vagrancy of Husband
B. Divorce Residency Requirements
    a) One spouse resident 90 days before filing.
C. Legal Aid Contact
    a) St. Louis: Room 409, 4030 Chonteau Avenue, 63110 (314) 652-9581

MONTANA:
A. Divorce—Dissolution Grounds
    a) No Fault:
        1. Irretrievable Breakdown of Marriage (and that spouses not live together for 180 days or that serious marital discord exists)
B. Divorce Residency Requirements
    a) One spouse 90 days residency before filing.
C. Legal Aid Contact
    a) Billings: 2822 3rd Avenue, N., 59711 (406) 248-7113
    b) Helena: 601 Power Block, 59601 (406) 442-9830

NEBRASKA:
A. Divorce—Dissolution Grounds
    a) No Fault:
        1. Irretrievable Breakdown of Marriage
    b) Fault: (none)
B. Divorce Residency Requirements
    a) One spouse resident for one year before filing.
C. Legal Aid Contact
    a) Lincoln: 800 Anderson Building, 68508
    b) Omaha: 1613 Farnam Street, 68102

NEVADA:
 A. Divorce—Dissolution Grounds
  a) No Fault:
   1. Incompatability
   2. Living Separately for One Year
  b) Fault:
   1. Insanity (2 years)
 B. Divorce Residency Requirements
  a) One spouse resident 6 weeks before filing.
 C. Legal Aid Contact
  a) Las Vegas: 900 West Bonanza Road, 89106 (702) 648-6970

NEW HAMPSHIRE:
 A. Divorce—Dissolution Grounds
  a) No Fault:
   1. Irretrievable Breakdown of Marriage
  b) Fault:
   1. Abandonment and/or Desertion (2 years)
   2. Adultery
   3. Alcohol Addiction (2 years)
   4. Cruelty
   5. Impotence
   6. Imprisonment (and conviction of felony)
   7. Joining Religious Group that doesn't Believe in Marriage and Refusal to have Sexual Relations for Six Months
   8. Separation without Support (2 years)
   9. Violence: Physical and Mental
 B. Divorce Residency Requirements
  a) Both domiciled in state when filed, or
  b) Plaintiff resides in state and defendant personally serviced in state, or
  c) Plaintiff domiciled in state one year before filing.
 C. Legal Aid Contact
  a) Concord: 136 North Main, 03301 (603) 224-3333

NEW JERSEY:
- A. Divorce—Dissolution Grounds
  - a) No Fault:
    - 1. Living Apart for 18 Months
  - b) Fault:
    - 1. Abandonment and/or Desertion (1 year)
    - 2. Adultery
    - 3. Alcohol or Drug Addiction
    - 4. Cruelty
    - 5. Deviant Sexual Conduct
    - 6. Imprisonment (18 months)
    - 7. Insanity or Mental Illness (2 years commitment)
- B. Divorce Residency Requirements
  - a) One spouse resident one year before filing.
- C. Legal Aid Contact
  - a) Newark: 463 Central Avenue, 07050
  - b) Trenton: 440 East State Street, 08608

NEW MEXICO:
- A. Divorce—Dissolution Grounds
  - a) No Fault:
    - 1. Incompatability
  - b) Fault:
    - 1. Abandonment and/or Desertion
    - 2. Adultery
    - 3. Cruelty
- B. Divorce Residency Requirements
  - a) One spouse 6 months domicile before filing.
- C. Legal Aid Contact
  - a) Albuquerque: 1015 Tijeras Avenue, 87101 (505) 242-3442
  - b) Santa Fe: 322 Montezuma Street, 87501 (505) 982-9886

NEW YORK:
- A. Divorce—Dissolution Grounds
  - a) No Fault:
    - 1. Final Decree of Legal Separation in Effect for more than One Year

b) Fault:
1. Abandonment and/or Desertion (1 year)
2. Adultery
3. Cruelty
4. Imprisonment (3 years)
B. Divorce Residency Requirements
a) Both residents before filing and grounds arise in state, or
b) One a resident for two years before filing.
c) One a resident for one year.
1. marriage occurred in state, or
2. grounds occurred in state, or
3. spouses lived in marital state in New York
C. Legal Aid Contact
a) Albany: 79 North Pearl Street, 12207 (518) 462-6765
b) New York: 335 Broadway, 10013 (212) 966-6600

NORTH CAROLINA:
A. Divorce—Dissolution Grounds
a) No Fault:
1. Separation (continuous 1 year)
b) Fault:
1. Adultery
2. Bestiality
3. Crime Against Nature
4. Impotence (at time of marriage)
5. Insanity or Mental Illness (with separation for three years)
6. Pregnancy (pregnancy by another man before marriage unknown to husband)
B. Divorce Residency Requirements
a) Plaintiff resident six months before filing.
C. Legal Aid Contact
a) Durham: 353 West Main Street, Box 2101, 27701
b) Winston-Salem: 202 W. 3rd Street, 27101 (919) 723-4301

NORTH DAKOTA:
A. Divorce—Dissolution Grounds
a) No Fault:

       1. Final Decree of Legal Separation in Effect for One Year.
       2. Irretrievable Breakdown of Marriage

  b) Fault:
       1. Abandonment and/or Desertion (1 year)
       2. Adultery
       3. Alcoholic (1 year)
       4. Conviction of Felony
       5. Cruelty: Mental and Physical
       6. Insanity or Mental Illness (5 years confinement)
       7. Refusal to Cohabit
       8. Wilful Neglect (1 year)

B. Divorce Residency Requirements
  a) Plaintiff a resident one year before filing.

C. Legal Aid Contact
  a) Bismark: 420 North 4th Street, 58501 (701) 258-4270
  b) Devils Lake: 1219 College Drive, 58301 (701) 662-8123
  c) Fargo: 15 South 21st Street, 58102 (701) 232-4495
  d) Minot: Box 117, 58701 (701) 852-3870

OHIO:

A. Divorce—Dissolution Grounds
  a) No Fault:
       1. Mutual Consent: joint filing and court approval of separation agreement covering property and custody.
       2. Living Apart for Two Years

  b) Fault:
       1. Absence (1 year)
       2. Adultery
       3. Alcoholic
       4. Bigamy
       5. Cruelty
       6. Fraudulent Conduct
       7. Gross Neglect of Duty
       8. Impotence
       9. Imprisonment (penitentiary)
     10. Insanity or Mental Illness (4 years confinement)

B. Divorce Residency Requirements
  a) Both spouses six months residency for mutual consent grounds.
  b) Plaintiff six months residency for all other grounds.
C. Legal Aid Contact
  a) Cleveland: 2108 Payne Avenue, 44114 (216) 861-6264
  b) Columbus: 1659 North High Street, 43210 (614) 293-6821

OKLAHOMA:
  A. Divorce—Dissolution Grounds
    a) No Fault:
      1. Incompatability
    b) Fault:
      1. Abandonment and/or Desertion (1 year)
      2. Adultery
      3. Alcoholic
      4. Cruelty
      5. Fraudulent Conduct
      6. Gross Neglect of Duty
      7. Impotence
      8. Imprisonment (for felony)
      9. Insanity or Mental Illness (5 years confinement)
      10. Pregnancy (pregnancy by another man before marriage unknown to husband)
  B. Divorce Residency Requirements
    a) One spouse 6 months residency in state, 30 days in county before filing.
  C. Legal Aid Contact
    a) Oklahoma City: 601 Mercantile Building, 73102 (405) 272-9461

OREGON:
  A. Divorce—Dissolution Grounds
    a) No Fault:
      1. Irretrievable Breakdown of Marriage
    b) Fault: (none)
  B. Divorce Residency Requirements
    a) One spouse in residence or domicile in state can file if couple was married in state, or

    b) One spouse in residence for six months before filing.
- C. Legal Aid Contact
  - a) Eugene: 1309 Willamette Street, 97401
  - b) Multnomah: Room 402, 732 Southwest 3rd Ave., 97204 (503) 224-4086

PENNSYLVANIA:
- A. Divorce—Dissolution Grounds
  - a) No Fault:
    1. Irretrievable Breakdown of Marriage (if both spouses file affidavit of agreement)
    2. Living Separately (3 years)
  - b) Fault:
    1. Abandonment and/or Desertion (1 year)
    2. Adultery
    3. Bigamy
    4. Crimes (specific crimes with a sentence of two years or more)
    5. Cruelty (endangering life)
    6. Indignities
    7. Insanity or Mental Illness (3 years confinement)
- B. Divorce Residency Requirements
  - a) One spouse resident for one year before filing.
- C. Legal Aid Contact
  - a) Philadelphia: 3111 South Juniper Street, 19107 (215) 735-6122
  - b) Pittsburgh: 200 Ross Street, Room 112, 15219 (412) 261-6010

RHODE ISLAND:
- A. Divorce—Dissolution Grounds
  - a) No Fault:
    1. Irretrievable Breakdown of Marriage
    2. Separation (3 years)
  - b) Fault:
    1. Abandonment and/or Desertion (5 years or less at Judge's discretion)
    2. Adultery
    3. Alcoholic

    4. "Because of Crime, Deemed to be Civilly Dead"

    5. Cruelty

    6. Drug Addiction

    7. "Gross Behaviour and Wickedness Repugnant to and in Violation of Marriage Covenant"

    8. Impotence (at time of marriage)

    9. Neglect and Refusal of Husband to Provide Necessaries

B. Divorce Residency Requirements

    a) One year for either spouse before filing.

C. Legal Aid Contact

    a) Providence: 76 Dorrance Street, 02903 (401) 331-4665

SOUTH CAROLINA:

A. Divorce—Dissolution Grounds

    a) No Fault:

        1. Separation (1 year)

    b) Fault:

        1. Adultery

        2. Alcohol or Drug Addiction

        3. Cruelty (Physical)

        4. Desertion (1 year)

B. Divorce Residency Requirements

    a) One spouse resident one year, or

    b) Both spouses resident three months before filing.

C. Legal Aid Contact

    a) Charleston: 119 Spring Street, 29403 (803) 722-0107

SOUTH DAKOTA:

A. Divorce—Dissolution Grounds

    a) No Fault: (none)

    b) Fault:

        1. Adultery

        2. Alcoholic (1 year)

        3. Cruelty

        4. Felony Conviction

        5. Insanity or Mental Illness (5 years confinement)

        6. Wilful Desertion for One Year

        7. Wilful Neglect for One Year

B. Divorce Residency Requirements
  a) Plaintiff resident when divorce is filed and until final decree is awarded. No residency requirement if married in state and couple never left state.
C. Legal Aid Contact
  a) Mission: P.O. Box 148, 57555 (605) 747-2241
  b) Rapid City: 300 West Boulevard, 57701

TENNESSEE:
  A. Divorce—Dissolution Grounds
    a) No Fault:
      1. Irretrievable Breakdown of Marriage (if uncontested, notarized property settlement with no service necessary and court finds written adequate provisions for child custody and support and fair property settlement)
    b) Fault:
      1. Abandonment and/or Desertion (1 year)
      2. Adultery
      3. Alcohol or Drug Addiction
      4. Bigamy
      5. Conviction of Infamous Crime
      6. Felony Conviction with Penitentiary Sentence
      7. Final Decree of Legal Separation in Effect for more than Two Years
      8. Impotence
      9. Murder Attempt of Spouse
      10. Pregnancy (pregnancy by another man before marriage unknown to husband)
      11. Wife's Refusal to Move with Husband and Absence from Him for Two Years
  B. Divorce Residency Requirements
    a) Plaintiff a bona fide resident, or
    b) One spouse six months residency before filing.
  C. Legal Aid Contact
    a) Knoxville: 1505 West Cumberland Avenue, 37916 (615) 174-2331
    b) Memphis: 200 Court House, 38103 (901) 527-9342

TEXAS:
  A. Divorce—Dissolution Grounds
    a) No Fault:
      1. Irretrievable Breakdown of Marriage
      2. Separation (3 years)
    b) Fault:
      1. Abandonment and/or Desertion (1 year)
      2. Adultery
      3. Cruelty
      4. Imprisonment (felony)
      5. Insanity or Mental Illness (3 years confinement)
  B. Divorce Residency Requirements
    a) One spouse resident six months in state, 90 days in county before filing.
  C. Legal Aid Contact
    a) Austin: 1713 East 6th Street, 78767 (512) 476-6321
    b) Dallas: 708 Jackson Street, 75202
    c) Houston: Suite 1909, 609 Fannin Building, 77002 (713) 225-0321
    d) San Antonio: 203 West Nueva Street, 78207 (512) 227-0111

UTAH:
  A. Divorce—Dissolution Grounds
    a) No Fault:
      1. Separation (3 years under separate maintenance decree)
    b) Fault:
      1. Abandonment and/or Desertion (1 year)
      2. Adultery
      3. Alcoholic
      4. Cruelty
      5. Felony Conviction
      6. Impotency (at time of marriage)
      7. Insanity or Mental Illness (permanent)
      8. Neglect to Provide the Necessaries of Life
  B. Divorce Residency Requirements
    a) One spouse resident three months before filing.

C. Legal Aid Contact
    a) Salt Lake City: 216 East 5th Street, 84111 (801) 328-8891
    b) Salt Lake City: 314 Atlas Building, 84101 (801) 328-8849

VERMONT:
  A. Divorce—Dissolution Grounds
    a) No Fault:
        1. Separation (6 months)
    b) Fault:
        1. Adultery
        2. Disappearance for Seven Years
        3. Imprisonment (3 years)
        4. Insanity or Mental Illness (5 years)
        5. Intolerable Severity
        6. Neglect and Refusal to Provide Maintenance
  B. Divorce Residency Requirements
    a) One spouse six months residency before filing and one year before final (2 years if insanity is ground)
  C. Legal Aid Contact
    a) Montpelier: 52 State St., Box 658, 05602 (802) 223-6306

VIRGINIA:
  A. Divorce—Dissolution Grounds
    a) No Fault:
        1. Separation without Cohabitation for One Year.
    b) Fault:
        1. Abandonment and/or Desertion (1 year)
        2. Adultery
        3. Cruelty (after year separation for cruelty)
        4. Final Decree of Legal Separation in Effect for More than One Year
        5. Imprisonment (1 year for felony)
        6. "Sodomy or Buggery Outside Marriage"
  B. Divorce Residency Requirements
    a) One spouse six months before filing.
  C. Legal Aid Contact
    a) Norfolk: Room 350, 147 Granby Street, 23510 (804) 627-5423
    b) Richmond: 18 North 8th Street, 23219 (804) 648-2821

WASHINGTON:
- A. Divorce—Dissolution Grounds
  - a) No Fault:
    1. Irretrievable Breakdown of Marriage
  - b) Fault:
    1. Abandonment and/or Desertion
    2. Adultery
    3. Alcoholic
    4. Cruelty
    5. Impotence
    6. Imprisonment
    7. Insanity or Mental Illness
    8. Non-Support (by husband)
    9. Separation (5 years)
- B. Divorce Residency Requirements
  - a) Spouses filing must be residents (no required time of residency)
- C. Legal Aid Contact

WEST VIRGINIA:
- A. Divorce—Dissolution Grounds
  - a) No Fault:
    1. Irretrievable Breakdown of Marriage (sworn complaint and sworn answers filed: required 60 day wait till final decree).
    2. Separation (1 year)
  - b) Fault:
    1. Abandonment and/or Desertion (6 months)
    2. Abuse or Neglect of a Child
    3. Adultery
    4. Alcoholic (during marriage)
    5. Cruelty
    6. Drug Addiction
    7. Felony Conviction
    8. Insanity or Mental Illness (permanent)
- B. Divorce Residency Requirements
  - a) Either spouse must be a bona fide resident before legal action is filed.

C. Legal Aid Contact
   a) Charleston: Room W-127, State Capital, 25305 (304) 348-8980

WISCONSIN:
  A. Divorce—Dissolution Grounds
    a) No Fault:
      1. Irretrievable Breakdown of Marriage (both spouses swear to ground or one states ground with one year separation or one states ground and court determines no reconciliation prospect).
    b) Fault:
      1. Adultery
      2. Alcoholic (1 year)
      3. Cruelty (Mental or Physical)
      4. Desertion (1 year)
      5. Impotence
      6. Imprisonment (3 years or felony)
      7. Separation (5 years)
  B. Divorce Residency Requirements
    a) One spouse six months residency in state and 30 days in county before filing.
  C. Legal Aid Contact
    a) Madison: 123 West Washington Avenue, 53702 (608) 266-3440
    b) Milwaukee: 211 West Kilbourne Avenue, 53202

WYOMING:
  A. Divorce—Dissolution Grounds
    a) No Fault:
      1. Irretrievable Breakdown of Marriage
    b) Fault:
      1. Adultery
      2. Alcoholic
      3. Cruelty
      4. Desertion
      5. Felony Conviction
      6. Impotence (at time of marriage)

       7. Insanity or Mental Illness (2 years post-marital confinement)
       8. Non-Support
       9. Personal Indignities
     10. Pregnancy (pregnancy by another man before marriage unknown to husband)

B. Divorce Residency Requirements
    a) Plaintiff 60 days residency before filing.

C. Legal Aid Contact
    a) Cheyenne: 1810 Pioneer Avenue, 82001 (307) 634-1566

Appendix C

GLOSSARY OF LEGAL TERMS COMMONLY USED
IN DIVORCE PROCEEDINGS*

Abandonment: See desertion.

Absence: Several states will issue a decree of divorce on the assumption of the death of one of the spouses. The spouse's disappearance must usually be taken as evidence of a presumption of death and the states usually require reasonable efforts to locate the spouse.

Acknowledged Illegitimate Child: A child who is born outside of wedlock whose paternity has been legally established according to the particular state's laws.

Acknowledgment: Admission of responsibility for one's acts. Satisfactory evidence of such admission differs according to each state's laws.

Action: A legal proceeding such as a law suit.

Adjudication: Formal court decision deciding the legal right of parties.

Adultery: Voluntary sexual intercourse or relationship of a married person with someone and a person of the opposite sex other than his or her spouse.

Affidavit: A notarized written statement under oath.

Affidavit of Regularity: A document signed by an attorney listing the major facts in divorce case and filed with the court as evidence that everything is in order.

Affidavit of Service: A signed and notarized statement by the person who presented the summons to the defendant. It establishes that the

---

*NOTE: This glossary is meant to offer only a layman's guide to commonly used legal words and terms which are relevant to divorce matters. The definitions cannot and do not claim legal accuracy. Each state has its own terminology and legal definitions of many of the words described in this glossary.

identity of the defendant was clearly established and therefore that the serving of the document was legal.

Alimony: These are the payments ordered by the courts for one spouse to furnish to the other spouse in a legal action for either divorce or separation. The payments are to furnish financial support.

Alimony Trust: The alimony funds are put in the third party's name. Usually used when large amounts of money need to be guaranteed to be paid regularly.

Annulment: A court decision terminating marriage on the grounds that it was never valid. The status of the spouses is the same as if the marriage had never occurred.

Antenuptial (Prenuptial): It means before marriage. A prenuptial property settlement means an agreement entered into prior to the marriage.

Appear: To be physically present in the courtroom or be represented there by an attorney in order to place yourself legally in the jurisdiction of the court.

Appeal: When a suit is taken to a higher court in order to correct some error by a lower court.

Arbitration Clause: A statement in a custody agreement that in cases of dispute there will be some structured arbitration.

Assets: Everything which can be made available for the payment of debts whether belonging to the estate of a deceased person or not.

Attorney at Law: A person licensed to practice law by the Bar Association of the state.

Bar Association: The state organization comprised of members of legal professions licensed by that state.

Bigamy: The criminal action of entering into a marriage while a former marriage is still valid.

Bona Fide: In or with good faith; honestly, openly, and sincerely; without deceit or fraud.

Breach: A failure to carry out a legal obligation.

Buggery: A carnal copulation against nature; a man or a woman with a brute beast; a man with a man; or man unnaturally with a woman.

Casual Mate: A cohabitant who lives with another person in a relationship of a relatively short time which lacks any indication of permanent commitment.

Child Support: Payments made by the non-custodial parent to either the parent having legal custody or foster parents for support of a child or children.

Cohabitation: Adults living together without being legally married.

Cohabitation Agreement: An oral or written agreement between cohabiting couples settling their property and/or legal rights.

Collusion: People plotting together to defraud. In divorces this usually occurs where adultery is legal cause for divorce and the couple pre-arranges to catch the other in the act so that the divorce can occur.

Common-law Marriage: A marriage that becomes legal without a state-recognized ceremony. These arrangements become valid marriages when a couple lives together as man and wife for some period of time which the state establishes as evolving such relationships into legally valid marriages.

Community Property: Property considered to be owned by husband and wife together. Usually property acquired after marriage.

Condonation: When a defendant claims a plaintiff's grounds are invalid on the basis that they had been aware of the situation for some time and had failed to act upon it. Usually when adultery is used as the legal reason in a contested divorce and the defendant claims that the plaintiff knew about it for some time.

Connivance: A defense used in divorces when one spouse is charged with making up the grounds for a divorce frequently through a plot with the other. Adultery is the usual circumstance and the plot is having one spouse "caught" by the other.

Consanguinity: A blood relationship.

Conservator: Someone court-appointed to manage another person's property.

Contract: A legal oral or written agreement with enforceable legal rights.

Convertible Divorce: A change of a legal separation to a full divorce after the period of time either specified by the state or under the specified terms written into a separation agreement.

Co-respondent: The third party named in an adultery suit.

Corroborating Witness: A witness summoned before the court to substantiate claims. This witness is neither the plaintiff nor defendant.

Counterclaim: After one spouse has been sued for divorce, the other may also sue on either the same or different grounds. Usually used to show equal or stronger reason for being the injured party.

County Clerk: The county's official custodian of files and records.

Creditor: A person who is owed something because they have given something of value.

Crime Against Nature: Sexual activities deemed to be outside the bounds of legal behavior by the state. The definition differs widely between states.

Cruelty: Mental or physical infliction of pain upon one's spouse. Frequently a grounds for divorce or separation. Actual damage usually need not have taken place. Threats frequently are considered reasonable grounds to establish cruelty.

Custody: Refers to the combination of rights, privileges, and obligations accorded to a person for the care and well-being of another.

Alternating Custody is the arrangement for the physical residence of the children which is provided in turn by each of the parents. It is a form of concurrent custody in that both parents continue exercising their parental privileges and responsibilities; although they do so independently and sequentially. In this situation it is common for the parents to have agreed to joint custody, which is the means of resolving major developmental decisions. The parent having physical custody makes all necessary day-to-day and significant decisions while the child is in his or her care.

Concurrent Custody is the general term which encompasses several arrangements, each of which legally affirms the continued parental role involvement in the upbringing of children by *both* parents after their separation or divorce.

Divided Custody is a term which has been more confusing in its use than it has been helpful. It has been most frequently defined as being the same as joint custody but applied in alternating custody situations.

Joint Custody is the legal arrangement in which separated parents continue the parental rights and responsibilities which they had during their marital relationship. From the child's point of view it is, perhaps, the most desirable form of concurrent custody because it allows and presumes that the parental powers will continue to be exercised co-operatively. Joint parental decision-making is encouraged in areas of social, health, educational and religious development of the children. In a joint custody arrangement there is a specific determination as to residential care. Day-to-day responsibility for the children may remain with one parent, may alternate on a periodic basis, or may be divided between the parents with one child in the daily care of one parent and the other child in the care of the other parent. Major decision-making by the parents is by concensus. Usually the parents provide that if they are unable to agree on an issue of significance to the children, they will seek assistance by competent counselors or the use of mediation.

Legal Custody is the term for the granting of authority and responsibility for the care, planning, and decision-making respecting a child. It usually encompasses the areas of socialization; and the provision of food, shelter, clothing, and other essentials for the security and safety of the child. If no specific designation of a physical custodian is made to the contrary, the legal custodian is also obligated to provide a home and the day-to-day guidance and decision-making for the child. Courts have repeatedly confirmed the right to delegate these responsibilities to another, so long as the provider remains responsible to the legal custodian, who must bear ultimate responsibility. Most custodial decrees provide for an award of legal custodial rights to one parent, but are silent as to the other. This is often interpreted to mean that the second parent has no rights other than what appears in the decree (usually only visitation) and the parent may be treated as a legal stranger to the child.

Physical Custody and *Residential Care* refer to the rights and responsibility for maintaining a home for the dependent on a day-to-day basis.

Split Custody is the legal arrangement whereby the physical custody of the children is divided between the parents on a continuous rather than alternating basis. For example, one child may be awarded to the care of one parent on a permanent basis, and the remaining child awarded to the care of the other parent. While each parent may exercise his or her rights and responsibilities as a sole custodian as to the children in his/her care, split custody invites the application of concurrent and joint custody concepts to maximize the continuing relationship of the children. Joint legal custody with split residential care appears to be the best legal description of this social arrangement.

Decedent: A dead person.

Decree: The final order of the court, the legal decision.

Defamation: The offense of injuring a person's character, fame, or reputation by false and malicious statements.

Defendant: The party sued or accused in a case of a criminal action.

Desertion: In divorce, the physical and voluntary separation of one spouse from another without mutual agreement.

Discretion of the Court: The privilege of the judge or court to take actions outside legal rules.

Dissolution (of marriage): The term currently used in many states instead of "divorce."

Divisible Divorce: When one state recognizes another state's decree of divorce, but does not go along with all of the custody, alimony, child support, and property division provisions.

Divorce: A court order, judgment or decree terminating a marriage. It may include property division, financial support, child custody, or these may be taken up separately.

Domicile Residence: The place where a person intends to have their true fixed and permanent home.

Dower: The surviving wife's property rights to real estate owned by her deceased husband.

Duress: Physical or mental force influencing another to do something they would not have done voluntarily.

Emancipation: The time at which a minor child reaches legal maturity or by the court's orders is no longer dependent on or answerable to its parents.

Encumbrance: A lien upon property, a claim against property usually financial, such as a mortgage.

Equity: 1. The net value of property. 2. Principles of fairness applied by the courts utilizing the spirit of the law rather than the letter of the law.

"Escalator Clause": A provision of alimony which assigns to the wife a particular percentage of any increase in income received by her husband following the divorce decree.

Estate: All of the property owned by a person during their life or after their death.

Express Contract: Agreement.

Family Allowance: An amount of money alloted by state law for a surviving spouse from the estate of a deceased spouse.

Family Court: A court with jurisdiction in marital disputes usually regarding dependant support. Also called domestic relations court in certain states.

Family Home: The home used by spouses as their primary dwelling place.

Fault: A legal wrong. In some states the act of committing certain legal wrongs can be grounds for awarding a divorce.

Felony: A serious crime as opposed to a misdemeanor.

Foreign Divorce: A divorce awarded outside the state in which a legal suit has been brought. It can be in another state or another country.

Fornication: Sexual intercourse between unmarried people.

Fraud: Deceit which is intentional.

Gift: A voluntary giving of something with all rights and title to another person without receiving anything in return.

Good Faith: Truthfulness of intentions, honestly presented.

Ground: The basis for a divorce law suit.

Gross Neglect of Duty: The intentional failure to perform a manifest duty in reckless disregard of the consequences as afflicting the life or property of another. Such a gross want of care and regard for the rights of others as to justify the presumption of wilfulness and wantonness.

Guardian: A person appointed by the court to manage another person or another person's property.

Habitual Intemperance: A habit of frequently drinking of alcohol, drunkeness.

Heir: A person who gains title to property upon the death of the previous owner. Usually a natural successor, such as a child. Also, refers to one who inherits by a legal will.

Homemate: A mate who shares a home with another where there is a serious personal relationship of some sustained length of time.

Homestead Exemption: A law that states a certain amount of the value in a family home to be exempt from creditors.

Impediment: A hindrance. In regards to divorce, a legal hindrance that makes a marriage illegal or invalid.

Implied Contract: A contract that is not written, but can be inferred from oral statements or the behaviors of the parties involved.

Incompatibility: Inability to live together because of misconduct, conflicting lifestyles, or personality clashes.

Infamous Crime: A crime which entails infamy upon one who has committed it. Crime such as treason, felony, or forgery.

Inheritance: The right to property ownership upon the death of another.

Index Number: An official number assigned by the county clerk to some legal matter. The index number must appear on all documents relative to a divorce or any civil suit which requires legal filing.

Injunction: A court order forbidding certain actions by the defendant.

Intangible Personal Property: Property that has no value by itself, but represents something of value, most commonly stock certificates or bank statements.

Intestacy (intestate): Dying without having produced a valid will or failing to dispose of certain property through a legal will.

Interlocutory Decree: A divorce decree that will not become final until some specified period of time. Until the decree is final, the couple is legally married.

Intestate Succession: The dealing out of a dead person's property according to state law as opposed to according to the terms of a valid will. Usually invoked when someone dies without having made a will that is valid.

Irretrievable Breakdown: Generally a "no-fault" divorce. The establishment that a marriage has deteriorated to the point that the spouses can no longer live together.

Issue: Decendant.

Joint Property: Community property or ownership in property by two or more persons which has as yet been undivided.

Joint Tenancy: Undivided joint ownership in property.

Joint Venture: A business or investment undertaken for profit by two or more people.

Judgment of Divorce: The final official decision which legally ends the marriage and specifically spells out the rights of the parties.

Judicial: Related to the courts, a court proceeding.

Jurisdiction: The legal power of a court to make judgments concerning a specific legal matter.

Jurisdiction in Personam (personal): Usually refers to situations where the two spouses reside in different states. A court with Jurisdiction in Personam can only rule on financial settlements, but not grant the divorce (the subject) (see below).

Jurisdiction in Rem (on the subject matter): Usually refers to situations where the two spouses are in two states. A court with such jurisdiction can grant a divorce, but not decide on settlement finances which require Jurisdiction in Personam (see above).

Laches: The laws establishing limitations of time before which or after which a legal action may not be brought.

Legal Separation: A court decree lawfully ending the living together between spouses although they remain married.

Legitimacy: Lawful birth. Usually being born within a legal marriage. Some states may call children legitimate children of their biological parents.

Lewd and Lascivious: Sexual acts socially unacceptable.

Liability: The legal responsibility.

License: A certificate of law granting permission, such as a marriage license.

Lien: A legal claim on personal or real property as security for a debt. A mortgage is a lien on a home.

Life Estate: An interest in property during a person's lifetime only.

Marital: Anything having to do with a legal marriage.

Marital Property: All property acquired after a marriage. A gift or inheritance may be an exception in states declaring separate-properties.

Mate: An unmarried person who lives with another unmarried person.

Meretricious: Legally a sexual relationship outside the marriage that has no legal status.

Minutes: The typed proceedings of a trial.

Misdemeanor: A minor crime.

Necessities: Basic purchases which furnish minimal standards of living, such as food, clothing, and shelter.

No Fault: A divorce granted without the finding of fault or misconduct by either spouse. Usually called dissolution rather than divorce.

Notarization: The verification of a signature on a document. Accomplished by having a notary public's seal placed over the signatures.

"Open and Notorious": A act committed in public.

Palimony: Court-ordered financial support between ex-mates. It is the equivalent of alimony, financial support between ex-spouses.

Partnership: An association of two or more people for a business purpose.

Paternity: The father, legally a court's statement or a father's admission that he is the biological father of a child.

Personal Property: All property, with the exception of real estate.

Personal Wrong: An illegal act against another individual.

Plaintiff: The party suing.

Polygamy: Having, at the same time, more than one spouse.

Precohabitation Agreement: An agreement concerning property or financial matters entered into between mates before living together.

Prenuptial Agreement (Antenuptial Agreement): An agreement concerning property and financial matters entered into by parties prior to marriage.

Presumptive Marriage: A marriage which is assumed to exist because the couple has lived together and/or has offered to the public the appearance or reputation of being married.

Probate: A court procedure to determine the validity of a will, as well as to provide for distributions of assets according to a legal will or according to the laws of the state regulating distribution of funds when there is no valid will.

Property: All real estate and personal property.

Putative Marriage: A marriage entered into by one person who was unaware of the legal conditions which render the marriage illegal.

Putative Spouse: The partner in a putative marriage who mistakenly believed that their marriage was valid.

Real Estate: Land, homes, land improvements and all attached fixtures to the land.

Real Property: Same as real estate.

Recrimination (Provocation): An accusation seeking dismisal of a divorce suit usually stating the plaintiff's actions were similar to those charged to the defendant as grounds for divorce.

Rehabilitative Alimony: Court-ordered financial support from one former spouse or mate to another to allow that person to establish skills to be able to reasonably earn.

Residency: The official residence of, or the territory subject to, a resident.

Retainer: The act of withholding what one has in one's own hands by virtue of some right. The act of a client in employing his attorney or counsel, and also denotes the fee which the client pays when he retains the attorney to act for him, and thereby prevents him from acting for his adversary.

Sentence: The judgment of the court upon a defendant following being found guilty of a crime.

Separate Maintenance: A reasonable amount of money a court decides will allow a spouse to meet financial needs until final settlement of divorce, annulment, or legal separation. Usually awarded monthly.

Separate Property: Property owned by one person before, during, or after marriage that is legally not owned by the spouse.

Separation Agreement: An agreement between spouses or mates dividing their legal and property rights.

Separation, Legal: Separation of spouses by a court order.

Separation, Voluntary: An agreement between spouses to live separately without taking any legal action.

Sequestration: The removal of property usually so that a court may deal with its legal disbursement.

Service of Process (To Serve): The delivery of court orders and summons as notification that they are being sued.

Sodomy: A carnal copulation by human beings with each other against nature. The sexual act as performed by a man upon the person of another human being by penetration of the anus.

Spouse: Wife or husband.

Statute: A state or federal law.

Suit (Lawsuit): A legal action.

Summons: Official notice a plaintiff serves by another person to a defendant in order to begin a lawsuit.

Temporary Alimony: Court-ordered payments from one spouse to furnish support to the other spouse prior to a legal separation or divorce.

Tenancy by Entirety (Entireties): Joint ownership by husband and wife which can be ended by death or some legal joint action, in which all ownership passes to the other spouse.

Tenancy in Common: Undivided ownership by two or more people where death does not automatically mean passage of ownership to the survivor.

Testacy: A person dying and leaving a will that disposes of their property.

Trial: The formal hearing before a court in which the plaintiff's case is presented and usually defense heard.

Verification: A confirmation of truth usually through a written statement or a statement made under oath.

Void Marriage: A marriage that is not legal because of some violation of the law at the time it took place.

Will: A document usually witnessed and written which provides for the disbursion of a person's property following their death.

Appendix D

GROUPED READINGS AND REFERENCES

A.   General Readings on Divorce
B.   Marriage Readings
C.   Adult Development and Single Life
D.   Single Parenthood
E.   Marital and/or Divorce Counseling and Mediation
F.   Divorce—Legal Aspects
G.   Divorce—Emotional Aspects
H.   Children and Divorce
I.   Custody
J.   Readings about Divorce for Children

A. General Reading on Divorce:

Baskin, Henry & Kiel-Friedman, Sonja. *I've Had It, You've Had It.* Los Angeles: Nash Publishing, 1974.

Blake, Nelson Manfred. *The Road to Reno: A History of Divorce in the United States.* New York: MacMillan Company, 1962.

Bohannon, Paul (Ed.). *Divorce and After.* Doubleday, 1971.

Epstein, J. *Divorced in America: Marriage in an Age of Possibility.* New York: E. P. Dutton & Co., 1974.

Jones, T. (Ed.). "Gateways: Passing Through Rituals of Transformation." *Quest 78* May-June, 1978, 120.

Kernberg, O. "Mature Love: Pre-requisites and Characteristics." *J. Amer. Psychoanal. Assoc. 22,* 1974, 743-768.

Krantzler, Mel. *Creative Divorce.* Signet (451-E8007), New American Library, Inc., 1975.

Plateris, A. A. *Divorces and Divorce Rates: United States.* Data from the National Vital Statistics System, Series 21. Number 29, DHEW Publication No. (PHS), 78-1907. Hyattsville, Md.: U.S. Department of Health, Education, and Welfare, March, 1978.

B. **Marriage Readings:**

Bach, G. R. & Deutsch, R. N. *The Intimate Enemy.* New York: William Morrow, 1969.

Bach, G. R. & Wyden, R. M. *Pairing.* New York: Avon Books, 1970.

Balogun, B. "Marriage as an Oppressive Institution: Collectives as Solutions." In L. B. Tanner (Ed.) *Voices from Women's Liberation.* New York: New American Library, 1971.

Bentler, P. M. & Newcomb, M. D. "Longitudinal Study of Marital Success and Failure." *J. of Consulting and Clinical Psychol. 1978, 46.* 5, 1053-1070.

Bergman, Ingmar. *Scenes from a Marriage.* New York: Pantheon Books, Inc., 1974.

Guggenbuhl-Craig, A. *Marriage Dead or Alive.* Zurich: Springer-Verlag, 1977.

Jackson, Don D., Lederer, William J. *The Mirages of Marriage.* New York: W. W. Norten & Co., Inc., 1968.

Laing, Ronald. *The Politics of the Family and Other Essays.* New York: Vintage Books, Random House, 1969.

O'Neill, N. & O'Neill, G. *Open Marriage: A New Life Style for Couples.* New York: J. B. Lippincott, 1972.

Rogers, Carl. *Becoming Partners: Marriage and Its Alternatives.* New York: Dell Publishing Co., Inc., 1972.

Rollins, B. C. & Bahr, S. J. "A Theory of Power Relationships in Marriage." *Journal of Marriage & the Family,* 1976, *38,* (619-627)

Weiss, Robert S. *Marital Separation.* New York: Basic Books, Inc., 1975.

C. **Adult Development and Single Life:**

Adams, M. *Single Blessedness: Observations on the single state in married society.* New York: Basic Books, 1976.

Edwards, Marie & Hoover, Eleanor. *The Challenge of Being Single.* New York: Tarcher-Hawthorne, 1974.

Edwards, Marie & Hoover, Eleanor. *The Challenge of Being Single.* Signet (#E8189).

Gould, R. "The Phases of Adult Life: A Study in Developmental Psychology." *Am. J. Psychiatry 129* (1972), 521-531.

Hunt, Morten M. *The World of the Formerly Married.* New York: McGraw-Hill, 1969.

Johnson, Stephen M., Ph.D. *First Person Singular: Living the Good Life Alone.* Signet (#E8048).

Rubin, Z. *Liking and Loving.* New York: Rhinehart & Winston, 1973.

Satir, Virginia. *Peoplemaking.* Palo Alto, California: Science and Behavior Books, Inc., 1972.

Sheehy, G. *Passages.* New York: E. P. Dutton & Co., 1976.

D. **Single Parenthood:**

Abarbanel, A. "Shared Parenting after Separation and Divorce: A Study of Joint Custody." *Am. J. Orthopsych. 49* 1979, 320-329.

Atkin, Edith and Rubin, Estelle. *Part-time Father.* New York: Signet, 1976 (Paperback).

Brandwein, R., Brown, C., & Fox, E. "Women and Children Last: The Social Situation of Divorced Mothers and Their Families." *Journal of Marriage and the Family,* 1974, *36,* 498-514.

Egleson, Jim & Janet. *Parents Without Partners: A Guide for Divorced, Widowed or Separated Parents.* Dutton, 1961.

Ross, H. L. & Sawhill, I. V. *Time of Transition: The Growth of Families Headed by Women.* Washington, D.C.: Urban Institute, 1975.

Schlesinger, B. *The One Parent Family: Perspectives and Annotated Bibliography.* Toronto: University of Toronto Press, 3rd Ed., 1975.

E. **Marital and/or Divorce Counseling:**

Bernstein, B. E. "Lawyer and Counselor as an Interdisciplinary Team: The Timely Referral." *Journal of Marriage and Family Counseling.* 1976, *2,* 347-354.

Coogler, O. J., Weber, R. E., and McKenry, P. C. "Divorce Mediation: A Means of Facilitating Divorce and Adjustment." *Fam. Coord. 28,* 1979, 255-259.

Coogler, O. J., *Structured Mediation in Divorce Settlement,* Lexington Books, D. C. Heath and Co., 1978.

Stuart, Richard B., *Helping Couples Change: A Social Learning Approach to Marital Therapy.* The Guilford Press, New York, 1980.

Suarez, J. M., Weston, N. L., and Hartstein, N. B., "Mental Health Interventions in Divorce Proceedings." *Am. J. Orthopsychiatry, 48,* 1978, 273-283.

Wallerstein, J. S., and Kelly, J. B., "Divorce Counseling: A Community Service for Families in Midst of Divorce." *Am. J. Orthopsychiatry, 47,* 1977, *14.*

F. Divorce—Legal Aspects:

Erickson, B., Holmes, J. G., Frey, R., Walker, L. & Thibaut, J. "Functions of a Third Party in the Resolution of Conflict: The Role of the Judge in Pre-trial Conferences." *Journal of Personality and Social Psychology,* 1974, *30,* 293-306.

Hirsch, Barbara B., *Divorce: What a Woman Needs to Know.* Chicago: Henry Regnery Company, 1973.

Milne, Ann, (Ed.), *Joint Custody: A Handbook for Judges, Lawyers and Counselers,* The Assn. of Family Conciliation Courts, Portland, Oregon, 1979.

G. Divorce—Emotional Aspects:

Bak, R. C. "Being in Love and Object Loss." *Int. J. Psychoanal. 54,* 1973, 1-8.

Braudy, Susan. *Between Marriage and Divorce.* Signet (#J7257).

Donelson, Kenneth & Donelson, Irene. *Married Today: Single Tomorrow.* Garden City, New York: Doubleday & Co., 1967.

Fisher, Esther. *Divorce: The New Freedom.* New York: Harper and Row, 1974.

Framo, James L. "The Friendly Divorce," *Psychology Today, Vol. 11, #9,* February, 1978.

Gardner, Richard A. *The Parents Book About Divorce.* Garden City, New York: Doubleday & Company, 1977.

Gettleman, S. & Markovitz, J. *The Courage to Divorce.* New York: Simon & Schuster, 1974.

Hunt, Morton and Bernie. *The Divorce Experience.* New York: McGraw-Hill Book Company, 1977.

Mannes, Marya, Sheresky, Normal. *Uncoupling.* New York: Viking Press, 1972.

Napotitan, C. and Pellegrino, V. *Living and Loving After Divorce.* New York: Rowsay Assoc., 1977.

Rosenberg, M. "The Broken Family and Self-esteem." In Ira L. Reiss (Ed.), *Readings on the Family System.* New York: Holt, Rhinehart, & Winston, 1972, 518-530.

Steinzor, Bernard. *When Parents Divorce.* New York, Partheon Books, 1969.

H. **Children and Divorce:**

Anthony, E. J. "Children at Risk from Divorce: A Review." In Anthony, E. J., and Koupernik, C. (Eds.): *The Child in His Family: Children at Psychatric Risk,* Volume 3, New York: John Wiley & Sons, 1974, 461-577.

Despert, J. Louise. *Children of Divorce.* Garden City, New York: Doubleday & Company, 1953 (Paperback).

Grollman, Earl A. (Ed.). *Explaining Divorce to Children.* Boston: Beacon Press, 1969.

Herzog, E. & Sadia, C. E. *Boys in Fatherless Families.* Washington, D.C.: Children's Bureau, 1970.

Hetherington, E. Mavis. "Girls Without Fathers." *Psychology Today,* February 1973, *6,* 46-52.

Hetherington, E. M., Cox, M. E., Cox, R. "The Aftermath of Divorce," in J. H. Stevens and M. Mathews (Eds.) *Mother-Child, Father-Child Relations.* Washington, D.C., National Association for Education of Young Children, 1977.

Tessman, L. H. *Children of Parting Parents.* New York: Jason Aronson, 1978, (3).

Tooley, K. "Anti-social Behavior and Social Alienation Post Divorce: The "Man of the House" and His Mother." *American Journal of Orthopsychiatry,* 1976, *46* (1), 33-42.

Wallerstein, J. & Kelly, J. "The Effects of Parental Divorce: Experiences of the Child in Early Latency." *American Journal of Orthopsychiatry,* 1976, *46* (1), 20-32.

Wallerstein, J. S. and Kelly, J. B. "The Effects of Parental Divorce: Experiences of the Child in Later Latency." *American Journal of Orthopsychiatry, 46,* 1976, 256.

Wallerstein, J. S. and Kelly, J. B., "The Effects of Parental Divorce: Experiences of the Pre-school Child." *J. Am. Acad. Child Psychiatry, 14,* 1975, 600-616.

Wallerstein, J. S. and Kelly, J. B. "The Effects of Parental Divorce: The Adolescent Experience." In Anthony, E. J. and Koupernik, C. (Eds.): *The Child in His Family: Children at Psychiatric Risk.* Volume 3, New York: John Wiley & Sons, 1974, 479-505.

Wallerstein, Judith S. and Kelley, Joan B. *Surviving the Breakup, How Children and Parents Cope with Divorce,* Basic Books, N.Y., 1980.

I. Custody:

Bodenheimer, B. M. Progress under the Uniform Child Custody Jurisdiction Act and remaining programs: punitive decrees, joint custody, and excessive modifications. *California Law Review 65,* 1977, 978-1014.

Derdeyn, A. P. "Child Custody: A Reflection of Cultural Change." *J. Clin. Child Psychol. 7,* 1978, 169-173.

Derdeyn, A. P. "Child custody contests in historical perspective." *Am. J. Psychiatry, 133,* 1976, 1369-1376.

Divorce, Child Custody, and Child Support. Current Population Reports, Special Studies Series P-23, No. 84. Washington, D.C.: U.S. Department of Commerce, June, 1969.

Goldstein, J., Freud, A., and Solnit, A. J. *Beyond the Best Interests of the Child.* New York: The Free Press, 1973, p. 38.

McDermott, J. F., Tseng, W-S., Char, W. F., and Funkunaga, C. S. "Child Custody Decision Making: The Search for Improvement." *J. Am. Acad. Child Psychiatry, 17, 1978, 104-116.*

Milne, Ann (Ed.) Joint Custody: A Handbook for Judges, Lawyers and Counselors, The Assoc. of Family Conciliation Courts, Portland, Oregon, 1979.

Morganbassor, M. and Nehis, Nadine. *Joint Custody An Alternative for Divorcing Families,* Nelson Hall, Chicago, 1981.

Ricci, Isolina. *Mom's House, Dad's House.* New York: MacMillan, 1981.

Steinman, Susan. *"The Experience of Children in a Joint Custody Arrangement,"* Amer. J. Orthopsychia. 5 (3) July, 1981.

J. Readings about Divorce for Children:

Adams, Florence. *Mushy Eggs.* (Grades 1-3) David and Sam are taken care of by a baby-sitter because their separated parents both work. G. P. Putnam's Sons, 1973.

Alexander, Anne. *To Live a Lie.* (Grades 3 and up) Jennifer weaves a series of lies to cover up the fact that her parents are divorced. Atheneum, 1975.

Berger, Terry. *A Friend Can Help.* Advanced Learning Concepts. (Early Readers) A girl tells her best friend her feelings about her parents' divorce. Raintree Publications, 1975.

Blume, Judy. *It's Not the End of the World.* (Grades 4-6) Karen tries to get her divorced parents back together and fails. Bantam Books, 1977.

Corcoran, Barbara. *This Is a Recording.* (Grades 5 and up) Marianne, a high school sophomore, goes to Montana to stay with her grandmother while her parents' marriage disintegrates. Atheneum, 1971.

Gardner, Richard. *Boys and Girls Book about Divorce.* A nonfiction discussion of sensible attitudes in divorce. (Grades 5 and up) Bantam Press, 1971 (Paperback).

Klein, Norma. *Mom, the Wolf and Me.* (Grades 5 and up) A girl struggles to adjust to her mother's new boyfriend. Pantheon, 1972.

Lexau, Joan M. *Emily and the Klunky Baby and the Next-Door Dog.* (Grades 1-3) Emily's divorced mother has so many responsibilities she doesn't have much time for Emily. Dial Press, 1972.

Lexau, Joan M. *Me Day.* (Grades 1-3) Rafer worries that his divorced father won't remember him on his birthday. Dial Press, 1971.

Mann, Peggy. *My Dad Lives in a Downtown Hotel.* (Grades 4-6) A boy learns to adjust to the reality that his father doesn't live at home anymore. Doubleday, 1973.

Pevsner, Stella. *A Smart Kid Like You.* (Grades 4 and up) Daddy's new wife is Nina's seventh-grade teacher. Seabury Press, 1974.

Richards, Arlene and Willis, Irene. *How to Get it Together When Your Parents are Coming Apart.* New York: Bantam, 1976 (Paperback).

Slote, Alfred. *Matt Gargan's Boy*. (Grades 3-5) A baseball story about a boy who feels threatened by Mom's new boyfriend. J. B. Lippincott, 1975.

Walker, Mildred. *A Piece of the World*. (Grades 4 and up) Calder spends a summer in Vermont while her divorced mother remarries and gets her new life together. Atheneum, 1972.

INDEX